Pe

Aug

Augment other INTs, especially OSINT

Assist tradecraft

The Grey Line

Modern Corporate Espionage and Counter Intelligence

Andrew Brown

Amur Strategic Research Group

The Grey Line: Modern Corporate Espionage and Counterintelligence

Cover Artist:
Kathleen Laval

Published by Amur Strategic Research Group

Discover other titles by the author on Amurstrategic.com

ISBN: 1466338709

First Edition 2011

This work is first dedicated to my family, for all of their love.

To the many treading on both sides of the grey line today, and to three in particular:

AE/Wintermute
AE/Seraphim
NI/Starlight

For your knowledge, insight and friendship.

Note: For obvious reasons many of the people who contributed their knowledge and experiences towards the writing of this book wish to remain anonymous. For that reason they are listed herein only by their cryptonym designation.

Table of Contents

The Grey Line: Modern Corporate Espionage and Counterintelligence

Prelude

"The future has already arrived. It's just not evenly distributed yet."
William Gibson

It is a warm spring morning in Northern California. A fit young man takes the elevator to the 7th floor of a nondescript office building where his company, Playtronics, has its offices. Like so many other startups located in the building, the office suites are intended to impress potential investors more than to provide actual work space for the yet to be hired programmers. Arriving early, he carefully checks and adjusts his equipment. This is a very important day. He and his team have been working towards this moment for months now. Endless hours of meticulous preparation, deep research and periods of manic activity all leading to this single day. Digital recorders activated he adjusts his headphones again and waits.

Across the street at the Boomerang Corporation headquarters, it is business as usual, save for one thing. The information technology staff is unveiling a new series of security protocols to protect their long awaited and massively expensive set of secured servers. Boomerang's senior executives are gathered in Conference Room B on the 10th floor, excited to hear the IT presentation about the innovative security set up. They have all read horror stories about computer hackers laying waste to other companies and can now rest easy in the knowledge that their systems are impervious. Today they will receive the pass codes to allow them access to their brand new impregnable system. There is, however, an extra attendee to this important conference that no one has invited.

From across the street at Playtronics, the young man smugly observes the action in Boomerang's Conference Room B via a very small remote-operated bug. No one notices the device planted in the flower arraignment on the refreshment stand next to the over-priced fair trade coffee. It had taken weeks to find the right personal assistant to take those flowers into the room. But it took even longer for the IT team to finally finish their penetration testing and activate the new security. All that work, and now it is about to be penetrated on the very day of activation by means which no one in the conference room, especially the IT security team, ever imagined. As the overpaid computer security guru droned on into his second hour, the only one paying even the slightest bit of attention anymore was Boomerang's uninvited guest.

Once the young man recorded the pass codes and operational procedures that he needed, with a weary sense of accomplishment, he quickly compressed the digital audio file and sent it off into the ether. Within 48 hours, the class A hacker on his team's retainer had completely compromised Boomerang's new impenetrable security system, stolen massive amounts of data and left an untraceable series of backdoors for future access. Terabits of data went streaming out via anonymous servers in Osaka and Leon. The young man and his team were long gone, the fake Playtronics offices were deserted and Boomerang was six months away from bankruptcy.

If you are thinking that perhaps you picked up a serial spy novel by mistake and have just double checked the cover of this book to be sure, don't be alarmed. The names and location in the above short story have been changed, but the actions described are all too real and occur all too frequently. Companies like "Boomerang, Inc." are targeted and penetrated to their core regularly. In the modern business world achieving total information dominance, by whatever means necessary, over rival firms like Boomerang allow competitors to lay bare a company's inner most secrets through an increasingly common practice...corporate espionage.

The Grey Line: Modern Corporate Espionage and Counterintelligence

Introduction

"Difficulties mastered are opportunities won"
Winston Churchill

Espionage and spies have been around for a very long time. The great military philosopher Sun Tzu devoted extensive portions of his works to the utility of intelligence in gaining advantage over ones foes. Spies are even mentioned positively in the Bible. Traditionally espionage has served nations, their secret services and militaries. State based clandestine intelligence groups work to further the vital goal of national security by discovering information which their strategic competitors and their allies wish to keep hidden.

Today numerous companies are beginning to adopt practices and develop resources, such as private intelligence arms, which were previously the sole preserve of sovereign countries. The main reason for the growth of corporate espionage is that companies are becoming more powerful and the costs of failure more extreme. Corporate competition for resources, access, market share and innovation is fueling a race for information advantage across the spectrum of human economic activity. Global sales for large multinationals often exceed the total economic output of all but the most developed nations. Both large and small companies have discovered a need for well funded political action arms, private militaries and now, advanced covert intelligence gathering capabilities. Adoption of covert intelligence practices can serve both defensive and offensive purposes. Increasingly, however, advanced intelligence gathering and other covert actions capabilities are being used offensively to gain advantage over rival firms.

State-run corporate intelligence programs have been in place for decades. The vast majority of such operations are focused on the United States and her companies. During the Cold War, the Soviets had hundreds of spies operating in the states, leeching out advanced military technology and other industrial secrets. The successful theft of American industrial technologies saved the Soviets years of research and development and other costs. A wide body of opinion holds that such military and industrial secrets are responsible for propping up the Soviet economy for years longer than would have been possible had the secrets of American companies stayed secret.

The Soviets were not alone in expending vast resources to spy on American industry. The allies of the United States were, and are, just as busy operating clandestinely around the country, stealing commercially valuable information to help their domestic concerns compete. State sponsored corporate intelligence is as pervasive today as it was during the Cold War. Indeed, with the information technology revolution, advanced materials R&D and blooming bio-tech industry, American companies, both large and small, have never been such attractive targets.

While state-sponsored corporate intelligence programs abound, this book's main focus is the growing field of private intelligence. Companies are increasingly and constantly developing and employing professional intelligence resources to spy on other companies. Corporations around the world engage in espionage against their rivals on a truly staggering scale. Conservative estimates place the level of loss to American companies alone at over 100 billion dollars a year and rising annually. Companies that engage in corporate espionage include some of the biggest names in the business world. Every year that list expands exponentially.

The tremendous benefits to a company that steals the secrets of its competitors are game changing. Whereas, the drawbacks to crossing the grey line to acquire commercially valuable data are few.

The Grey Line: Modern Corporate Espionage and Counterintelligence

The practice of privately funded corporate intelligence is an omnipresent threat to businesses around the world and in the United States in particular. This trend shows no signs of diminishing. Those that choose to willfully ignore the danger of information theft and direct action make extremely soft targets for the growing cadres of private industry spies.

The purpose of this book is to explain what corporate intelligence is, how it is practiced, who the targets are and how companies can protect themselves. Make no mistake, corporate intelligence is a real and growing threat to companies across the entire business spectrum. How targeted companies choose to deal with the threat of corporate espionage may well determine their fate in the hyper-competitive 21st century business world.

Disclaimer

This book consists of two main sections. First the art and practice of espionage is examined. Understanding what spies actually do, how they recruit sources inside of companies and penetrate their technical defenses is a crucial first step in building an adequate defense against modern corporate espionage. The second section of this book explains how a company can build passive and proactive defenses against corporate intelligence operators. Taken together this resource will provide a broad understanding of the threat faced by companies as well as the scale and practices of such activities.

Much of the material found in these chapters may seem like a 'how to' guide for corporate spooks. In no way is this book endorsing the act of covert intelligence gathering against companies or individuals. The acts that make up private covert operations are, by and large, illegal in almost every nation around the globe. The resources provided herein are meant to inform and forewarn the reader, and are not to be used by private law-abiding citizens maliciously. The first thing that readers will have to do is discard what they think they know about private intelligence. Hollywood has not prepared you for the realities of the modern corporate espionage. In this book we will detail exactly what it is that modern corporate spies do, how they operate against private targets and what steps can be taken to mitigate this risk for individuals and corporations alike. Knowing how an enemy thinks and operates is, after all, half of the battle.

Using Corporate Intelligence

Companies absolutely require massive quantities of timely and accurate information to compete in the trench warfare like environment of modern international business. In this age of information, the appetite for data is insatiable. Intelligence, regardless of how it is obtained, is the life blood of corporations large and small. The better the information a company has access to, the more likely they are to succeed in the cut-throat international business world. A large number of legitimate corporate intelligence companies operate well above the grey line and have proven to be a vital adjunct to internal company information gathering. The practical utility of such information gathering companies is difficult to over-emphasize.

However, on the other darker side of the grey line, a growing number of groups operate covertly to ferret out commercially valuable data for their clients. Companies across the globe routinely employ less than honest persons to provide secret information about their competitors that is not available via legal means of discovery. The pressure within companies to capture information about their rivals is the mainspring behind the growth of covert corporate intelligence in the modern business world. This competitive pressure is not going to diminish and thus the existence of covert intelligence gathering capabilities can only grow in the future.

Benefits of Corporate Intelligence

Information is power. The more of this raw power a company has, the more successfully they can compete with rivals at home and abroad. As more companies discover the significant benefits of using covert means to penetrate and strip their rivals of secret information, they quickly and regularly start to employ these tactics. Morality in business can be summed up as what a company can get away with at any one time. The risk/benefit calculus of corporate espionage is heavily tilted in favor of those that employ this tactic.

The simple truth is, corporate espionage works. It works so well that the number of companies regularly employing corporate spies has seen dramatic increases every year for decades. Imagine the benefits of total informational awareness of every move that competitors planed to make before they made them. Achieving that kind of strategic dominance is what clandestine corporate intelligence, and only corporate intelligence, can provide. The temptation of having this kind of knowledge and power over the competition has proven to be more than many companies can resist.

Drawbacks to Corporate Intelligence

Stealing data and conducting direct actions against a business competitor is illegal, period. The individual acts that make up corporate intelligence gathering and direct action are almost all illegal everywhere a company may operate. Just to name a few types of laws broken, corporate espionage violates trademark, intellectually property, fraud, breach of contract, theft, criminal breaking and entering, copyright, the Foreign Corrupt Practices Act and many other local and international laws. Residual moral constraints, in addition to the potential for legal blow back, are what have kept universal acceptance and employment of covert corporate intelligence action somewhat in check. As the historical tide ebbs on the nation state as the defining center of human organization, and as corporations become ever more powerful, notions of right and wrong with regard to corporate action are shifting dramatically.

Corporate empowerment of this kind can already be seen in countries where the government has been more or less shaped to serve business interests first. Companies emerging from such environments prove to be more willing to employ covert intelligence gathering, private military groups and other direct actions against their rivals. These resources are no longer considered the sole tools of state power. Former US Secretary of State Henry L. Stimson once quipped when shutting down America's only non-military intelligence operation, "Gentleman don't read each other's mail." Today such naiveté seems ludicrous for a nation, indeed almost criminally dangerous. As companies increase global competition and find utility in taking up the tools of states, a similar adherence to antiquated moral norms in business becomes just as dangerous.

Despite the blatant illegality of corporate espionage, there are rarely any instances of discovery, let alone prosecution. Companies that engage in acts of espionage take great pains to protect themselves from legal liability. The desire for legal insulation and plausible deniability is the corner stone of the growing covert private intelligence industry. The general lack of interest or priority by countries around the world to police or bring to trial corporate espionage cases, even if discovered, is another reason that this industry has been allowed to flourish.

Perhaps the most important factor which makes corporate espionage a relatively safe and risk free activity, is that the target company rarely uses precautions to prevent or take the actions needed to uncover a penetration. If information theft is discovered, the victimized company is more likely to cover up the news of the invasion than resort to public exposure of their lack of security. The very motivation of a company to deny the reality or extent of corporate intelligence action is the espionage industry's best protection against prosecution.

Trends in Corporate Intelligence

If private covert corporate intelligence groups were listed on the NASDAQ, analysts would rate these as "buy now" stocks across the board. This clandestine industry has nowhere to go but up. Covert intelligence groups are being fed by two major trends. The first is the growing demand from private industry for real time commercially actionable intelligence about their rivals, regardless of the source. The information revolution does not just involve YouTube and iphones. The unending appetite of companies for the advantages gained by information dominance makes corporate intelligence from both sides of the grey line, a very marketable item.

The second trend pushing private intelligence growth is the end of the global war on terror (GWOT). When the Soviet Union collapsed there were a huge number of out-of-work spies dumped precipitously onto the market. Vast numbers of unemployed KGB, Stasi and other agents went straight into the private sector, possessing a very narrow, but potentially valuable skill set. This espionage talent dump in the 1990's created a massive swell in private intelligence activity targeting companies around the world. The main target for corporate intelligence has been, and remains to this day, companies located in the United States and her first world allies.

After September 11th, the USA and other Western nations went on a spy hiring binge. Scores of very clever people were scooped up by the CIA, MI-6 and other national intelligence organizations. These agents were highly trained and sent out across the globe to sharpen their skills against some very hard targets. However, after ten years in the counter terror trenches, these skilled operators are opting into the private sector market every year in vast numbers. A new renaissance is taking place in the private intelligence world. This new burst of activity comes from the large cadres of trained intelligence agents emerging from under the skirts of Western state intelligence as the GWOT slowly winds down. Huge numbers of highly trained American, British, French and other spies are looking for work in a private sector that provides few legitimate well-paying outlets for such specialized skill sets.

Integration of spies into private enterprise is leading to a golden age in corporate intelligence. Fueled by the perfect storm of increasing demand and a steady supply of skilled covert operators, the world of private intelligence is growing by leaps and bounds. A reassessment by Western business people of the utility and acceptability of corporate espionage is opening new markets for operators from across the globe. When highly skilled and available talent is paired with skyrocketing demand, you have a ready mix for explosive growth. Corporate intelligence is absolutely no different than any other industry when it comes to growth, and is set to continue on this path well into the foreseeable future.

Intelligence Groups vs. Freelancers

Corporate espionage operatives can be organized into two main categories, spies that work for an intelligence group (either in-house or private) and those who operate freelance. In the past, freelance corporate espionage operations were much more common than what is found in today's market. While they do exist, freelance operators are steadily being replaced with larger, better organized and well-funded professional groups. The reason for this change is due to access and resources. As a freelance spy, the biggest problem is not in generating the intelligence, but in selling it. In the modern business world, as more companies develop their own in-house intelligence capacity or rely on better equipped professional intelligence groups, the list of potential clients is steadily shrinking for freelancers. Conducting successful intelligence operations is more expensive and technology intensive than it used to be. Currently, modern corporate intelligence operations often require the use of advanced technical teams and, perhaps most importantly, skilled computer hackers. Specialized operational materials and cover identity costs are also on the rise. These personnel, services and resources require money and connections to acquire. Skilled covert operators, seeing this trend, have started to band together to pool talent and resources in order to increase operational efficiency and profits. Just like any other industry, increased efficiency in synergistic groups has led to the demise of the smaller or less capable individual intelligence cadres. Terms like demise or die off are figurative, but sufficed it to say, most corporate spies today operate within the fold of a clandestine intelligence group or as part of an in-house corporate intelligence team.

More and more we see international companies creating in-house intelligence gathering capabilities. The teams are covert in nature and will not be found listed under "our corporate spies" in a company's records or order of battle. In most cases, an in-house covert operations team is described as either a tertiary subsidiary within a corporate group or as a stand-alone consulting firm funded as part of a company's black budget.

The utility of maintaining an in-house intelligence capability versus contracting out work to a private intelligence group is twofold. First, an in-house intelligence team can be specifically tailored to the requirements and targets of their parent company. This means that the company can create and maintain a group precisely fitted to their specific information gathering needs and keep skilled operators on staff long enough for them to provide extra value through experience targeting a select group of rival firms. The second, but by no means less important, aspect here is security. Keeping intelligence operations in-house acts to generate loyalty among company operatives and can more easily keep them in line. In-house teams also reduce to the bare minimum the number of people in the loop, which is always a good thing when it comes to keeping secrets.

The Intelligence Cycle

The way that spies operate in the private sector is very similar to how they work when employed by the state. The pattern of intelligence operations can be summed up as the intelligence cycle. The first step in this cycle is to identify a need. The client company is generally informed on the overall activities of their rivals. From this basis of knowledge, they determine the kind of inside information they are seeking. Often the desired degree of information awareness on rivals can only realistically be obtained by illicit means.

Once a spy is assigned to gather certain protected information they move on to the next stage, collection. The process of actually obtaining secret information through clandestine means is what espionage is all about. Professionally trained spies are needed because they are adept at the covert acquisition of information. They operate individually or in small teams and their training gives them a significant edge against law enforcement and internal corporate security assets. Once a spy uncovers the information they are tasked with providing, they transfer that data back to the client company for the next stage, analysis.

The company takes the stolen information and uses it to advance their own business interests or to formulate action against their rivals. After information has been assimilated and acted upon, the cycle repeats with the company using their new found understanding of the rival firm to create further intelligence taskings for their private spooks. The circular simplicity of the intelligence cycle belies the complexity of the many arcane arts and illicit acts that make it function. For companies trying to avoid being penetrated, understanding the intelligence cycle and actively working to disrupt it is the key to their defense.

The Future of Corporate Intelligence

Where will corporate intelligence be as an industry in ten years? In fifty years? If present trends are any indication of future action, corporate intelligence activity will be an omnipresent feature in the business world of the 21st century. Certain features of corporate intelligence will play a greater part in the mix, such as the in-house deployment of advanced cyber weapons to penetrate or attack other companies directly. An increase in direct action by companies against their rivals outside of the net is also a likely trend. The advent of the internet has revolutionized intelligence gathering and will undoubtedly play an increasing role in the acquisition, communication and analysis of intelligence. For counter intelligence, the game will become even more skewed against them as technology places more advantages in the hands of the attackers.

Corporate intelligence is here to stay. It is already a major force in the business world today. Though little talked about, espionage is a vital aspect of corporate operations for many firms across the globe. Companies that do not take steps to mitigate the potential damage such covert actions can inflict on them, will operate at a great disadvantage against those companies who construct efficient defenses. There is no such thing as a perfect defense against corporate intelligence. Even purpose-built intelligence organizations like the CIA get penetrated to their core from time to time. No private company can hope to match the level of internal defenses that national intelligence organizations possess.

For the corporation of the future, and indeed for companies today, the best that can be achieved defensively is the emplacement of obstacles and delay in the path of corporate spooks. This is why companies should immediately begin to take a more proactive approach to corporate intelligence. The odds are so stacked in favor of the offense in corporate intelligence that to play a strictly defensive game is to lose before you even start. Companies that embrace the strategic use of corporate intelligence, whether offensively or defensively, will be infinitely more capable of competing in a market thick with spies.

As you read this book, keep the above injunction well in mind. Corporate intelligence is a murky and dark world filled with unsavory characters and jaded spies, but it is the shape of things to come. Companies have a limited window to prepare themselves and their defenses to meet this emerging threat. The efficient use of intelligence by companies, just like nations, can mark the difference between survival and destruction today and more so in the future.

The Grey Line: Modern Corporate Espionage and Counterintelligence

Part I

Intelligence Collection

"Few men have virtue to withstand the highest bidder"
George Washington

Information is the corner stone of human existence. It is the ability to generate, remember and disseminate knowledge and experience which has allowed the human species to evolve to our present position in the world. Knowledge sharing has elevated us over the course of millennium, but during this evolution human beings also acquired the ability to lie and to keep secret information which we did not want others to know. As societies developed there arose the necessity of creating in-groups and out-groups. These segregated groups have always been defined by their access to information. Some bits of information are guarded more closely than others. Concurrent with the very primal human desire to keep secrets, emerged the need by others to discover them. From this need has emerged a group of people who have made it their profession to uncover secrets and share that knowledge with others who seek it for national, personal or business reasons. These men and women are spies.

In our modern world, after the information revolution, society and business have become awash in vast oceanic levels of data. This unceasing flood of data has not changed the overall basis of human interaction, the delineation of difference through access to information, fundamentally. However, it does add an additional need for clarification and context which, in many cases, only a human source can provide.

The majority of modern commercially relevant information is freely available and can be gathered through open source research into whatever area one explores. With the availability of open information there has been a corresponding raise in the amount of secret information which nations, organizations, companies and individuals desire for whatever reason to keep hidden. It is this undisclosed information which others seek to possess that has created the need for professional intelligence operators and drives their actions.

In no other realm has the open secret of active intelligence operation been more prominent and yet so poorly understood than in corporate espionage and private intelligence gathering. National intelligence organizations and their various operations, real or imagined, are a constant source of fascination for a public drawn to the perceived power of the secret world. There is no doubt in the public mind that there are significant forces, controlled by individual nation states, at work today concocting and carrying out a wide array of secret information gathering and other clandestine activities. Yet ask the same public about corporate or privately run intelligence and they can name precious few real world examples. Generally, they out and out relegate such activity to the realm of fiction. The unfortunate or fortunate truth, depending on which side one happens to be on, is that private intelligence targeting corporate entities is real and pervasive throughout the business world. The costs to companies that find themselves unprepared are staggering. Even for companies that invest wisely in counter intelligence assets and have a strong policy of deterrence and active defense, few resources exist outside of the company to prevent or disrupt company-on-company intelligence operations. The reality of corporate intelligence and the silence that surrounds it is one of the key areas that will impact corporations and individuals around the world.

Intelligence can be anything, from the top secret designs of a latest generation fighter aircraft to company gossip and a person's favorite ice cream flavor. Intelligence is simply defined as knowledge held by one and valued, but unavailable, to another. For obvious reasons, some knowledge has greater relevance to certain parties than others. All groups and people, whether as large as a nation or as small as an individual, place limits on the information which is considered appropriate to share with others.

The creation of in-group and out-group information sharing protocols is the first line of defense against information leakage. Limited access to information is the prime motive force for spies and their varied activities. By designating a piece of information as "secret", people on the inside know not to share it cavalierly with those who are on the outside. A need for covert means of extracting inside information exists because knowledge is power. Nowhere is this axiom truer than in the modern business world.

While a tremendous amount of information can be obtained through overt means about any given subject, often relevant and commercially useful information is held to be secret and can only be obtained by more covert measures. This concept defines corporate intelligence as gleaning protected information held within a company that can only be obtained through covert means.

The allure of secrets is as old as society itself. Breaking trust to obtain secret information has gone hand-in-hand with the keeping of secrets over the long ages of humanity. People engage in covert information gathering on a daily basis among their peers, often with mixed results. When the practice of information gathering is applied to organizations and companies it enters into the realm of corporate espionage. Spying is often called the second oldest profession and with good reason. The anti-social aspects of uncovering secrets, the lying, cheating and subterfuge, come as naturally to a select few as certain similar aspects of the oldest profession do to others.

There are many myths and illusions about how information is gathered covertly by people, companies and nations. If you believe

Hollywood, intelligence collection mostly involves very attractive people engaging in heart pounding daring do, matching wits with cunning adversaries in exotic locations and exchanging pieces of microfilm over martinis and baccarat. The truth is a great deal more mundane but no less damaging to the target because of it. Gathering of covert intelligence generally involves a tremendous amount of research, covert asset development processes and dry application of technical measures. Moments of crushing anxiety and fear are bookended by preparation and tedium. Much like war, the extraction of closely guarded information from protected sources is fraught with potential dangers, never ending cycles of trial and error and a great deal of hurry up and wait.

The first step in gathering intelligence covertly is to clearly identify exactly what kind of information is sought. The client usually has a specific idea of the kind of information that they would find useful. Given the vast oceans of data created everyday by a major company and one can easily understand the need for clarity of purpose and specific targets for a spy. Imagine commercially valuable intelligence as akin to a few grains of gold in a beach of ever shifting sand.

Once a spy knows the specific genre of intelligence to target, the next step is to determine where and by whom that information is held and then decide the most efficient and safest means of extracting it. Obtaining information is done through open source research, technical means, suborning of human sources within the target organization or a combination of all three. After the target is determined and approach set, the next critical stage is to lay in the covert infrastructure for extraction. When the information extraction process involves the use of grey or illegal means, preparations for an operation are done covertly. Undetectable extraction can be extremely time consuming and must be attended to carefully, lest the spy leave traces of the operation for the opposition to work with if the process is detected. Spies are paid to be discreet and not leave trails back to the hiring firm. Subtlety and deniability are the reasons companies hire trained spies to operate covertly for them.

Once the ground work is in place it is time to actually implement the established operations plan. Using whatever human sources or technical means that plan may call for, the actual extraction and delivery of information is usually rather swift when compared to the long process of preparation. Extractions can be continued as long as is necessary, assuming that the sources of the information remain covert and in place. Clandestine activities are, by their nature, caustic to even the best laid plans. The ability to use hard won experience to improvise effectively in the face of uncertainty is another reason that companies use trained spies. Once the target information is extracted, the spy still has to move the data and escape the area of operations intact and undetected.

Accessing information has been made simpler and more covert with the advent of the internet; the best espionage tool ever invented by man. The heavy lifting still falls to a skilled and resourceful spy to carry out but with modern tools like the internet their job has been made a great deal easier and infinitely more covert. Receive a target, develop access, acquire the data, move the data, sell, get paid and get away, find the next job and repeat. This, in a nut shell, is the intelligence cycle for spooks in the corporate world of today.

The development of covert intelligence sources, when targeting business, like when targeting government or military agencies, involves many steps and a great deal of technique to effect. Most of these operational processes are illegal. By its very nature, the trade in covertly generated data is illicit. Operations to find, develop and sell information are invariably carried out under multiple layers of secrecy and security. Legitimate business intelligence firms do not cross the grey line into covert intelligence or utilize illegal information gathering techniques. However, such firms are merely the candy coating on an entire clandestine industry operating on the darker side of the grey line.

Covertly pilfering data and many of the individual processes that make such an act possible are illegal nearly anywhere in the world. Defenses as well as penalties within countries vary from the massively draconian to the unaccountably lax. Whether technical penetration of a target system, suborning of a human source, technical interception of communications or whatever other means a spy may use to covertly obtain information without explicit authorization, it should never be forgotten that there are laws against and penalties for these actions which require the acts to be carried out clandestinely.

The need for intelligence, particularly in the modern business world, has never been stronger. As ever greater numbers of large corporate entities emerge to vie for intrinsically limited resources and market share, the demand for quality information will only increase within companies that wish to succeed. Markets are deeply competitive and only getting more so as international competition increases. While much information can be obtained on the lighter side of the grey line, companies which cross over and work with covert intelligence assets hold a tremendous advantage over those who do not. It is this advantage, or at the least the perception of advantage, that is driving the growth of the modern private covert intelligence industry.

The penalties imposed upon a corporation engaging in covert intelligence work are quite nominal, short term and do not serve as much of a deterrent. Target rich environments such as the United States remain astoundingly open and unprotected, offering a wide range of easy targets for corporate spies and those who derive advantage from them. It is a combination of these factors, business advantage, ease of access and lack of penalty that are shaping the corporate intelligence world into a vital part of the business landscape in the present century.

Sources and Methods of Intelligence Collection

Human Intelligence (HUMINT)

Human intelligence is information held by or obtained through a person. It is a very simple definition for a very complex and arcane art. Obtaining information from a human source is at the core of almost all intelligence gathering activities because it works. People hold knowledge and secrets. It is from people that secrets can frequently best be obtained, even in our interconnected high-tech world. It is individual people too who hold the keys to computer based information systems and this makes them the primary targets for corporate spooks.

Seeking information through human sources contains many potential pitfalls. Human beings can be as shifty and dishonest as those who seek to obtain secrets from them. People are also fragile creatures needing constant attention and care in order to be useful over long periods of time as covert information sources.

The initial contact and approach to a potential covert information source is critical. The means of bending a source to a spy's will and suborning them to their purpose is eerily similar to the first stages of a romance. Each party has their own interests and needs. Meshing together conflicting interests into a single forward movement is an extremely delicate process, as any spy or would be Romeo can tell you.

Once a spy identifies and hooks their information source, the care and feeding of the new asset often proves to be the most trying aspect of the entire operation. Simply put, what a spy asks their source to do in secret is to lie, cheat and steal for them. These types of actions cut against the grain of cultural and ethical norms for most people, making them prone to insecurity, remorse, guilt, fear and other emotionally destabilizing states. Psychologically propping up and reassuring an agent in place is one of the spy's most critical duties.

Human intelligence offers superior advantages in the field of corporate espionage. With a well-placed human asset, the spy possesses all of the access that source has within their company. This includes, but is not limited to, all network and technical access and provides invaluable context for the information that is obtained from inside. A human source can also act as a talent spotter for further asset recruitment. Covert sources can be used to gather basic information on the security and structure of a company, identify others for recruitment, steal secrets directly, access a company's internal systems and perform direct action tasks that only a person on the inside can accomplish.

The use of human sources within a target company is the primary means of covertly extracting valuable information in corporate intelligence. The costs of recruiting and running a human source within a target company often prove to be but a fraction of the value in information that such an inside source can provide. People would be shocked at just how cheaply a trained spy can turn an employee. Costs, of course, are all relative. Even if a source demands hundreds of thousands or even millions of dollars for the information they can access, if the information that they provide allows the sponsoring competitor company to scoop billions in business, it is a relatively small price to pay. Sources are rarely aware of the real commercial value of the information that they have access to. A single file can be the genesis for informed decisions which have ramifications measured in billions. The real costs of running a clandestine intelligence operation lay in the operative spies and the necessity for redundant and covert infrastructure to support them.

Despite the myriad costs and potential pitfalls of recruiting a human source within a company, most firms invest little or no resources towards hardening their staff against conversion. Regardless of how much a company spends to defend their internal digital information and resources, if the staff can be compromised all other defenses are moot. The sheer breadth of access that a human source can provide and the fact that they are often left completely uninformed and unprotected by their companies, makes recruiting a human asset the preferred method a spy has to breach a company's defense.

Technical Intelligence (TECHINT)

Technical intelligence is the gathering of information via technical, or nonhuman, means. This can be aided by human sources within an organization, but in its purest form is an outside attack on the communications, data systems, or other technical aspects of an organization.

Collecting technical intelligence can take the form of bugging, tracking, compromising computer systems, the interception of communications or any means that involves non-human sources of information gathering. There are several advantages to technical intelligence over human intelligence as well as many drawbacks. The main advantage of technical intelligence gathering is that most firms only harden a fraction of the potential penetration vectors and leave the rest to the mercies of a technical savvy spy or one with recourse to specialist help.

As technology evolves, more information is held on external memory sources. People, companies and nations have invested heavily in protecting these machines and systems from external attack. The weakest link in any security system will always remain the human element, and this goes double for computer defenses. Information systems and security protocols are only useful if they do not overly impede daily use. It is through those people authorized to access and hold information that a spy most easily obtains covert access. One can use the human penetration agent to gain covert access to a system, thereby bypassing much, if not all, of the complex of built-in defenses.

Attempting to compromise computer systems from the outside, while by no means impossible, is a difficult and highly sophisticated task requiring significant expertise to do effectively. However, once a system is compromised, there is virtually no limit to the scope of information that can be obtained. The persistence of technical penetration also means that a system can be open to the spy over a longer period of time than may be the case with a human asset. Another advantage to systems penetration is the very covert nature of the action. Few, if any, other people will be aware that a spy has covert access. If the penetration is done correctly that means fewer traces and a lower potential for being caught.

A key advantage to technical information gathering is the strange psychological quirk that consumers of covert intelligence have which holds that raw information from the source, for example an intercepted telephone conversation or data taken directly from a compromised computer system, is more trustworthy and therefore of higher value than information obtained via a human source. Despite the fact that data is infinitely easier to manipulate than people, information coming from a covert technical source is often held in higher esteem. "Paper over people" is something of a mantra in intelligence organizations both national and private.

This belief opens up some very interesting avenues of defense for companies who wish to protect their most valuable data and can lead to a great deal of pressure on intelligence agents who are often called upon to obtain hard copy proof of their human source derived intelligence.

Open Source Intelligence

Open source intelligence is information obtained through ordinary overt means and open sources. This is an often overlooked area of intelligence gathering since it involves no covert operations to obtain. A commonly held opinion within the intelligence community is that the more difficult the process is to obtain information, the truer that information has to be. The savvy intelligence operator, however, will quickly realize that a tremendous amount of valuable information is simply out there on the net waiting to be plucked and used. Open source intelligence is most often obtained directly from the internet, at conferences, via published trade materials and from the company itself. This is one of the most powerful tools in the arsenal of the corporate intelligence agent. Overt open source research engenders little or no risk of detection and can yield tremendous amounts of commercially valuable information which often gives as clear a picture of a company's actions as any form of covertly developed internal information could.

There is an old adage that a good spy is a good researcher and that the Central Intelligence Agency could learn more by reading the New York Times then the Times could learn from reading CIA cables. This has held true time and again and is an avenue that should never be over looked by the corporate intelligence agent or, for that matter, by those inside of a company trying to thwart the spies.

Another area in which open source information has become useful is in the preparation work needed to conduct covert operations against a company or an individual. Countless people place a massive amount of personal data about themselves online every day. Previously private information is freely accessible and can be used to target sources and develop an approach tailored by personal information against a specific target individual. A quick check of open sources such as Facebook, linked-in, twitter, and eHarmony can provide a corporate intelligence agent with virtually all of the personal information they need to effectively operate against a targeted individual or even an entire company.

Direct Action

Aside from the suborning of a human source within an organization, using technical means to penetrate a company or open source research to gather information, there are other means a corporate intelligence agent can use to gather intelligence about an organization or individual. Alternate techniques involve direct action to obtain intelligence materials. Collection of information by direct action against a company or person can be highly effective but may entail a significantly increased risk of discovery to the spy. Breaking into a company or an individual's home to steal information, collecting personal or corporate trash for examination, direct actions to change policy and other methods all fall into this category and will be discussed in detail later.

There are various means of gathering intelligence, each with their own unique benefits and drawbacks. An adaptable intelligence agent knows how and when to use the most appropriate method or methods to obtain the desired result. The first step in any intelligence gathering action is to identify and work towards a specific collection goal. The means by which that particular goal is achieved is a matter of choosing which tool best suits the situation.

Human Intelligence

Human intelligence means using a Joe, mark, source, asset, or whatever a spy chooses to call their suborned human source on the inside, to obtain information on behalf of their client. Wittingly or not, using an inside person to gather information, gain access or recruit others for the spy is the oldest and by many measures, the most effective means of collecting information covertly.

The benefits of human intelligence, or using a human source, are numerous. Chief among them is that all systems, from the nation state to the company, are nothing more than collections of people with varying degrees of rightful access to information. By suborning an individual within an organization with the proper access, the spy can gain a direct route to the information that they desire straight from the source. Not only are human assets conduits for direct information transfer, but they are also full of secondary information about the organization, people within it and can provide invaluable context for the information being passed along.

One of the most appealing factors of using human intelligence sources in corporate espionage is the ease with which people can be turned to a spy's purpose. Everyone, from the lowest cleaning person to the highest chief executive, has weaknesses and needs. Identifying their needs and weaknesses will allow a clever intelligence agent to easily manipulate a person with access to the information that they seek. Unlike state organizations, people who work for companies often have a much lower degree of attachment or loyalty to their organization which makes them infinitely softer targets for recruitment. Not having to deal with sentiments of patriotism, religious fervor and ideological betrayal is one of the key features that make targeting companies a safer and easier game than states or terrorists. Today's employees are highly mobile, often underpaid, overworked, accustomed to changing jobs regularly, feel under the down-sizing or lay-off ax and therefore are less likely to hold deep rooted or sentimental attachment to the company or trust for the people in it.

Another key difference and advantage for corporate spooks over their state based brethren is that they are not subject to recruitment barriers by their employers. In most state intelligence organizations, there exists a highly detailed code defining the type and background of persons who can and cannot be approached for recruitment. Government guidelines are often based more on political expedience than on operational effectiveness. Such handicaps are rarely applied to corporate operations. The field of covert recruitment is open to a much wider cast of characters in the private world than would ever be available to a state sponsored intelligence agent.

Key Benefits of Human Intelligence:

- Direct access to information
- Ease of turning vulnerable sources within an organization
- Access to total range of potential clandestine sources
- Human sources can provide context for information unavailable within the raw data
- The ability to create cutouts and a "fall guy" in the event of trouble
- The possibility of using a human source within an organization to circumvent technical data collection counter-measures
- The chance to look an asset in the eye and detect falsehood
- The possibility of using that asset to spot and recruit others within an organization for direct actions against the target company
- Persistence and mobility within a company of a recruited source, the ability to maneuver the source to the area that the spy wishes to penetrate.
- Sources have a right to secret information as part of their function within a company so little suspicion will fall on them for accessing that information on the spy's behalf.

There are distinct limits to the usefulness of human intelligent assets. Primarily, it may prove difficult to recruit a source within the narrow circle of people who have direct access to the specific information that a spy seeks. One thing to remember is that not just the senior echelons in a company have access to commercially valuable information and protected internal systems. Secretaries, IT staff, cleaning people, assistants, family, lawyers, lower level coworkers and many others can gain access overtly or covertly to virtually every part of a company's data network or other intelligence nodes. Sources are prone to lie, fabricate information, have doubts and guilt or be turned against the spy by the opposition. Human assets are fragile beings who require a significant amount of care, particularly if they are in place over an extended period of time. Due to the fragile nature of the human psyche and sheer bad luck, human assets are the most likely avenue by which corporate intelligence agents are caught.

When a person has made the decision to lie to their employer and their peers, it can be quite empowering and potentially habit forming. The power of holding secrets over others and the utility of deception imparts an almost narcotic like high. This sense of power can bleed over quickly into attempts to deceive the spy on the part of the source. The tendency for a human intelligence asset to lie, make themselves seem more important than they are or provide false or misleading information to please or punish their handler is always there and needs to be protected against at all times. Knowing precisely the asset's ability to conduct covert acts and level of access to certain kinds of information is a critical aspect of proper asset handling. It is always necessary to maintain a tight rein on intelligence sources and if possible, double check their information against other sources to verify the information received.

Drawbacks of Human Intelligence

- Difficulty of recruiting sources within the narrow circle of people with access to the information that the spy seeks
- The possibility of fabrication or inflation of data from the source
- The necessity of direct contact with the source for recruitment and running
- The fragility of human beings when faced with the pressure of a double life
- The potential for counter intelligence to use sources to feed false or misleading information to the spy

The essence of being a competent corporate spy is not just in the preparation work, the tradecraft and knowing how to take care of oneself in the field, it is in the care of one's recruited assets.

A properly maintained asset in place can yield all of the vital information a spy requires and do it in such a way as to remain undetectable for years. Assets, however, are civilians prone to breaking down emotionally and physically from the stresses of leading an operational double life. This vulnerability is one of the main drawbacks to using a human intelligence asset in place. If an asset falls apart, they can be detected. If the insider is detected or defects, not only does the spy not obtain the information that they are seeking, but they too can be caught. At the very least, the target organization will realize that there is an immediate threat and increase levels of defense in response, making the spy's job much more difficult.

Given its wide and international usage, detection, arrest and prosecution of corporate espionage agents is remarkably rare. Discovery is almost always the result of careless or disintegrating human assets being turned by the opposition to expose their handlers. When an intelligence agent is using human assets to penetrate an organization, they are well-advised to use tight trade craft at all times and keep a close eye on their human sources to detect the possibility that they are under opposition control.

Signs that an Intelligence Asset has been Turned or is Ready to Crack

- The asset is suddenly extremely nervous and anxious when communicating or meeting with the handler
- The quality or quantity of information being provided by an asset changes suddenly
- The asset becomes evasive about their behavior and recent actions

- The asset becomes smug and superior in their attitude to the handler
- The asset insists on meeting in person in a location or time of their, not the handler's, choosing
- The asset tries to warn the handler by subtle sign or action that they are under control
- Good tradecraft means teaching the source some simple key words to use when communicating with their handler to indicate that they are under opposition control.
- Use occasional spot surveillance of the source to ensure that they are at liberty and operating for, not against, the spy.

Given the list of disadvantages and fragility of human nature, one might ask why an intelligence agent would choose to use human sources at all when almost any category of information sought is available via technical means or through the company's own computer network. The short answer is complexity and technical knowhow. Breaking into an organization's computer system, tapping a target cell phone, or any of the myriad technical means of modern covert data collection require a certain degree of expertise and specialized equipment which the intelligence agent in the field may not possess. There is also a high probability of encountering tight internal systems security. Most companies in the world invest very heavily in protecting their technical infrastructure, particularly their computer systems. The typical spy does not have the expertise or access to staff capable of breaching systems to the degree necessary for obtaining the information required, or if they do, the cost may be too high. This lack of technical expertise or resources leads back to using a human source.

If a spy can recruit a single person with access to the information systems that they need, they can usually completely bypass all of the security measures that a company has placed in the path of outside intruders. One lesson that corporations have yet to learn is that no matter how state of the art their technical defenses are, the weakest link is always going to be the human element. Time and again, companies have been penetrated to their very core by employees who are left completely defenseless and unmonitored against the advances of a corporate intelligence agent. It is a known fact that corporate espionage regularly costs companies hundreds of billions of dollars each year around the world. And yet effective internal security and counter intelligence operations in most companies are practically nonexistent. Private businesses operate in such a laughably poor state of preparation to defend against the predation of trained and resourceful intelligence agents that in most cases there is little challenge in breaking through a company's internal security.

Thus, when an intelligence agent examines their goals and the defenses of the target company, they choose the easiest path to the target information, which in most cases is through the recruitment and running of a human asset within the target firm.

Long Term Versus Short Term Recruitment

Another key issue to look at when examining the human intelligence source is the difference between recruiting for long-term operations in place or for a more short-term target specific operation. The criteria can change dramatically when looking for a short-term agent versus a longer term one. Short-term agents are, for lack of a better term, disposable. The spy uses them and then leaves once they have the information that they need. These project specific assets do not require nearly as much time and cultivation, training and observation as do the longer term sources.

With shorter term sources, stability often doesn't matter as long as they can provide the quick access that the spy needs. With a long-term asset, the spy has to be much more careful. First, psychological stability becomes a primary concern when selecting their target source. The last thing an intelligence agent can afford is for an asset to self-destruct while they are being run. A destabilized asset has the ability to attack the spy, set them up with the opposition, or alert the company to what is happening. An out-of-control asset can bring down an entire operation in the blink of an eye. It is important to know as much as possible about the potential source before recruitment and to monitor them closely while the operation is in process.

Short term operations generally require fewer moving parts inside an organization and can be created in a more condensed period of time. With limited goals, there will be little need for elaborate plans within plans or multiple assets within an organization operating in chorus. A longer term operation, which maintains agents in place, is a delicate balance and requires more intensive asset cultivation, care and back ground preparation to pull off successfully. Ideally the spy quickly gathers the necessary inside assets and places a technical pipeline out of the company for information. Human sources are pared down to the bare minimum and operate with a lower detection profile while continuing to siphon off the required data. Each operation is unique; there is no way to tell beforehand about needs which may emerge with any particular situation. This is why it is always necessary for the agent to remain flexible in their approach. Prior to engaging on a project, one must decide exactly what the targets are and not get greedy.

Recruitment

Numerous freelance corporate intelligence professionals throughout the world operate independently and generate intelligence which they try and sell to companies, states and individuals. However, given the complexity and costs involved in mounting corporate intelligence ventures, the majority are sponsored directly or indirectly by companies.

So how does one go about finding a corporate spy? Many multinational businesses, particularly outside of the USA, already maintain a discreet covert operations capability in-house under various guises. The common cover for such a group is listing the operatives as part of a legitimate business intelligence research section under a tertiary subsidiary or as a standalone consulting firm. Legitimate business intelligence, the gathering of open source information about the activities of rival companies and other competitors within a given industry, is a vital and growing field in today's international business world. In some instances, the same divisions within a company that engage in legitimate information gathering also conduct off-the-books covert operations. In the United States, companies are at a significant disadvantage, because historically the very concept of covert in-house intelligence gathering is generally repugnant to the character of American business. It just seems so nefarious and unfair. Many also feel that covert operations open the door to significant corporate liability issues in the event of discovery. This stigma does not exist to the same degree among foreign competitors.

The use that states have for corporate intelligence is a great illustration of the above point. America is the ONLY country among the industrialized nations of the world which does not utilize its national intelligence apparatus (CIA, FBI, NSA, DIA, NRO, etc.) to conduct corporate espionage action against foreign economic targets for the benefit of its domestic companies. Another way to look at this is to say that Japan, China, Korea, France, Germany, England, Holland, Switzerland, Spain, Brazil, Argentina, Russia, Israel and most others directly task their state intelligence organs (among them some of the best in the world) to develop corporate intelligence, which they pass straight along to companies at home. The advantages reaped by foreign companies over the years from such massive state-sponsored intelligence activities are incalculable. Imagine if the CIA, let alone the NSA with its massive communications intercept and computing capabilities, were to have divisions which spied on the companies of other nation states and sent that information to Dow Chemicals, Ford

Motor Company, CITI Group and others. The advantage to American companies from such information would be incalculable. The activities of foreign state intelligence organs in support of domestic corporations and the lack of response from their targets, particularly in the US, have shown overseas companies the advantages of covert intelligence gathering.

In the past the majority of corporate intelligence action was state-based, yet in today's international business world the action has moved to private intelligence firms and in-house assets. Companies recognize how effective good intelligence can be and use it constantly. What has changed is that state intelligence agencies have for almost a decade now focused more of their energy into combating international terrorism and other transnational crimes than corporate intelligence, creating a coverage gap. This gap in business intelligence received from the government is being filled in by the companies themselves. Many have found that it is more efficient to create or sponsor their own intelligence groups that they can target as they see fit and not to wait for handouts from the state. This independent hiring bleeds over to personnel. Thousands of highly trained people who have spent entire careers conducting corporate espionage, principally against US targets, upon leaving state intelligence agencies are now available to work in the private sector. Companies in other nations have their pick of the top agents from the state sector to staff their in-house or private intelligence gathering sections. Some nations have larger private than state pools of corporate espionage trained personnel. For example, Japanese companies select the majority of their corporate espionage team recruits directly from top colleges and train them in-house to spend entire careers overseas spooking for major corporate concerns. Sweden and Canada are two more examples of states that have larger private than state intelligence pools. In general, most overseas companies take their people directly out of the state intelligence apparatus and put them to work collecting corporate intelligence against their rivals. This highly trained and mobile manpower pool gives companies, who hold little compunction on using them, a significant advantage against soft corporate targets in the USA and elsewhere.

The world of corporate espionage in America is much murkier. Recently, with the ongoing war on terror, there was a significant hiring drive among the various US intelligence agencies and now with that conflict winding down, a large number of these trained intelligence professionals are flooding the private sector. This trend has lead to a mini boom in the number of private intelligence shops sprouting up around the country. Many of these private intelligence companies specialize in working with the Defense and Intelligence organs of the US government, but an increasing number are beginning to switch over to full-time corporate espionage activities. The money is better and the risks fewer working against soft corporate targets than those selected by the US government.

Under such benign sounding headings as "Business Intelligence" and "Market Research" departments, these companies operate legitimate research arms while maintaining covert espionage capabilities available for a price. US companies have seen the advantages gained by their overseas competitors using covert intelligence and some have decided to engage in their own crossing of the grey line. Unfortunately, this number is still miniscule when compared to the long list of their international competitors who regularly engage in such activity.

By utilizing a series of cut-outs and semi-legitimate front companies, major firms are virtually untouchable legally for the actions of the corporate intelligence groups which operate on their behalf. The obvious trend in the business espionage sector is explosive and continuing growth. For US companies tired of being constantly outmaneuvered by their foreign competitors, the shift to active engagement in intelligence collection and covert direct action is inevitable and ongoing.

For a company new to the world of corporate intelligence finding a covert group with the right kind of capabilities is not difficult. A good place to start is in-house with your business intelligence and market research people. Firms that operate covert intelligence gathering staffs are like Remoras, they need to stay close to their corporate clients to attract work. In all likelihood, if an executive discreetly approaches someone who has been in the legitimate business intelligence world for a time that person will know who to call. If that doesn't work, then talk to the IT security people. Spies are not in the yellow pages, but they do maintain extensive contacts in the legitimate corporate world in order to generate business. A great deal of the initial approach will be innuendo and based on wink and gesture, but with a small amount of perseverance and a realistic budget, finding and engaging the services of corporate spies is not as difficult as one might imagine.

As a new customer it is considered bad form to out and out ask for a private spy. One must be discreet and hold with the decorum of these kinds of things. Instead of directly asking a business intelligence consultant to meet their secret pet ninja, a realistic and subtle approach needs to be taken. First, explicitly describe what the firm is looking for. A discreet way of handling this is to request something that could be considered legitimate business intelligence, for example "how many of the new type X cars will Toyota produce next year and what will the capacity of their hybrid batteries be?". Certain kinds of very useful information are simply not available through overt research. The answer will inevitably be that the legitimate intelligence arm is unable to produce such data because it is held secret by the rival company. This is where the executive asks for reference to a company or individual who can provide such information. So far, all is legal.

When contacted covert intelligence firms invariably present themselves as "business intelligence" or "market consulting" boutiques, with corporate headquarters conveniently located overseas of course. If the sponsoring company is willing to pay the price, and companies do pay high sums for hard business data all of the time, they can begin to negotiate. Once the covert intelligence firm has vetted the hiring party and researched the request, they come back with an initial budget and tentative timeline for the operation to retrieve the sought after information. Agree to this and move the money through channels as they specify. Once a tasking is received from the client company for information or other action, the planning, implementation and delivery of the target data is now the responsibility of the corporate spies. Once the money is sent the covert machinery of corporate espionage begins to hum along. Congratulations, you have now hired yourself a real life corporate spook.

How the consultant generates the information which they launder back to the hiring company is not considered the legal responsibility of the originating firm. Data laundering in all its wonderful varieties, covered in detail later, is carried out through such a wide array of cut outs and front companies that it is impenetrable to all but the most industrious investigators. In the extremely unlikely event that such activities ever do make it back to the door of a hiring company, quasi legal actions have a tendency to be laid at the feet of "an overeager mid-level employee whose actions were unknown to management". In virtually every case of corporate espionage in America, there has been no blow back from any traced corporate espionage action. Smarter American run corporate espionage firms are "based" overseas. US government investigations of corporate espionage, the few that ever even make it out of the starting gates, shut down the instant they touch on covert actions carried out by "allied" countries. Nominally basing a corporate espionage firm in a country such as Canada, Israel, France, England or Japan adds a further layer of obfuscation and protection to an industry that is already more byzantine and covert than the drug trade.

Identifying Needs

Every consumer of intelligence product has their own unique needs. The first step in the intelligence collection cycle is to identify and prioritize the client needs. Often this is done in advance by the company which hires the intelligence group to do its spying. The consumer knows what is needed for their competitive edge and will present the wish list to their in-house or contracted covert intelligence arm. From this point, it is up to the spies to generate the information that will fill those needs. It gets a bit more complicated for freelance espionage agents or other groups who come into possession of commercially valuable information which they in turn attempt to sell to a company.

There are a number of very significant hurdles for a freelance corporate espionage agent. Simply approaching a company and offering to sell them the secrets of their competitors will often result in the would-be spy getting thrown out of the building or worse. While a small number of freelancers do operate quite comfortably outside of private intelligence group control, the industry is a rather narrow one. For the most part, freelance corporate intelligence is the preserve of criminal gangs, sting operations and disgruntled walk-ins.

In other countries where the local companies are more accommodating to covert intelligence operations walk-ins are generally more acceptable and are taken seriously. A walk-in is a person who has access to commercially valuable information and wishes to sell that information on their own. These are usually quite rare but it is certainly not unheard of for a disgruntled employ to hawk their inside knowledge to the competition for a few pieces of silver. Because law enforcement rarely runs dangles against companies to entrap them in corporate espionage cases, walk-ins are considered a safe, effective, and rare bonus.

It can be just as difficult for criminal groups to directly approach companies seeking to peddle illicit information. In countries where organized crime groups play a significant role in the legitimate business world, the membrane separating the business and criminal underground can get fairly thin. In these nations, intelligence generated by criminals is more readily accepted by corporations, many of which have long standing relationships with their local criminal organizations. This can prove to be quite advantageous for these companies since criminal groups are already well versed in operating covertly, are comparatively cheap and have recourse to information collection methods that, while effective, are not often engaged in by professional intelligence agents. The obvious downside to this resource is that if criminals get arrested for unrelated activities they may attempt to blackmail their corporate backers for favors. The degree to which a company chooses to engage with traditional underworld sources is dictated by how comfortable that company feels with the groups and how securely the groups are entrenched within the country of operation.

On a side note, criminal resources are often employed by larger professional private intelligence firms to set up collection sieves for corporate intelligence. The classic example is for an intelligence group to work with an underworld organization to set up high class prostitution rings and "safe" drug sources. Business people get caught up in such honey and powder traps each year in rather embarrassing numbers. For organized crime already operating any number of such illicit services, creating a tailored team of trained prostitutes and drug dealers is easy and cheap. Intelligence professionals train the women and men to work in this capacity, specifically to target certain kinds of high level corporate employees for the purpose of ferreting out specific kinds of valuable information. These traps are also used to generate blackmail materials useful to turn employees who get taped engaging in acts they wish to keep secret.

A strong division of labor between intelligence operators and criminals is exceedingly common and highly effective. Poorly trained employees of major companies fall for these ploys in droves, which mean that such honey and powder traps can pay for themselves many times over within weeks of being set up. Bacchus has drowned more souls than Poseidon and Aphrodite has broken more empires than Athena after all.

For the freelance covert intelligence agent, unless they develop a relationship with a company in advance, it can be very difficult to sell whatever information they uncover. The rejections, difficulties and dangers of trying to sell black market data have relegated the true freelancer to the fringes of the private intelligence world. The majority of corporate espionage is thus conducted at the behest of a company (or its shell) for a specific purpose through established persons within the private intelligence industry. The initial intelligence tasking may come from the client or as an offer from the intelligence company itself. The first step in the corporate intelligence cycle, like the state-based intelligence cycle, is identifying needs.

The needs of a company with regard to intelligence are varied. Knowledge is profit, dominance and power. Companies often prove more than willing to pay whatever is necessary to gather all of the information that they can, both overtly and covertly. They just want to feel that they are safe in doing so. From the company perspective, there are specific item of information that realistically can only be obtained through covert actions. Once the extent and nature of the data is identified, whether from the company or the private intelligence side, the general request is parsed into specific intelligence gathering goals.

When a private intelligence firm knows the type of information or action required, the intelligence provider then examines the target organization for weaknesses and determines what is needed to gather the requested information. This process generally requires time for the intelligence provider to research the target company thoroughly and possibly make initial probes to test their security. After the company and its defenses are examined, steps are taken to identify exploitable personalities among those with access. Based on a plan of data extraction, negotiations with the ordering company begin to determine the level of payment and overall time lines of the operation. Compensation for covert action can vary widely, but generally runs from tens of thousands of dollars into the tens of millions, depending on the difficulty of extraction, level of defense, and value of the information or materials to be obtained. After the preliminary target identification has been completed and price set, the private intelligence firm puts together the team which will conduct the actual operation.

Looking for Sources

The first step in gathering intelligence is gathering information. This sounds completely intuitive, but it is the one stage in the process where the most mistakes are commonly made. Done correctly, foundational intelligence gathering can vastly simplify the entire collection process. Once the spy is tasked with gathering a certain item of intelligence or more generally with penetrating a company, the process becomes one of discovering means to achieve that objective. In later sections, technical and other means of gathering intelligence or conducting direct actions are covered, but below is how a spy develops human intelligence resources within a target company to obtain their take.

When you are hunting people, like hunting any other big game, the first priority is to know your adversary. In corporate espionage, the adversary is man and the knowledge needed is an understanding of human nature, weaknesses, needs and responses to stress. One of the key elements that make up a good spy is the ability to get into the heads of other people. Empathy may not be a trait that most would associate with espionage, but when looking for a person to lie, cheat and steal on your behalf, an ability to engage the target asset on a deeply personal level can be critical. For the intelligence agent searching for a target individual within an organization, the first step is finding your man or increasingly often your woman. It is critical to first develop a deep level of personal information to base selection upon.

Remember that when searching for access to information, certain intelligence does not always rest solely within the company that is targeted. For example, if a spy is looking for plans to a new type of solar panel, a number of outside sources such as parts suppliers, lawyers, printers, trash collection and IT support companies will have the same access to target information as employees in the company. Any of these potential access points could possess the target data and can often be penetrated more easily than the company itself. Companies require outside service providers and depending upon the company's level of security awareness will freely distribute important data to smaller service companies which possess less internal security than might be found at larger, better protected, firms. Sub-contracting services are a significant weakness with many companies and are exploited by corporate intelligence agents to supplement or simplify the collection process regularly. The further removed a person is from the direct consequences of theft of a particular piece of information, the less attachment they will have to it and the lower the level of protection they will place upon it. Outside venders for major companies often do not have the resources to provide the same elevated levels of internal security that are deployed within a larger enterprise. Generally, the employees at these smaller companies are easier to turn since they do not have a direct stake in protecting the secret information of a faceless client company.

Continuing the example of targeting a new type of solar panel this technology will likely be closely held at the source, especially if it is a small start up, which are notoriously difficult to infiltrate because the employees have been working together for years to finally bring the technology to market and whose future profits and placement within the industry rest with it being a success. A good spy may be able to find a weak link within the organization, but it will almost certainly be a challenge. Most of the difficulty bleeds out of this particular assignment if the spy can simply go to the industrial print shop down the road that the startup uses or the IT company that handles their server maintenance and find an underpaid staffer or part-time worker, who for a few hundred dollars will give the spy whatever they want. People in smaller service firms may not even know that the information which they hand over is valuable or even secret. Such part-time and underpaid secondary employees are less likely to question a legitimate sounding request for the data if the spy chooses to approach under a false flag or resist effectively if offered cash.

Physically breaking into secondary support companies, such as the law firm holding the patent application for our new type solar panel, is likely to be easier than breaking into a primary target company as well. The mentality at most secondary service companies holds that there is nothing of interest for anyone to steal and security costs money, which none of their clients directly ask them to spend, so why guard or lock down the offices after hours? If data is stolen the first place investigators, in-house or police, focus on is within the targeted company. This detour gives the intelligence agent further time to get away and cover their tracks when they gather information through a secondary firm. Another point is that, if theft is detected within a secondary company the opposition may not be able to pin point exactly which client firm was targeted, further delaying the pursuit.

Always remember that one of the keys to good intelligence work is flexibility and creative approaches to any given problem. If the task is to steal information item "A" then approach it by first thinking about stealing "A" and not just about infiltrating company "A", as these are not always the same thing.

Assuming there is no other alternative to obtaining the information that the spy requires than to break through security within the main target company it is back to square one and the need to develop an asset within that company. Some larger companies are aware of the potential security risks of using outside vendors to service secret information and so have invested in developing in-house capabilities to cover the process of creation, dissemination and storage for highly classified data. In such heightened security cases, the only approach is to penetrate the target company itself to reach the data. Once a spy has exhausted means of extracting information obliquely through softer secondary approaches and determined that the best approach is to develop a human asset with the necessary access internally, it is time to go source shopping.

How to Source Shop

In this day and age, looking for vulnerable links within an organization has become much easier than it was even a few years ago. This is due to the advent of the internet and more specifically, to the boom in social media. In the past, a spy would need to conduct surveillance of the target company then individual employees to determine who would be a good inside source or actually penetrate the target themselves. The initial goal would be to develop an access agent who could give them information about company personnel. Access agents, those who spot better placed potential sources instead of seeking information directly, are key ingredients in the penetration of target companies. Common examples of access agents include a gossipy secretary or other low level employee with details of the personal lives of the senior staff. While the utility of a well placed access agent is by no means extinct in today's world almost everyone in a company, particularly if the company is in the US, places vast amounts of personal information online, making it available to any corporate spook with basic internet knowledge. With minimal technical skills, a spy has access to nearly every detail that they could wish for on people working at a specific firm. Sites like LinkedIn give immediate access to critical startup data such as who works for a specific company at any given location and their background. By taking this basic personnel information, a spy can use other sites like Facebook and twitter to gather large amounts of more personal information to look for specific targets.

People truly have no idea the wealth and utility of data that they regularly make available about themselves online, just ripe for the picking by intelligence agents the world over. Everything from up-to-date resumes, personal beliefs, political views, family relationships, pictures and juicy tidbits such as addiction indicators are just a few clicks away. What before took weeks or months of intensive surveillance, cultivation of access agents and meticulous deduction now can be done on an iphone over an espresso at Starbucks. By now there is probably even an app for clandestine source mining for the iphone. By no means has the internet completely replaced old fashioned shoe leather in the intelligence world when it comes to developing information about potential sources. What modern technology and the internet has done for corporate spies is to make the life history and personal views of nearly every person of conceivable interest instantly accessible without the need for covert investigation. The act of initial target selection is now a faster and more efficient process than it ever was in the past.

The majority of covert intelligence companies and state corporate intelligence organs actively engage in passive surveillance of potential target organizations. By using the internet they are able to sit back and build extensive files on potential sources within organizations they see as likely future targets. This preliminary screening is a common practice among national intelligence agencies that target US economic interests as well as in the private intelligence industry. A quick scan of the social network connections of mid-level employees with US defense contractors and other high tech firms would likely reveal several of their "friends" to be front profiles for national and private intelligence agents keeping tabs on them for potential future use. Passive net based surveillance is a pervasive fact of life in modern corporate intelligence. By keeping tabs on potential sources within regularly targeted companies, the private intelligence firm can eliminate a great deal of the initial process of source recruitment by accessing their own short lists of attractive targets. Efforts required to maintain these prospecting lists get easier all of the time as more powerful data mining tools become available to private intelligence companies and individual spies.

Once a spy has narrowed the field using open source social networking and other web based tools, a number of deeper penetration options present themselves. For example, hacking email, can be as easy as gathering sufficient information from Facebook to guess the prey's security questions. The ease of email penetration can be seen in the regular hacking of Hollywood media faces and covert attacks on senior US political figures by other countries. If a group of junior varsity hacker kids can do this to dozens of world-famous and protected individuals, just imagine what teams of trained intelligence officers backed by significant resources and class A hackers are doing daily to completely unprotected corporate employees.

If an employee uses a difficult to guess password, there are other options like brute force attacks, hijacking home wifi, employing targeted phishing scams (so called spear phishing), or simply calling and asking for the target's password. Often the simplest attacks work best. It is ironically comical how often even trained employees will disclose sensitive personal information over the phone or respond to tailored phishing scam type emails. Once a spy has a single password, they gain access to every protected site that an individual uses it for. The most common computer security issue that average citizens have is the tendency to use the same password across multiple sites. Only the most security conscious of individuals use multiple passwords. People also rarely change their passwords as often as they should to prevent meaningful exploitation. Gaining access to an individual's email account can also give the spy the keys to other very informative sites. Think about your own email password, is it the same as the password for your bank site? Is it the same for your social media and personal web pages?

Is it the same for the hobby, personal interest or adult sites you may belong to? What level of information about yourself can be gained if someone were to have access to all of these internet sites that you regularly use? When a spy gains access to a person's email, bank site and other nodes they open a window into that person's thoughts, consumption patterns and interactions with others, often going back years. Reading the backlog of emails to and from another person is akin to reading their diary. Employees also keep staggering amounts of classified data in their personal and company email inboxes. More than once, an intelligence acquisition project of high level sensitive information was completed just by breaking the simple lock on an employee's personal email account. Material obtained about a person through their internet connections can be put to immediate use in judging their potential value as a source and in determining the best vector of approach to turn them. It can also be used to develop compromising personal information to compel action as well.

Additionally, a tried and true means of acquiring information about a potential source is to tap their phone. Modern cellular communications are just as vulnerable to covert interception by tech savvy spies as their analog cousins were in the past. Indeed modern wireless communication is even easier to tap in many regards as it often requires no direct physical wires and can be done by intercepting wireless signals from a safer distance. People talk on their phones incessantly and by listening in covertly, a spy can develop a very good picture of the target's life. The means of tapping into land lines and cell phones will be covered in greater detail later but suffice it to say, the process is substantially easier to accomplish than people may want to believe. Breaking into a home wifi network to covertly monitor the target's internet usage is another valuable tool for monitoring potential sources. The means of tapping into a wifi network, while quite technical, has proven to be another effective means of gathering information, including potentially compromising information, about a potential source. Standard security measures may be fine for keeping a neighbor from piggybacking your home wifi, but are no defense against a technically adept intelligence agent.

The technology behind listening devices and video surveillance has undergone a remarkable revolution over the past 20 years. Once audio and video surveillance required physical penetration of a home or office to install rather unwieldy bugs and guys hunched over in smoky rooms listening to bulky reel to reel recorders. Today's surveillance simply requires micro bugs or insertion of special programs designed to turn everyday technology into listening devices or even video surveillance tools. Further refinements of covert listening technology can digitally screen recorded conversations for key words or phrases, making the process even easier.

Think about your office or home right now. How many microphones (potential covert listening devices) do you have installed already? If you cannot think of any, the next few lines should be a revelation. Every phone, assuming it is digital, can be turned into a bug, the cell phone you keep on you constantly can easily be reconfigured to act as a covert transmitter, signals from a baby monitor or home security camera can be hijacked, your laptop and home PC with wifi and built-in web cameras and microphones are completely vulnerable to being turned into covert listening devices, the list goes on. All of these everyday items and more can be turned against the user without any need to physically penetrate a home or office to plant covert devices. If it is necessary to implant physical devices on site then the technology behind stand-alone surveillance tools has shrunk them dramatically over the past few years and made them much easier to install and hide as they are small enough now to be virtually undetectable.

Technical means of gathering information about an individual can reveal who they are, what kind of person they think themselves to be, their desires and needs and many of their darkest secrets. With this kind of inside information, the spy can make a much more informed selection of a potential source. An approach armed with deeply personal information allows the spy to turn an employee more easily and with far less risk of rejection. Having personal secrets has the secondary benefit of making the spy seem all knowing to a potential source, which can be a very powerful psychological lever. Given the pervasive nature of many technical means of observation, the spy can closely monitor their recruited agent in real time to check for any sign that they are fabricating, have been doubled back or are becoming unstable.

As with any other technical operation there are drawbacks, such as the need for technical knowledge and very specific, sometimes illegal or illegally modified, tools. The technical knowledge issue can be redressed through training or by hiring an individual who possess the specific skill set that the spy requires. The potential rewards of covert technical observation have to be weighed against the risk of detection. Technical penetration requires the user to access systems or intercept signals in unorthodox ways and manners which can potentially leave traces. Implanting technical access may require actual physical penetration which carries its own set of risk factors that often mitigates against their casual use. Real time monitoring of technical penetrations carry the risk of trace back to the spy, catching them red handed. As with any aspect of an intelligence operation, the utility of technical penetration and monitoring to gather information about an individual must be weighed against the defenses of the target and the potential for detection.

Access Agents

In some instances, the best way to find a human source within an organization is to use another human source to talent spot for the spy. Both people and machines these days hold secrets, but only other people can provide the spy with context. When a source scouts for and provides information on other potential sources, that source is called an "access agent." Access agents have been used throughout history to spot other better-placed sources for intelligence agents. The classic example of an access agent is the gossipy secretary, who over a few drinks or for a small fee will give the spy dirt on anyone and everyone in their office. The best kinds of access agents are those who hear everything, know all of the skeletons and have a good feeling for the mentalities of others. One competent access agent can lay open an entire organization and the lives of everyone in it. Their data and insights can also provide context for the spy and help filter information received from a source for falsehoods.

As needed, over the long run it is possible to riddle a company with access agents. However, in the beginning it is best to start by looking for low level employees that service the upper echelons of a company from which the spy wishes to recruit their primary source. Executive assistances, paralegals, low-level IT staff, junior execs, and mid-level employees with a grudge can provide fertile ground for the recruitment of access agents. These types of employees hold a vast quantity of inside information on other employees at all levels within a company. Their daily contact with other potential assets lets them investigate on a more personal level. Preliminary access agents are generally underpaid staff that has been with a company for some time.

A good rule when looking for an access agents is to start with those people who are centrally placed inside of a company, hold little access of their own, but have personal problems such as addiction, depression or debt. A number of corporate intelligence agents use the so called "single parent rule". When seeking access agents (as well as primary sources) within a target company, they first look for employees who are single parents just squeaking by financially. People can self justify just about any action, if taken to improve the lot of their children. By providing a small amount of extra income or other support, again and again these kinds of sources will bend over backwards to bring the spy who recruits them all of the information that they seek and then some.

While single parent personal assistants are by no means the only access agent a spy may target, they do make up the most common class of initial penetration agent many spies employee. Employers who cut salaries or lay off support staff, but give ostentatious bonuses and privileges to their senior managers and officers, create entire classes of bitter and easily turned access and primary agents among the lower echelons. Happy employees who feel appreciated and are fairly compensated are difficult to turn. However, fearful, resentful, underpaid and unappreciated employees will flip for pennies.

Access agents do not necessarily come from the bottom ranks of a company. Recruiting from the bottom is the most common approach, but some targets require a spy to look for inside information from higher income or more senior sources. Higher ranking sources are more difficult and costly to recruit, but once on board they can make for superb assets. The main reason for this discrepancy is that the higher placed an organization source is, the more they have to lose from discovery. If such a valuable source is obtained, they often prove to be tireless workers for the spy until they are no longer needed or mentally burnout.

A third source for access agents is from outside of the company. Consultants, wives, girlfriends, external service staff and others who exist symbiotically with company personnel are a ready source for use as access agents. These access sources are often knowledgeable but less protected than actual company employees. If the target source is already selected, an external asset can help to provide detailed personal information as well as maintain passive monitoring during the running of the source to detect issues before they may be apparent to the spy.

The major drawback to using access agents is the very nature of the people who make the best access agents in the first place; they talk. Keeping an access agent from telling everyone they know about what they are doing can sometimes be a challenge. It is best to approach such indiscrete people obliquely and under a false flag. Giving gossips or egocentric people a juicy secret like their role in a covert intelligence action can be too much temptation. They may have little loyalty to the company, but will show less or no loyalty to the intelligence agent who recruits them. If there is even the hint of danger or counter measures put in place to detect intelligence penetration, access agents can get easily spooked. When they are frightened, they have little compunction about exposing the agent at the first signs of trouble.

Discovering access agents, turning them and getting them to uncover intelligence operations is a primary means used by the opposition to disrupt collection actions. Therefore, it is prudent to keep all but the most firmly turned access agents at arm's length once the spy has the information they seek. When dealing with access agents, it is a common ploy to lay down a smoke screen by asking about multiple personalities in the company, not just about the primary targeted one. Never take an access agent into deep confidence. Access agents are tools which need to be utilized judiciously and carefully.

Direct Contact

In some instances, use of third party access agents or technical means of discovery to find a good source within a target organization is unnecessary. If an agent has worked in the sector before and knows the players, they can determine who to approach simply based on past experience. If the security situation is lax, the agent might also consider insinuating themselves into the target environment to gather data on potential sources through direct contact.

Hunters often cover their approach to the prey by masking their own scent with that of the target animal. This allows the hunter closer access and a better shot. A spy may also find utility in developing direct contact with a potential source before they make the approach to turn them into an asset. Direct personal contact is used in intelligence circles as spies are trained to gather information about a target and make judgment calls about the possibility of turning them and can do so best through direct personal contact. Such direct access is covertly gained by running in the same social or business circles, "accidently" meeting the potential source and developing a friendship. National spy agencies prefer this direct contact method and it is one of the reasons that their intelligence officers are thinly veiled as diplomats or sheep dipped as embassy staff of one kind or another. A spy can also choose to approach their target more obliquely by posing in some kind of service capacity such as drug dealer, procurer, fixer, lawyer or side business partner.

Developing a personal friendship with a target source prior to the approach is a pragmatic way to determine their strengths and weaknesses and to build a bond with the target to better affect recruitment. Insinuating themselves into the target's social circle is extremely useful because it provides the spy with a valid reason to regularly observe their asset once they have been turned as well as a direct conduit to people who know the source well and can alert them to subtle changes. Such direct penetration can also provide the spy with a powerful cloak against suspicion when done correctly. As the Russian master spy Richard Sorge, operating for years under cover as a Nazi journalist and academic in Japan, once put it, "The best way to be above suspicion is to be beyond suspicion". Penetrating the social circle of the intelligence target and joining the "in-group" can give the spy a very powerful shield when working on a target company. Sorge knew all about the power of working from the inside with veiled purposes. The German ambassador himself came to bail Sorge out when he was caught by the Japanese for espionage. To the day of his death, Ambassador Otto professed his undying friendship with and conviction in the innocence of Richard Sorge despite the mountain of evidence and even Sorge's own later confession.

Covert operators seeking insertion into the business and social circle of a potential target individual need to study the habits and customs of the group and adopt them as their own. Of the innumerable means of going about this, the best approach is usually the simplest. By conducting through background research into the activities, associations and lifestyle of a target, the spy should be able to pick a proper venue for insinuation. Background work to discover a target's interests is easily done today through technical means and the internet. Google the person of interest by name. Look at the target's Facebook, Linked-in or personal web page. What do they list as interests, what pictures do they post? Remember that what people claim they do and what they actually do are often two very different things. An overweight executive who proclaims on their match.com profile that they love rock climbing and marathon running is not likely to be found shopping at the local Nike store. If possible, crosscheck self-proclaimed interests with actual purchasing patterns, vacation choices, memberships, interest in certain web sites and email with friends. If the spy has access to a target's home, covertly or overtly, they can look at the pictures on the wall, the condition of their interest specific gear and overall wardrobe selection. These profiling indicators, when taken as a whole, should paint a pretty good picture of the lifestyle of the target for the spy to analyze and adopt as part of their own approach.

Interests extend across all activities. Perhaps the target is not into sports but Swedish cinema; not ballroom dancing, but cocaine and strippers; not flower arraigning, but Persian history. People are strange creatures and the limitless variety of their individual tastes runs from the generally blasé to the absolute extreme of human ingenuity. Generally speaking, the more money and power an individual has the more exotic and potentially compromising their interests. A spy wishing to approach a target through their interests, should study the chosen subject of their source thoroughly and become adept at them.

Once the spy has identified a suitable interest set, then it is time to do yet more research. In order to place him or herself into a particular circle of people, a spy has to know the lingo, where the activities take place, key players, history, the rules and best practices and then become proficient enough to obtain valid entry into the circle. To approach a target via their interests, the covert operator needs to truly make it their own interest.

Most people, not just targets of corporate intelligence operations, do not appreciate a newbie trying to break into their social circle. After preparation through research and practice, comes the time for actual insertion. Find a family member or friend of the target and become their friend first. It is easy to suspect a newcomer who attaches themselves immediately to you, but few people suspect someone who is referred by a third party and friend.

Upon becoming a regular fixture of the group, the spy can insinuate themselves with the target individual with less risk of detection. Study the target, their behavior within the group and their interactions with others. If the subject wants a follower, then shower them with praise and stroke their ego. The kind of personality that requires the overt adulation of others is one with a weak ego and can often be turned with the promise of revenge against perceived slights by those above him in the company that "don't appreciate his true brilliance" or by a simple need for the approval of others regardless of source. For stronger personality types, an approach based on a wide set of mutual interests (well-researched before hand) will often yield better results because strong people are always on the lookout for kindred spirits who share a similar level of inner strength. In the end it is all about coming to know the target individual inside and out through deep research and interaction. An approach will present itself once the spy studies and knows the target well enough to win their trust and friendship.

Another tried and true avenue is to approach the target through their wife, husband or a significant other. People who harbor secrets tend to have a higher level of native defense than those who do not have as much to protect. Direct access can be complicated by suspicion, where introduction and access to an individual through another person will appear more natural and less suspicious to the target. Look at the target's social media friends list, their main email correspondence and their love interests for a pool of people to approach first. If the spy discovers that the wife's best friend has a profile up on match.com, then bite the bullet and start courting her. Maybe the target's best friend from college loves trout fishing. The spy can get tight with him and create an opportunity for everyone to go out together.

Searching for Weakness

When approaching the issue of extracting secret information from a company by developing a human source on the inside, the first thing to look for in a potential source is human weakness. There is an old saying, "No one breaks up a happy home"; that is, it is next to impossible to get a happily married individual to cheat on his or her spouse. The reality of happiness often precludes the possibility of betrayal. By its very nature, espionage is an act of betrayal. Spies look for unhappy target sources. A predicable indicator, this mental attitude accompanies the existence of exploitable weaknesses in character and actions on the part of the target.

Keep in mind, the nature of weakness varies with difference in cultural practice and norms and from individual to individual. The very definition and severity of any given infraction changes depending on the society and culture of the potential source. For example, a Chinese business man who goes to a whorehouse with colleagues after his business meeting, or a Silicon Valley tech who is in fact gay, but not yet out, are neither really defying their environment norms and are correspondingly less open to exploitation through these "transgressions". There are always rules within rules when it comes to accepted behavior within any society. Knowing these internal sets of norms will help immeasurably in defining what can be used to get close to a target or can be used as leverage to turn them by coercion, if necessary.

An interesting example of how using bad behavior to turn an asset can backfire on a spy occurred during the Cold War. A married US diplomat was the subject of a KGB run honey trap in Eastern Europe. They used a very attractive young Polish secretary at the embassy to lure him into an illicit affair. What they didn't realize was that he had an understanding with his wife on this very subject and that nearly everyone else at the Embassy was also engaged in this kind of activity which made it almost expected behavior within his social group. When the KGB confronted him in the swallow's flat after a tryst with photos and home video, his response was to ask them for prints of the better photos for his collection. After the extortion attempt by the KGB, the diplomat immediately informed the CIA station at the embassy. It was decided that he should be run as a double agent. The covert operation went brilliantly and gave the CIA insights into the sources and methods of the local KGB station for some time. It is the mark of an amateur to make assumptions in the intelligence game. A professional will look at all angles at play and make sure that any approach used has a maximum potential for success.

In US society, there are still actions which are generally held to unacceptable and reprehensible. Violation of a cultural norm or societal rules, can lead to an opening for the searching intelligence agent. Some of the most common are listed below.

- Extra marital affairs (particularly when there are children involved or religious strictures against such in the family; this is doubly true for homosexual liaisons)

- Sexually fetishistic activities, many of which are legal, but few are socially acceptable among certain classes of peers. This type of activity can usually be detected by monitoring the target's internet viewing habits and reviewing their purchases.
- Use of prostitutes. Sex is still considered a fairly taboo subject in America and few actions are more compromising than to have a sex tape or other photographic evidence of promiscuity around. Illicit sexual encounters are one of the easiest situations to artificially create to entrap an individual and have been proved highly effective against targets from more prudish cultures.
- Drug use, as socially acceptable as certain kinds of drugs and their casual recreational use are, drug use is still illegal. Drug use or addiction offers great potential for coercion. Abuse of narcotics is also a certain sign of malcontent in an individual and can be used as a positive indicator for recruitment potential.
- Compromising emails or other social media in which an individual bashes their company or coworkers. Such incriminating evidence is often readily available if the spy takes the simple step of hacking a target's email account.
- Illegal or criminal activity of any sort.

Nearly everyone engages in some kind of infraction against social norms or laws, so this type of activity can be a powerful piece of information to hold over a person. People take great care to hide their more embarrassing actions, but these defenses are generally geared toward preventing accidental or casual detection. Unless the target is extremely security conscious, a trained espionage agent will have little problem ferreting out many of the target's secrets and vulnerabilities in short order.

Trans National/Cross Cultural Operations

Another very important aspect of source recruitment is the simple ability of the spy to operate in a foreign cultural or social setting. Much of the espionage activity conducted in the US against American companies has been carried out by non-native agents of foreign governments and companies. This is a significant handicap which is overcome by foreign operatives in several ways. First, is the hiring of spies who have experience in foreign nations and are familiar with the culture and norms of the United States or other target countries. The second is training, whereby the agent becomes versed in the minutia of a culture and how to operate effectively in that society. This aspect often includes mentoring with other more seasoned agents and a great deal of in-country practice. The third means of overcoming this handicap, is to target foreign nationals working in a specific company. National identity and solidarity, not to mention coercion through family and friends left behind in the country of origin, is a very powerful motivating factor for many assets and is widely employed.

There is an old saying that every Jewish person living overseas is a sleeper agent of the Mossad, Israeli intelligence. As much of an overstatement as this obviously is, the sense of kinship and desire to defend ones homeland is very strong, particularly among ethnically and culturally monochromatic societies. There has been a rash of cases involving Chinese espionage efforts against American defense contractors carried out by native Chinese assets within these companies. This is by no means unique to Chinese intelligence efforts in the US. The same sense of ethnic solidarity is used by many other nations to turn employees in the US and abroad. One thing to remember too is that this same sense of national solidarity can be used on Americans working overseas as easily as it can on native Koreans in San Francisco.

Many allies and friends of the US take advantage of this patriotic mind set to shamelessly target companies in America. Rarely is real exception taken on the part of the United Stated government, as long as espionage actions do not cross the magic line of spying against government defense and intelligence agencies or key defense contractors. Germany, France and Japan, nations covered under the US military defense umbrella, rarely conduct such operations against the US defense structure but concentrate their main efforts on economic targets. Espionage action carried out by state agencies against American companies is rarely punished by authorities in the US, even if discovery is made, simply because it would cause a crimp in foreign relations with these allies if such activities were ever publically disclosed out of all proportion to meaningful gain. Loses to individual companies, regardless of the scale, are not seen as worth the potential for temporary embarrassment and friction in international relations.

Another avenue, taken to lessen the difficulty of operating in a foreign area for overseas companies, is the use of private American intelligence firms to conduct the espionage on behalf of an overseas company in the United States. Espionage agents on the ground, unless they are part of an in-house team, rarely know the name or nationality of the client who will ultimately receive the intelligence that they generate. The nature of the espionage game is deniability. Companies involved with covert intelligence gathering take endless precautions and use a series of cut-outs to insulate themselves from the front line agents. Using US state intelligence trained America agents to penetrate targets in the US on behalf of foreign companies is not a new practice. Native born and trained operatives are gaining popularity as more GWOT period agents are leaving the American intelligence world and as foreign companies experience the effectiveness that these operators can bring to their penetration efforts.

For an American operator working overseas, the story is a bit different. One of the major hurdles that the US intelligence world has faced over the years is that despite the rich ethnic tapestry in America, there has always existed a deeply held conviction that non-Caucasian intelligence agents were prone to being turned if used against nations of their own heritage. The persistent idea that Chinese-Americans were Chinese first and American second or having grown up in Iran, a person was more likely to feel guilt about spying on their former country than a Midwestern farm boy who had undergone 2 years of intensive Farsi training in Virginia continues to handicap American intelligence community effectiveness to this day. Steps are being taken to remedy this short-sighted and frankly racist approach to the recruitment of intelligence officers in the US but it takes time to build a pool of effective intelligence agents, especially with the shifting mosaic of US intelligence targets.

Police intelligence agencies are more effective in recruiting officers who have the necessary linguistic and cultural backgrounds to penetrate criminal organizations run on strict ethnic lines. Not being protected from scrutiny of their hiring practices under the moniker of national security, police organizations accept and use recruits of all backgrounds and nationalities in the US. Interestingly, police-trained agents are now a prime source for recruitment by private sector intelligence firms in the US and are often used to target overseas companies and non-US citizens.

Conducting intelligence gathering efforts against foreign targets on their home soil is, rather counter intuitively often much easier than targeting their branches in America. For a very long time, American companies were not engaged in any form of espionage activity against their foreign competitors. However, as production, research and development of key technologies and centers of gravity in the business world moved overseas and foreign companies begin to compete more effectively against US firms this has started to change. In sectors where espionage has the potential to play a decisive role, US companies are waking up to the realities of what foreign companies have long known, "espionage works". Because of a historic lack of intelligence action on the part of American companies against their foreign rivals overseas competitors are often caught unprepared to defend themselves against this new wave of penetration efforts by American companies. The recent corporate espionage activity on behalf of American firms has exposed a state of vulnerability in overseas companies who were not prepared to defend their interests against trained American operatives. Once the threat from American based private intelligence efforts is discovered, however, overseas companies will retool their defenses to meet this latest challenge. This hardening of defenses will happen very quickly as many foreign companies are already engaged in a covert war with their own domestic competitors and live in a world where defense against covert penetration is already of paramount business concern.

Target Recruitment Criteria

If identification of a potential intelligence source is about research, both initial and in depth, the final selection process for recruitment is done by narrowing the target pool of candidates down based on distinct criteria.

Access

The first and most important criterion in selecting a source is "does the person have access to the information that is sought or can they gain access through another person?" If the answer to this question is 'yes', then they are worth pursuing. If the answer to this primary question is 'no', then no matter how juicy or easy a target might be, it is best to leave them be. Soft targets may appear worth collecting, but in most espionage operations it is best only to recruit assets essential to the completion of the assigned tasking. If the operation is conducted to retrieve a specific piece of information the more complexity or more moving parts there are the higher the likelihood that the operation will be compromised and fail. If the goal is not just the extraction of single bits of information, but to gain access to a range of corporate operations over extended periods and in-depth, then a wider selection of sources are potentially more valuable. Even if weaker sources are not directly recruited for a specific task, they are well worth cataloging for possible future exploitation.

Access can be broken down to two basic categories: direct and indirect access. Direct access to targeted information or systems is the ideal for any source. The dictates of an operation necessitate the use of the most appropriate tool for that particular job. While direct access sources are sought out on principal it never hurts to remember that they are not always the only possible route into a company's secrets. The key is to be objective when looking at how to achieve the goals laid out for a particular operation.

Direct access means that the source has a legitimate reason to possess or obtain the information that the spy requires. There will be no suspicion aroused if the source requests target information or access to secure parts of the company's systems since this is a regular function of their role within the organization. Exceptions breed suspicion in any organization. For example, a low-level employee that deals with client services has no legitimate reason to access IT protocols or new product development designs. If they ask for something out of the scope of their work, unless internal security is lax enough that such requests are not monitored, such activity will likely raise significant suspicions.

If the source can be burned after a single use, then they can be used from any position to gain access to target information or systems. Be careful using such onetime sources since the probability for detection is much higher, could lead back to the spy, expose the operation and compromise the covert access vector once installed.

However, if the assignment calls for a simple snatch and grab, a spy can often save time and energy by recruiting and using anyone who can potentially snatch the data or access that is immediately required.

The main drawback to finding a direct access source is the relatively low number of people who are given unfettered access to certain kinds of information within an organization. The pool of potential targets is smaller, so the spy must select a viable candidate for recruitment from a more rarified group. People with direct access to information are generally the long-term employees within a company with a high level of trust to handle such sensitive information. This secure positioning and level of trust can make such potential targets more difficult to recruit.

Recruiting high level executives is made easier by appealing to their ego. There are few who reach senior positions within an organization by being meek natured. Even with a limited executive pool of targets, the very personality profile of those in leadership positions lends itself to more exotic vices and needs. Sometimes bored or egocentric top executives can be easier to recruit than more salt-of-the-earth employees who live pay check to pay check. Upper level executives tend to be mobile between companies and can be turned with the simple promise of a move to a higher position with a different company. Running a false flag operation posing as a recruiter from another firm is a ploy that has worked time and again against even the most hardened of senior executives to obtain information illicitly.

It is important to remember that not everyone with direct access to information has to be a senior researcher or company vice president. Consultants, executive assistants, IT personnel, designers, engineers, accountants, legal aides, temporary workers and many other categories of employees may have direct access to targeted information. In general, mid-level employees are easier to gain access to and to turn than higher level employees. Day-to-day workers are also cheaper to recruit, run, control and are more easily disposed of after an operation has been concluded because they have fewer resources and connections to fight back. Key to running an efficient extraction operation is to keep an open mind when searching for target individuals with direct access.

Indirect access to information is the other half of the primary target criteria. Indirect access means, that while it is not normally part of an employee's duties to access certain kinds of information, their doing so will not result in too much suspicion being raised. Types of employees with this kind of indirect access might include consultants, lawyers, IT personnel, assistants, printers, accountants, certain types of managers, researchers, repair and maintenance staff and many others. There is a great deal of crossover between people with indirect access and lower level employees with direct access. Be aware that people will claim and promise access, even if they do not have it, when they are pressured or offered money for cooperation. Always make sure the employee can actually deliver the level of access that they promise before activating and tasking them. Some untrained employee caught breaking into the president's office will not stand up to scrutiny and alerts the company to an active intelligence operation against them. Misjudgment or misuse of sources is a sure way to get caught or make the company harden their defenses to the point that it becomes too difficult to obtain the target intelligence.

Another aspect of access, direct or indirect, with sources is the potential to use an employee's access to an office or plant technical tools or to bring the intelligence agent physically past security to conduct onsite operations. Using an asset in this way, to gain actual physical penetration of a target firm, can open all kinds of doors for intelligence operators. An asset, if placed high enough or in the right section, can also "hire" a spy to come and work at the target company. This employment allows the spy to gain access to systems or information that they might require directly and in person. Placing a trained intelligence operative into such a situation can yield immediate access to secret information or secure systems. An operative working onsite is an extremely efficient means of completing a mission, but it does place the agent at the mercy of the internal security apparatus of a company.

Target Vulnerabilities/Needs

When considering a source for recruitment, the spy must carefully consider the vulnerabilities and needs of the target individual. Not all recruitment needs to be adversarial or based on coercion. In fact, the most effective recruitment is when the target believes the covert actions to be in their best interest and works for the spy of their own volition. Both exploiting vulnerabilities and feeding needs are means of turning and controlling intelligence sources.

State intelligence organizations teach that while every source turns for their own individual reasons, or combination of reasons, the genesis of betrayal can be covered under the acronym MICE. MICE stands for money, ideology, coercion and ego. These four factors cover the primary motivating forces that compel people to betray trust. Each asset uses their own amalgam of the above four motivating factors to justify their betrayal. Knowing which proportions of each of the four will appeal to an individual target is the key to turning them successfully.

MICE (Money-Ideology-Coercion-Ego)

Money

Money, or the desire for money, is the root of all evil, or so the good book tells us. Never has this been truer than in the present age of competitive consumption, endemic debt and status through material possessions. Money, or more typically the lack there of, is one of the main sources for betrayal in corporate intelligence as it is in state sponsored espionage. People feel that they need money to live, but also that money itself is the key to their self worth, happiness and the image and attractiveness that they project to others.

State run intelligence organs, particularly of the American flavor, consider money as the primary and most reliable means of recruiting and controlling intelligence assets. The logic goes that money, mercenary greed, is a more honest and less ethereal form of control. Greed is considered an easier motivation to understand and manipulate than the others. This has, in innumerable cases, been proven out, but the mindset that places money as the end all and be all in espionage can prove unsuitable as motivation for those that value other things beyond lucre or are awash in enough money that it would be pointless to use it as he prime lever of control.

In the corporate espionage world cash is king. Money is the most common reason that people turn on their employers and steal information for others. The amount necessary to buy an individual varies, but as a general rule, very few people will turn down cold hard cash in exchange for information, if there is enough of it on the table. Psychological attachment and loyalty to a company and coworkers rarely exceeds personal greed on the part of an employee. Sources dress up their mercenary actions with a wide variety of justifications, but in the end the lure of lucre is too powerful for most people to refuse. While the saying, "everyone has their price" is certainly not universally true it has proven to be the case in the vast majority of corporate espionage operations.

Ironically, this desire for compensation holds as true for top level executives as much as it does for lower level employees. The top tier people do not necessarily need the money that they are given for espionage actions, but rather tend to use it as a measure of their worth in the eyes of their handlers once they are turned. A psychological dependence and validation is very common between intelligence agents and their sources. By using money as a tangible reward for services rendered, it is quite easy to stroke the ego of, and thus control, a top level source within an organization.

For lower level employees, the lure of money is its ability to enhance their lifestyle. The easiest way to impress a potential low level source is to take them out and lavish them with attention, presents and money. People, particularly in the United States, are awed by the power of money. They literally worship what they perceive as the reality altering power of wealth. Since birth, people in America are bombarded by a continuous money/consumer centered message through advertising and media portrayals of the happy smiling rich. The fact that money is being used as a tool to exploit them and to compel illegal action is lost on most people since they tend to believe that they deserve the "free" money that is given to them. The siren appeal of cash should never be ignored when targeting corporate employees.

The majority of people in the corporate workforce do not feel that their employer pays them anything close to what their services are really worth. This is an extremely common sentiment in the corporate world and one that can be used as a lever to pry loyal employees away from their employer and gain willing cooperation. Appealing to the unfairness of an employee's position and pitiful remuneration for slaving away all day, proves to be a very powerful draw on mid and low level employees. Taking the money in trade for information or other services is not just a way to make extra income off the books, but is a subtle rebellion against a system that is keeping the employee down in their own mind. The use of money is not just a straight exchange for information and services, it serves as a psychological lever and has yielded extremely beneficial results among employees of all levels within an organization.

In many cases of corporate espionage, the small amounts paid for information that is worth hundreds of millions of dollars to the competitor, would make people gasp. People are cheap to buy. An average employee can be turned for a few thousand dollars. Higher level employees rarely rate more than a few hundred thousand dollars, no matter how many secrets they bleed. In exchange for these, relatively small, sums turned employees will hand over information worth millions of dollars in immediate and future revenue to their employers without batting an eye.

Walking up to an executive assistant at a major corporation who makes $50,000 dollars a year and works like a dog for an undeserving and dismissive boss and asking them to make extra copies of some of the evil tyrant's documents in exchange for $10,000 dollars is a quick and easy approach which works nearly every time. There was a case where an IT security specialist at a large corporation turned over the keys to the entire system in exchange for money to buy a limited edition Voltron Force action figure (total value $3,000 dollars). Cost to the company for this breach in security, unknown, as the only person searching for covert security penetrations was the one who received his doll in exchange for unfettered access.

For obvious reasons it is difficult to make companies understand that their best possible defense against corporate intelligence is to make their employees happy and pay them well. Companies will spend millions of dollars annually on computer security, not to mention untold sums on executive bonuses, but stiff the executive assistant pool on annual raises or their Christmas bonus. Corporate spies are aware of these acts and will use the lure of easy money and revenge to tempt disaffected employees. The sheer number of successes generated from this simple approach makes it the favorite for quick and easy recruitment in companies around the world.

The proven effectiveness of simple money payoffs makes it a powerful tool in the corporate intelligence arsenal. Where people would have serious qualms about betraying their country or their loved ones for mere money, employees view selling out an employer as little more than karmic retribution for corporate greed and an excellent way to supplement their own personal income. Corruption of this kind is not considered to be a crime, or at worst, a victimless crime in the eyes of most employees. For the above reasons money has becomes the most common inside source recruitment tool of the corporate spy.

Ideology

When people think of the term ideology in relation to espionage, they often will recall those dupes who spied for the Soviets because they blindly believed the utopian vision of world communism back in some ancient antiquity. In fact, ideology serves as a major force in the modern espionage world, if in different guises than the motivations of yesteryear. Ideology is one of the least trusted, but most powerful motivating forces available to the spy.

Ideology, as a motivational force, is most trusted by those whose systems are based on ideological purity. The Soviets during the Cold War, the Iranian secret services in this age and various terrorist organizations all look for ideological recruits because they fit perfectly into their own world view. Conversely, systems that value other more tangible motive forces tend to have a visceral distrust of ideological motives in potential assets. American intelligence, often against the will or desire of the source, insists on paying assets for the intelligence that they provide, for example. In the world of corporate intelligence, the various trust issues of national intelligence services do not really come into play.

Getting a source to spy on their company based on an idea depends on how it is presented to the person. Ethnic solidarity is a form of ideology that plays a huge role in corporate espionage activity, particularly among immigrant populations in the US. Appealing to a sense of redressing imbalances of power between the US and one's home country continues to be used all of the time by intelligence professionals. This happens particularly in research and development arms of a company, where employees betray secrets back to the home country or original employer for little or no remuneration. The Chinese employ national interests and ethnic solidarity as a coercion tactic with ethnically Chinese employees in America, mostly in the defense and scientific communities, all of the time. Other nations use this same tactic effectively to steal secrets from American industry and business for use at home. Corporate intelligence under the false flag of US national intelligence has been known to regularly motivate American workers within foreign companies to turn over secrets to the "CIA" and Uncle Sam.

Another ideological ploy, which has the power to make employees betray their companies, is when there is questionable or even criminal activity occurring within that company. Under a false flag as an investigative journalist, NGO activist or undercover government regulator, employees are easily induced to give a spy wide ranges of information about the affairs of a company if they believe they are doing the right thing and possibly helping poor innocent people. Appealing to a sense of righteousness and morality can be a very strong motive force and yields a stable source at almost any level within a target company. This form of ideological conversion has proven to be particularly effective against companies in the heavy industry and bio-medical fields.

Ideological conversion of a source, if handled correctly, can yield strong assets who volunteer to undertake nearly any kind of action on behalf of their handler. If a person believes strongly enough that they are doing the moral and right thing, they willingly go to the ends of the earth with a smile on their face for the spy.

Coercion

Since time immemorial, coercion has been used as a tactic for extracting information from a person. It is a psychologically traumatic action to take against another human being and can lead to deep instability of the source but, like torture, it continues to be used because it works.

Coercion, as a tactic for recruitment of intelligence sources, works well because people fear shame. People fear the opinions of their peers, disgrace, and the consequences of their past should such actions ever see the light of day. The average person has a mountain of little secrets that they do not want others to know. People do not lead blameless lives and even if they do, it is possible to create a situation which may be construed as compromising in order to force compliance.

In the modern American culture, the merest hint of scandal or appearance of impropriety is often enough to cost a person their job, family, reputation, wealth and all else that they hold dear. As banal as such personal scandals may be to a seasoned intelligence agent, threatening exposure of culture-based shame and little secret misdeeds can move ordinary people to do extraordinarily uncharacteristic things. With the myriad skeletons that even normal people have rattling around in their closets, it is not difficult for the trained intelligence agent to uncover secrets that the target individual would prefer stay hidden.

People hide personal and business secrets from others in their life all of the time. Unless they happen to live with a person who is highly intuitive or a trained investigator, defenses against discovery are usually only sufficient to deter casual detection by those within their immediate social circles. One of the reasons that private investigators often have an easy time uncovering infidelity is that people never think that anyone else is actually watching. An old saying goes that "paranoia is simply reality on a finer scale". A hyper-vigilant mind set is extremely taxing on the human psyche. Knowledge that people are out to discover one's secrets may sharpen a person's defenses and keep their secrets buried deep for a time but constant paranoia is not a state conducive to long-term mental health or one that is very easily sustainable. It is certainly not the common mindset of average citizens going about their daily lives working at a company in everyday America.

When put under the microscope of close investigation, covert or overt, there is almost always something that comes to light quickly which can be used to coerce a person into taking actions for a spy. Corporate espionage is an easier realm to use an exposure of secrets approach in, because it generally takes less coercion to make people betray their company than it would to betray their country or their family. If this coercion tactic is chosen, it usually leads to quick control over almost any target with only a minimum of research and digging necessary.

If the spy approaches an individual with evidence of some misdeed and asks them to spy in exchange for silence, there is the risk that they will collapse mentally or immediately betray the agent to the authorities hoping for a reprieve. People simply react differently to pressure and these psychological diversities are the greatest drawback to the use of coercion as a means of recruiting an intelligence source. Occasionally people meekly do whatever the blackmailer asks, with a minimum of fuss, while others prefer to fight their way clear no matter the cost. Initially source candidates try and come up with some means of removing the threat to their lives other than doing what the intelligence agent asks, regardless of how minor a task it might be. Forcing compliance in the face of such fearful resistance is the task of the intelligence agent.

Judging the response of someone to pressure before the spy makes their approach is crucial to successfully using the coercion tactic. Using leverage over another person is a dirty business, but can be extremely effective as long as the target can be made to behave. When the spy puts pressure on a potential source, it is advisable that they maintain passive or active surveillance to make certain the unsure new source is complying, on task and not mentally falling apart.

Among the worst things that can happen is when a source becomes mentally unstable under pressure from coercion. There have been extreme cases where an intelligence asset under coercion to produce information even attacked and killed their handler. A more likely outcome of disintegration under pressure is where the person becomes remorseful over their actions and confesses to their employer or to the authorities. The ease with which someone under coercion can be turned against their handler is another drawback to this approach.

When done properly, coercion can give the intelligence agent access to almost anyone at a company with little fuss, at low cost and quickly. Because the spy holds significant leverage in the mind of their source, the spy can set the parameters and duration of the relationship. The source can be run for as long as they are mentally stable enough to take the strain. In many cases of coercion, an asset begins to identify with the person blackmailing them more than the target of their intelligence gathering actions. This common form of Stockholm syndrome indigenous to intelligence activities can be leveraged, if cultivated correctly, into turning a coerced asset into a kind of ideological or egotistically motive one. The asset begins to see the blackmailer as their protector and the intelligence target as the enemy. This disturbingly common reaction is one to be fostered if the spy intends to utilize their coerced source over an extended period of time.

Coercion as a motivational force is generally used to obtain short term objectives. Quick penetrations lend themselves to the use of coercion for two reasons. First, most sources held under coercion will only be mentally stable enough to keep up appearances for a short duration of time. After disintegration begins, they are of little use, easily turned and may provide false or misleading information in order to punish the handler. Second, if a spy stumbles across enough information to coerce a direct access source, there is no need to cultivate a long-term source within a target entity. The use of quickly converted coercion assets helps cut out a great deal of the time and cost of running an agent using the other motivating factors.

When recruiting under a different motive factor such as money or ego, the spy needs to develop leverage to use on a source in the event they develop qualms about their betrayal or try to get out of a promised action. As back up to other more stable forms of motivation, discovering and holding onto compromising information about the source for potential coercing later is an elementary move.

An example of delayed coercion is the CIA practice of making sources sign a receipt for payment. Anyone with an ounce of sense would see the trap of having their fingerprints on a receipt that says "I receive money from the CIA". But almost invariably, after a while, sources get so accustomed to dealing with their handlers and addicted to the money that they sign. With such physical evidence in hand, the CIA owns them. Covertly videotaping meetings with a source is another classic trap set to develop leverage over an already operational source.

Coercion can be a very powerful motive factor, but also has distinct drawbacks attached to its use. If done correctly it can streamline the entire intelligence collection process and adds a certain layer of protection to the spy. Very few informants willingly go to the authorities after they have been blackmailed and the blackmailer has received what they wanted. The risk of source collapse is the main drawback to this form of recruitment, but can be mitigated if handled intelligently. Coercion or the potential for coercion adds control and leverage over the source and should be developed as a safety measure even if the source operates willingly.

Ego

Ego, as a motive force for spying, is the least easy to define of the four main springs. Yet, ego can yield the most pervasive and powerful control over a source for the spy. Using a person's ego as a tool for control can be very tricky and requires constant upkeep. Once fully engaged, a source becomes fervent in their actions on the spy's behalf and is willing to engage in whatever their handler suggests. One of the main drawbacks of controlling a source through their ego is the asset's tendency to take too many risks as they play the game that the spy sets up. The temptation to secretly beat their peers is always there and can lead a source to do too much too fast for operational security. If the spy can reign in an actively engaged source and keep them working within safe limits, ego can drive the asset to great lengths on the spy's behalf. A source's ego makes them see spying as something they are doing for themselves, not just for the agent. Since it becomes a game they play against people at their organization and against the world at large, they are more prone to stability and tend to take precautions, if properly controlled, to remain in the game longer.

Stroking someone's ego to get them on your side is something that people do every day with coworkers, friends and lovers. It is an act that everyone is familiar with and one that we fall into naturally. Using this ego building act to control and influence another person to conduct espionage may run contrary to common sentiment, but can be an extremely powerful psychological tool for a spy. As with sexual attraction, people do not want to believe that someone can possibly use flattery, appreciation and friendship to intentionally manipulate them. People want to believe that such core emotions and actions are sincere and are not something the can be faked for nefarious purposes. Despite all rational knowledge to the contrary, when a person works the ego of another the feelings elicited and control gained are rarely questioned.

Because the ego motivating factor is self-generated within the source, it can be fed over time and remain stable as long as the source can be reigned in from precipitous actions. This stability and self-starter mentality is what makes this motivating factor so powerful. The source themselves feels wronged, smarter, more capable, and better than those small people around them who conspired to keep them down.

With this kind of a mind set, it is a simple step from thinking that you have been wronged to doing something about it. The intelligence agent just has to provide an outlet for this feeling and stimulate the person with small gestures along the way. The source will create their own internal narrative and justifications for their actions. Revenge for perceived slights and misplaced feelings of superiority are the main wellsprings of an ego motivation.

Consistent ego cultivation and small gestures are generally all that is required of the intelligence agent to develop a psychological dependency from the source. Small gestures can include a wide range of acts. For good ideas a spy could visit the many dating advice sites on the web as the act of building love and building psychological dependence from an intelligence asset is eerily similar. Much like a romance, or in many espionage cases, a bromance, the littlest things get remembered. The smallest gesture counts for so much in the potential source's seething mind, that only small appreciative pats on the head are needed. Pay for all the meals, buy small gifts, and always remember birthdays and important anniversaries. For some reason, the first time they steal information for the spy is almost always a very important date in the mind of an ego driven corporate intelligence source. Simple gestures such as these put the spy on their way towards becoming the main source of approval in the life of their asset.

Another great way to stroke the ego of a source, especially a female source, is to listen to their small talk and proclaim value in the advice they give. This works for both genders, but particularly well on the fairer sex. The act of listening attentively to someone is often what the source was searching for in the first place and can easily make them psychologically dependant, loyal and willing to take extraordinary risks on the spy's behalf.

Everyone needs to feel important and valued by others. If a potential source has any idea of their self worth, particularly an overly inflated sense of that same self worth, then they yearn for an involved relationship like the one between asset and handler. If a potential source expresses feelings of being isolated, underappreciated or lonely, they are susceptible to this ego manipulating form of persuasion.

There is a flip side to all source recruiting and managing methods, and the ego is no exception. The positive aspects of the ego form of recruitment are that much of the persuasive work is already done in the sources own head, so there is little for the spy to actually do. Because the source is doing this seemingly of their own accord, they will be much more cautious and a better actor when on location at work. The down side of this kind of recruitment is the psychological dependence that develops on the part of the source. They tend to need constant upkeep and reassurance that the spy is happy with their work. They may exceed orders and gather too much in the belief this is what the handler will reward best, which can be potentially hazardous to the operation. If the spy can successfully mitigate the risk factors and deal compassionately and effectively with the source, then the ego is one of the most powerful internal levers of control that exists in the espionage world.

Mental Stability

Mental stability as a criterion for the selection of an effective intelligence source has been touched on previously, but simply cannot be overstated. Once recruited, the source's mental health is of the utmost importance to the operation. Mental stability is often the only difference between brilliant success and dismal failure. Failure to properly assess the stability of a source prior to recruitment is one of the key elements of disintegration in intelligence operations.

A potential source may need money badly, be happy to work for the "homeland", have identifiable vices, or possess a chip on their shoulder and a grudge against the boss, but conditions like this are also found in people with the least amount of self control and psychological stability. Lying, cheating and avarice may be natural facets of the human condition, but when directed by a third party towards a specific goal, these behaviors can lead to intense stress and a corresponding corrosion of mental stability.

When examining a potential pool of sources, there are some essential traits to look for to best determine their mental state prior to recruitment:

- Obvious signs of self destructive behavior, such as being a weekend warrior, abusing drugs or other vices, lack of emotional control and overreacting to simple stressors.
- A predilection for dependant relationships most visible in their mating habits; maintained long term friendships; spending an inordinate amount of time online in virtual worlds; and a history of dependence issues.
- Socially adequacy. Do they mix well with others, are they comfortable in normal social settings, do they have abnormal social hang-ups or habits, are their daily actions considered to be weird or suspicious to their coworkers?
- Serial promiscuity and addiction. Do they have trust issues, are they capable of developing normal social relationships, do they have deep seated inadequacy issues?

Examining key mental stability factors is a basic part of the initial analysis of every potential source. The traits are by no means disqualifying issues for an intelligence asset. In fact, the opposite is true. The intelligence agent is looking for people with weaknesses and issues which can be utilized to bend the source to their will. It is all a matter of degree. For instance, too much instability can manifest itself in resistance to the handler, potential defection to the authorities or other negative actions.

A competent spy is well versed in human psychology. Even with limited experience or second-hand knowledge of the subject, they are able to judge their potential source's mental stability and suitability to the task. One reason why covert operators are generally unable to maintain long-term relationships of their own is not just the secrecy of the job or the ability to apply their training and trade craft to cover the tracks of infidelity, but rather that they are trained to be good listeners and tend to habitually probe and manipulate the wills of others for their own advantage. This is not a very positive trait to take home to the wife and kids. When applied to the recruitment of a potential intelligence source these faculties must be on their highest settings to detect subtle mental issues before they can become a problem. Spies take their skills and secretive nature to amazing extremes, often more for personal aggrandizement than for any conceivable security rational, but when operational the skill of a spy marks the difference between success and prison.

Access to Other Sources and Critical Information

A further consideration in the selection of a potential intelligence source is their access to other more valuable sources. Under the rubric of development of access agents, a spy learns to use a direct access intelligence source to pump out information on others working in the organization. Used as part of the initial debrief once recruited, this increases a source's value many times over for the spy. People possess great quantities of information of use to an intelligence agent, without even realizing that it is worth something. Relationships within an office, layout and level of security in a building, merger or layoff rumors, and good old-fashioned cubicle gossip can be of extreme value to an intelligence agent, particularly in long-term or ongoing operations within a single company. Gathering this sort of inside dirt is an important part of any operation. Any unusual activity might indicate moves made by the opposition showing that an operation has been compromised. Picking up trace evidence and weaving it into an intelligible narrative is a key intelligence operator skill. As any veteran of the grey line will tell you, information, no matter how trivial to the source or secondary it may seem, is always of value.

Level of Protection

The final area to examine when searching a potential source pool is the different levels of protection offered to each candidate. This is generally more applicable to high security defense industry firms or jobs which require clearances where employees are routinely screened, polygraphed or otherwise protected. The level of internal security at a company is of critical importance to a spy, particularly if they are operating against a hardened corporate target. While the level of internal defense against espionage activities is nearly nonexistent in most companies, there are a limited number that do have selective protection measures in place. If an intelligence agent is assigned to penetrate such a firm, correctly judging the level of opposition and finding potential sources less likely to under high levels of scrutiny or protection is key.

For private intelligence operatives working against corporate, non-defense related targets, the chances of running into a seriously hardened company are extremely remote. Companies that provide effective counter intelligence protection are almost all deep into the US defense and intelligence fields, which mandate these higher levels of security. By no means is such security insurmountable, but it does require that extra care be taken in the selection of potential sources. Not only will counter intelligence programs be in place to monitor employees, but the personnel themselves often come out of the military or state intelligence apparatus and are versed in common espionage practices. Very few private sector firms operating outside of the orbit of the US defense industrial complex feel compelled to spend the money on adequate counter intelligence programs. Corporate security is severely lacking at many American firms, despite the fact that such programs easily pay for themselves by stopping loss to hostile corporate intelligence programs, often within months of commencement. Companies are generally unaware of the extent of the private and state sponsored corporate intelligence programs ranged against them. Lack of meaningful protection makes common corporate entities very soft targets. With low levels of internal security and staff training, the security check stage in the assessment process is often quite abbreviated for corporate spies. One of the first areas a corporate spy will look into when tasked to penetrate a new company is the state of their internal security apparatus. No spy should ever just assume that a target company is unprotected. Even if no counter intelligence programs seem to be in place one should always proceed with caution, companies do sometimes hide their true capabilities, and lack of basic preparation is a very uncool reason for getting caught.

Placing and Running Intelligence Agents in Theater

Once the research and potential source analysis phase of recruitment is completed, it is time to actually break the proverbial seal and move against a target. Let's examine what it takes to place an intelligence agent into the field and what they do while out in the cold. After all, not just fidgety assets get operations blown, but spies can also give away the game through lack of proper tradecraft and slipshod operational security. So how does a spy move into enemy territory and conduct intelligence operations under the noses of state and internal corporate opposition forces? What is it like operating in an unknown area against harsh deadlines and unwilling sources? What exactly does a spy do all day? It is certainly not all hot bikini-clad women, dry martinis and gun play Mr. Bond.

The Right Spy for the Mission

If one has access to a number of different potential intelligence agents to work on a specific project, as is increasingly the case with the flood of new talent into the corporate intelligence market, choosing the right person to carry out the mission is a matter of selecting the agent with the skills needed to best complete the job at hand. Companies and individuals who are new to the corporate intelligence game may have little choice as to who they hire, but with more candidates, you can narrow down the list of potential agents to those who possess the specific skills best suited to each mission. The following are some of the more important agent selection criteria to consider.

Experience

Espionage, like any other professional field, requires its practitioners to possess unique skills honed through practice. The more experience a field operative has, the more likely they are to complete a mission successfully and efficiently. Familiarity with the stresses and difficulties of operating in the shadows gives an agent confidence. Experience develops insights and resources to effectively deal with the unexpected which inevitably arises during the course of an intelligence assignment. There is no substitute for real life experience in the world of espionage.

Familiarity with the Operational Theater and Culture

Being familiar with the setting and culture is particularly important when conducting operations in foreign countries or in unique environments. Even the most experienced espionage agent will find it very difficult, if not impossible, to deal effectively with people that he or she cannot understand in a location to which they have never traveled. Cultural and linguistic knowledge of a target area can be crucial to the success of a mission. Knowing the layout and rhythms of a city are also very important for the efficient application of tradecraft. During the Cold War the KGB used to put teams of agents on every American diplomat at their embassy in Moscow. One of the clues they used to determine who was working for the CIA was to focus on embassy employees who took long walks or went jogging around the city regularly. They knew that the CIA trained its people to constantly better their knowledge of the areas in which they operated and one of the best ways to get in-depth knowledge of a city is to walk through it or run along its trails and streets. Knowing the ins and outs of a location and culture can help an agent remain inconspicuous when operating undercover and can be a vital ingredient for success. Knowledge of the local culture and language will allow the agent to interact effectively with the people, better detect the opposition, develop local sources and blend in with the local population.

While it is not always necessary to be a native of whatever area one is operating in, having the tools to deal with locals and a basic knowledge of the environs is a very valuable asset for any spy. As a rule of thumb an agent sent to work overseas should possess at least rudimentary language skills and do research of the intelligence site and on the ground recon to become familiar with the target location and culture before they start the collection process.

Knowledge of the Target Industry

A spy does not have to be a trained aerospace engineer to spy on Boeing, but a solid foundation in the particular target industry is a great advantage to the intelligence agent when working against a company. A keen understanding of the demographics of the people who populate the company and backgrounds and conditions of the work place will all help determine who is best to target for recruitment. A grasp of the professional terminology and unique mores of a target industry will smooth the approach to the target. Finally, foundational knowledge of the technology or specific type of information sought will help to prevent source fraud and gives the operative an idea of the scope and value of primary and collateral information that is obtained.

Professionalism of the Spy

Not all spies are created equal. Intelligence agents are just people selected for their predilections and capabilities who have been professionally trained to do a very specialized type of work. Intelligence operators have the same strengths and weaknesses that plague the rest of humanity. It is important when selecting a spy for a particular mission that the employer assesses that agent's level of professionalism and current mental state.

Corporate espionage agents are often recycled from their respective national intelligence agencies. This does not mean that they are the dregs or rejects of those same agencies, however, in many cases they may have left for cause. An agent can burn out, just like a source, from the continued stress or specific incidents of the job. Thus, it is very important that they be assessed and deemed ready to take on a new mission before they are sent back into the wilderness. While agent collapse in the field of corporate espionage is rare, carelessness and oversights can occur if the agent is not at the top of their game. The level of opposition faced by corporate spooks is, in almost all cases, far less than those of state agencies, but the stress of living under cover and conducting espionage activities can be tremendous and corrosive even against the softest of targets. A professional spy will maintain discipline and proper operational security wherever they are tasked to work. The level of an operative's professionalism can be judged by the manner in which they have carried out previous assignments and the state they are in to start the new assignment.

Matching the Spy to the Target Culture and Industry

Matching people and places can be especially important when you are running an operation against a limited target base or in a different country. Foreign cultures have norms radically different from those in the US. For example, running a female agent against a Saudi oil company or a Chinese arms manufacturer places them under the additional handicap of those nations' sexual bias and can limit their ability to manipulate sources and thus their effectiveness in the field. There was a case where a known homophobic agent was used to recruit a homosexual head of division in a major US company. The turned division head was more than ready to give up everything he had on that company's overseas operations, but was totally alienated by the agent's attitude and walked before the data was delivered. These examples are not to say that a female operative is not capable of breaching a Saudi oil company or a racist field agent can't effectively recruit a foreign national. However, since corporate espionage is a for-profit clandestine operation, it is always prudent to match the appropriate agent with the task to give them the best chance of success in their mission. Political correctness has no place in the dark world of for profit espionage.

Finding a Spy who is Available and Interested

The espionage industry is growing rapidly and intelligence agents who have good track records are in constant demand. Finding a suitable top end spy to take on the mission may mean postponing the start date until they are finished with their present task and will certainly require paying them adequately for their time. Since corporate espionage is, in its component parts, basically an illegal act, it is highly recommended that when hiring a spy, budget what is necessary to get the very best. Discretion and loyalty cannot be assumed in a world where everyone is trained to lie and manipulate others professionally. In the world of espionage, as in so many other areas of life, you really do get what you pay for. Do not expect a stable of highly skilled espionage agents to be available at your beck and call unless this is something your business is willing to pay to develop and maintain. Quality spies are rarely free from other commitments, but are worth the wait and expense.

Operating with Teams

Even the most hardened spy knows that operating with backup is preferable to flying solo. For security or vanity reasons, some espionage agents do prefer to work alone, but in the real world most never get that luxury. There are several valid reasons for using espionage teams instead of solo operators. The first is that few individuals possess all of the requisite skills to effectively complete complex corporate intelligence tasks alone. It takes as much time to develop the skills needed to identify, recruit and turn people efficiently as it does to learn how to breach computer security systems. Therefore, a team of people with varied skill sets is often necessary.

It can be a challenge to find an agent who can work well with others, manage a team or at times also be managed. It takes a rather complex and strong-willed personality to be a spy, so in many cases these personality types come into conflict when forced to work together over extended periods of time, especially if not carefully managed. It is vitally important that the person who assembles a covert team understands the nature of the individuals that make up the team and avoid placing people who have different temperaments or bad blood on the same project.

One item of note, under no circumstances should the hiring party come into direct contact with the intelligence operator who is out there committing illegal acts on their behalf. This precaution is for the safety of all parties involved. A junior executive at whatever corporation has a great deal to lose and will almost certainly flip on the spy the instant they are pressed by a police organization. For the hiring party, a spy who knows exactly who they are working for instantly gains leverage over that company. Spies can very easily use their skills to turn around and extort the firm even before the tasking is completed. It is always advisable that the parties remain anonymous and maintain a number of cut outs between themselves.

Moving to the Target Location

Once a task has been assigned and a spy chosen, it is time to move the intelligence operator into the field. This can be as simple as flying an individual to Seattle from California or as complex as mounting a long-term team effort in Beijing. Laying down the infrastructure for an operation is all relative to location and target.

If the operation is to be mounted in America, as most corporate espionage operations are, a team of people familiar with the country and able to speak the language helps. The same holds true for undertaking operations overseas. The team members should be capable of operating efficiently in the environment into which they are sent. If this is not the case, then the prospect of successful completion of the mission is greatly reduced. It is possible to use local facilitators to overcome some of these handicaps, but such assistance is hard to find and notoriously casual in their loyalty.

Once a target organization is selected and a location determined, moving the assets into place requires that they have some form of cover. A cover need be nothing more elaborate than a plausible reason for the individual being in a certain area. In the old Soviet Union, the Russians intentionally set up entire cities around specific strategic war industries to prevent penetration by Western intelligence. One could not very easily come up with a valid cover to go wandering around Tankograd. This was efficient from a counter intelligence perspective, but was horribly inefficient economically.

Some countries still operate with internal passports and high levels of suspicion against foreigners. In the US, where the vast majority of corporate intelligence gathering takes place, no such movement or access restrictions apply, so creating a cover generally requires about as much time as it takes to print out and laminate a decent fake ID.

In today's modern world, the issue of cover has become much simpler. Companies, in order to keep their employees happy, generally set up their facilities in larger towns and cities. America has no internal passport controls and people move freely about the country for any number of different perfectly valid reasons constantly. Cities can provide wonderfully effective camouflage for intelligence operations. While perhaps a bad thing for overall social cohesion, the sheer size of most cities and people's aversion to nosing around the affairs of their neighbors, is the ideal environment to operate as a spy.

Determining a feasible cover depends on the approach the spy intends to make on a specific target. If they are trying to befriend a high level executive, then operating undercover as a fry cook at MacDonald's is obviously not the best means of gaining access. Cover should be established in such a way that the spy is protected from casual detection and can pass off normally as what they purport to be.

A workable cover requires documentation and backstopping. Backstopping a cover means that you provide legitimate background so that in the event the cover is ever checked, it will not immediately register as false. This can be a complex process requiring significant resources, but has been made simpler thanks to the modern information based society. State and national agencies that control identity documents and other similar functions are notoriously easy to hack into.

Listed below are the basic elements of an effective cover identity. A quick note, a spy should never use their real identity operationally. A cover provides a fire break in the event of discovery. False identity barricades exist to make it more difficult to trace an agent if the authorities get onto the operation. Cover is a snake skin to be shed once the operation is completed so that any trail the authorities follow stops cold with the dead cover identity. These are all basic elements of the tradecraft that helps to keep a spy alive and out of prison.

Drivers License

By far the most common form of standard identity in America is a driver's license. The very commonality of this identity makes it one of the simplest forms to forge and to back stop. To acquire a valid government issued driver license in most states, requires only an older license and some proof of residency. An older license can be duplicated on a quality printer set up in minutes. Proof of residency, which is generally just a bill addressed to the person giving an address within that state, is also easy to replicate. Rarely are these artifacts checked and all can be back stopped effectively to prevent casual detection. Several states are much softer in their requirements than others and are used by a preponderance of espionage agents in the US because of it.

With a shiny new driver's license in their pocket, a spy can go out and pick up almost any other form of ID that they might need. A driver's license does not have to be obtained legitimately, it can be picked up by theft or purchase from someone who shares similar physical characteristics or from any decent forger. The vast majority of forgers in the US do not service common criminals; they by and large service the illegal immigrant population. The cost for a full set of false, but well-made and even backstopped in the state system, papers is remarkably low these days. The connections to a local forger can be obtained with time spent in front of a large hardware chain where day workers hang out, a bit of foot work and a few hundred dollars.

Passport

The guidelines for obtaining a valid US passport are more stringent than for a driver's license. If a passport is not called for during an operation, it is rarely worth the time and trouble of obtaining one. If, however, the spy intends to inhabit a cover identity for an extended period of time or is targeting an individual who travels a great deal, then it may prove necessary to include a passport in their suite of operational cover identity documents.

Passports are best obtained through the use of backstopped state identity papers. An expedited passport can be issued very quickly. Because of the sheer volume of passports issued out of a major center like LA or New York, unless the spy's other documents are obvious forgeries they can receive a valid US passport in as little as 48 hours. Theft or purchase of a passport is also a valid option.

Unless professionally backstopped, forged passports should only be used a limited number of times because border controls are some of the most wired and difficult areas to pass through these days. Thanks in large part to America's war on terror passport controls have become something of a hurdle to modern spies. By no means unbeatable, entering the US on a fake passport can be a nerve wracking experience. When spies have to cross a border on false papers they often will take a valium or other sedative to calm themselves, especially if they are new to the field. Border agents are trained to examine the individual more than the document itself. Anyone who shows excess signs of stress or uncertainty is liable to receive a much more through check. Dressing well and looking the border agent in the eyes while chatting them up are simple but effective means to ally suspicion. These men and women after all have to deal with literally thousands of people everyday none of who are criminals or terrorists. Engaging in small talk and taking flights that arrive during the very early morning or late at night, when the guards are more prone to fatigue, is another common method to make the border passage safer. A quick tip for making small talk with officials or others who the spy may wish to distract is to animatedly discuss very dry or uninteresting subjects. People are naturally averse to spending extended periods of time hearing about matters which do not interest them and will desire to have the person going on about such things out of their presence as quickly as possible. As an example when faced with a border crossing start smiling and recounting in detail with the guard all about the fascinating accounting work you were engaged in wherever you came from or how well your, select odd but orthodox religion, missionary work went. Being overly friendly but terrifically boring will get the spy past official scrutiny faster than almost anything else.

Passport controls will become ever harder to slip through in the future because of identity documents becoming wired and more extensive use of biometrics. All of these high tech defenses can be beaten, but it requires increasingly elaborate forgeries and such precautions as stick-on coverings for the fingertips and other exotic apparatus.

In most cases, if the spy is caught traveling under false documentation, they will simply get deported unless they are in the system under a warrant or on a federal watch list. Even then, communication can be very slow between federal authorities and border stations, especially the more remote border points. A spy caught at the border should pretend to be anything other than an espionage agent. The best bet is to go for the mundane, feign an accent and pretend to be just another immigrant trying to sneak in and breathe the sweet free air of America. Border agents are only human, so if you play to their expectations, they are not likely to look any deeper. The undocumented spy may be shuttled quickly on to a plane back to Eastern Europe or bus to Latin America, but at least they won't be in an FBI office.

If necessary covert border crossing is an option for the espionage agent. This is a last resort but one that is quite easy to affect if the need arises. Even with high tech defenses and billions of dollars spent each year the present border situation in America is a joke. Hundreds of thousands pass undetected through the southern US border every year. The cost of a coyote to bring the spy in from Mexico is low or they can simply tool up at REI and walk across themselves. The best bet for intelligence agents wanting to sneak into the US, though, is from the North through Canada. Canada has much more lax entry protocols and security than the US so sneaking in there is easier. Once in the great white north a short bit of hiking will bring you right across the border. Have a car waiting on the other side and one can move from country to country in hours completely clandestinely. One word of advice on clandestine border crossing, if the spy is going to walk across illegally do not bring anything which may implicate yourself in deeper criminal activity. Do not carry drugs, guns, exotic equipment or other goods which will cause the police or border agents to further investigate. If goods need to be smuggled into the US for an operation, hire a professional. The drug cartels and human traffickers both north and south in the US are extremely good at getting people and materials into the US undetected. They are expendable and easy to contact. Getting caught at the border with a sniper rifle or memory stick filled with cyber weapons is a great way to come to the attention of law enforcement.

Credit Cards

Credit is a marvelous universally available thing in America that allows the common man, or woman, to spend like a rock star at only 30% compound interest. Credit cards are also the most frequently stolen, easiest to fake or acquire through covert means piece of ID there is. Do not expect to get an American Express corporate card just by asking for it. However, with a decent cover document suite (state ID, social security card and fake birth certificate) a spy can apply for, and easily receive, a number of high interest rate cards delivered within days, right to their door. The idea is not to steal money with the cards, but to have a normal looking wallet, which in the US means at least 3-5 current credit and debit cards. Credit card companies maintain an army of investigators and collection agencies who are often better at tracking a thief through multiple identities than the FBI. The last thing a spy wants is to have a collection agent show up at their supposedly safe house during an operation over unpaid credit debt. Remember, pay your bills and never think of operational cash or credit as a license to shop.

The US is switching more and more to a cashless society which makes the possession and use of credit cards a must for the spy. Ever look at how many people in front of you at Starbucks pay for that 3 dollar latte with a card? In order to blend in, a spy should try their best to look and act just like everyone else. If the cover and back stop identity in use are weak, then rather than jump through the credit approval process and possibly get detected use prepaid credit cards, available at most drug stores and lower income area retailers. These look exactly like the real thing but are pre-loaded with a set limit and can be purchased with cash at the register. Pre-paid credit cards, burner phones and fake net nodes will be covered in greater detail later as part of modern tradecraft tools for operations in the US. These are vital tools used by spies and other nefarious types regularly because they allow the spy to remain off of the grid and therefore more operationally secure. Operational security is all about a layered defense.

Cell Phones

While the US has not come as far as a country like Japan, where you can use your cell phone to make credit card purchases, ride the train, transfer money between individuals and as a valid form of personal ID, cell phones are so common and useful, that to be without one would arose comment from others faster than almost anything else. Obtaining a cell phone can be done anywhere in the US and generally costs very little. In addition to their contract phone services requiring a certain degree of background and credit checking, every carrier provides prepaid options for almost all popular phone models. Pre-paid phone service will cost more, but is generally the more cautious choice. People cannot tell from the outside appearances whether a phone is prepaid. Picking up a high-end prepaid requires less background checking, gives the user a greater degree of security, and is easier to purchase without leaving a trail. Pre-paid cell phones can also be had for cash, so called burner phones. A further covert option for cell phones is to buy one from a grey market source. Such phones are generally only useful for a limit amount of time but are as completely secure and untraceable as such devices can be.

Having a high-end smart phone, like a latest version iphone, is a very useful status symbol recommended for most operations. Never use any feature of a phone to deal with operational information if that number is known to others or can be traced back. It is always a good idea to purchase multiple phones to use in different aspects of the operation. One phone should be used for contacting each individual source and kept strictly quarantined from other operational aspects. Use a different phone to contact the operational cutout or other team members. A separate back up phone is useful for emergencies or as a fall back. Finally, a personal burner phone should be employed for any other business that might come up.

Professional tradecraft demands that the spy keep various aspects of the operation separate. The easiest way to compromise an entire espionage ring is to use the same phone to manage all aspects of it. Phone records, call lists, texts, browser histories and GPS information are stored indefinitely by the provider and are easily accessible to the authorities. If the operation goes wrong, the last thing the spy wants is a trail leading back to them and their assets and real time GPS tracing through their phone for the police to follow. Operational phones need to be changed out at regular intervals in order to prevent information leak due to tapping, eavesdropping or cloning as well.

Pocket Litter

If an everyday civilian were to open up their purse or wallet, you would find a wealth of personal tidbits and random paper known as "pocket litter." According to standard police training, one sure sign that something is criminally suspicious or amiss is when a questioned individual has an empty or almost empty wallet. It just screams "I am different and probably up to no good".

During the preparation and insertion phase of an operation, it is always a good idea for the spy to spend some time generating a bit of pocket litter. Go ahead and open up your wallet right now and see what you have in there aside from that raft of credit cards and your driver's license. Chances are your pocket litter consists of old ATM receipts, pictures of your significant other and kids, supermarket member cards, an under-used gym membership, library card and maybe a coffee punch card or two. This is the kind of common stuff that everyone carries around with them for no good reason. Therefore, a prepared spy collects the same day-to-day evidence of normality as a basic part of their cover.

Pocket litter may be a useful adjunct to day to day operations but when a spy goes out to meet their assets they often travel sterile, without any form of compromising ID or pocket litter. When one goes operational, meeting an asset covertly or performing other illegal actions, carrying pocket litter or other forms of traceable ID can be very damaging if caught. It is easier to make up an excuse for not carrying anything than to give away little bits of potentially useful evidence that show the area where the spy lives, their bank and account information, the coffee shop they frequent, or their current address. If the spy is ever caught, obscuring the trail or record of movement between them and the operation can give their employer and team the time they need to sweep their connection and get away.

Suffice it to say, the goal is normality in day to day life and sterility during an operational period. Average Joe citizens carry certain kinds of documents, cards and pocket litter on their person, so in order to avoid suspicion and blend in when on location, an undercover spy will strive to fit that pattern. Do not carry multiple forms of ID in the same wallet but do place several different identities, especially the emergency ones, away separately just in case.

A workable cover is one that is easily assumed. Spies often use their real first name or a variation of the name, as a common trick to cut down on confusion. During an operation, the intelligence agent should have a primary identity that they use with their source and a secondary identity used to lay in infrastructure such as safe houses, phones and to make purchases. A third or back up identity is necessary in the event of emergency. In the event of discovery, each identity should be unique and separate, not just in names and dates of birth, but also in physical appearance and reflected personality. This makes tracking much more difficult for authorities.

Another important cover point to remember: Never do anything which is illegal, unless it is absolutely necessary to the mission. More than a few intelligence agents were caught because they went out during a deep cover mission and banged some prostitute or bought drugs for personal use from an undercover narcotics officer. All of sudden they are in police custody. A thin cover or inherent nervousness alerts the authorities that these people are not who they would appear to be and the questions mount. Occasionally, it is necessary for the mission to engage in illegal activity with or for the target source. Some of the most favored lures and rewards of assets are drugs, girls and other illicit goods/services. Under no circumstances should such actions be taken for personal reasons while operational. There will be plenty of time to indulge once the mission is complete.

The keys to an effective cover are usability, anonymity and effectiveness tailored to the mission needs. When operational, it is critical that the agent live within the cover. Breaking cover and arousing suspicion is an easy, and not very cool, way to get exposed and caught.

Safe Houses

The spy's living space is where they are most vulnerable because that is where they spend most of their time and where they sleep, when they sleep. Establishment of a series of safe houses, that are actually safe, is an essential part of any operation. The duration of an operation and the manner in which it is carried out will dictate the best type of safe house arrangement for each mission.

On short term assignments, where the spy will not have to entertain or deceive a source, a discrete hotel or short-term rental may be the best option. For in-and-out missions or when operating in another country, there may be no options other than a hotel or rented room. The first places that counter intelligence forces and police look for spies, or other criminals, is in hotels and motels. There are many options available to a creative spy wishing to remain anonymous in a city for a short period of time and each should be considered when starting an operation to find the best.

Internet Home Share and Vacation Rentals

This is a new phenomenon and one that has proven to be extremely useful for the short term spy. In hotels and other common travel lodgings, one is required to present some form of ID, a credit card or other traceable form of payment. Cash in this day and age has become increasingly suspicious. The usual hotels and motels are also linked to the police as a common first step in their search procedures. However, a large number of legitimate online resources exist for house sharing and short-term vacation flat subletting that are not on any list. Short-term rental owners will not blink at cash, require no ID and are virtually untraceable. This alternate housing market is an excellent option that requires little searching and a wide variety of cover homes. A suitable and even nice spot can generally be found online in minutes. Since this housing arena is a relatively new mode of safe house operation, many counter intelligence and most police forces remain ignorant of their existence and possess no means of effectively checking them. Additionally, if the person whose home or flat the spy is letting is out of town on vacation, the chances of them seeing information about any investigation involving the spy becomes correspondingly remote. A further benefit to this kind of arrangement is the ability to use the address, telephone, and internet connection of the absent owner to conduct an operation under an additional layer of security and anonymity.

Squatting

This does have certain risks attached to it, namely the owner returning from a trip to find a spy camped out in their house. But if the spy needs a quick totally untraceable nest for a very short period of time, the squatting option can be the perfect fit. This safe house option is most effective in anonymous cookie-cutter neighborhoods or large apartment complexes where neighbors work during the day and are less likely to know or care about each other. A more desperate measure used to obtain a very short-term home is to either kidnap or kill the occupant and take over their house or flat for the needed duration. Of course, in either case the extreme crime committed to get a place to stay far exceeds the crime of espionage (but not some of the other potential functions of the intelligence agent which will be discussed later) and should only be used in the most extreme of circumstances.

Staying with Friends or Connections

Staying with friends or connections is an option, especially if the friend is in the same line of work or they can be trusted. If only in town for a short span or the spy can keep the owner in the dark about their activities, this has all of the benefits of anonymity that a spy could wish for. The obvious drawback is that the friend may require significant recompense for allowing the operational use of their home if they know what is going on or they may inform on the agent during the operation if they do not. Another potential drawback is that if the identity of the spy is discovered, like any other criminal, one of the first places that the opposition will look is the obvious such as the flat of a former girlfriend, college roommate or ex-wife that just happen to be in the same city.

Camping, Staying in a Recreational Vehicle or Houseboat

Counter espionage agents and cops watch the same spy movies that everyone else does and tend to neglect potential locations that are out of character for a spy. Operating outside of character is an excellent way to stay off of opposition radar. Staying in a low-rent neighborhood, the countryside or mobile lodgings breaks profile and is easily overlooked during an initial search. This makes such rural or transient locations a viable option for the short-term spy. Staying in a cabin in the woods, a recreational vehicle or even in a tent in the forest (depending on outdoor skill and the climate) is hard to beat when it comes to staying off of the grid. The drawbacks are lack of infrastructure, although many camp grounds these days do have cell reception and free wifi, and the need for specialized equipment. Staying in a recreational vehicle or house boat, on the other hand, gives the spy a roof, kitchen, shower, full access to telephone and internet services and mobility in the event of discovery. The camouflage potential of acting out of character for a spy should not be overstated here.

Long Term Operations

For longer term operations, the creation of safe houses is a more complex and costly process than it is for shorter term ops. Corresponding risk factors are greater in long term operations if proper cover is not maintained. A long-term safe house needs to have several things going for it. The location needs to be unconnected to the operational identity being used by the spy and it needs to be secure and functional. If a spy uses a safe house to recruit and run an asset, that house should be furnished and have a lived in look. Magazines in the bathroom, clothes in the closet, knickknacks around the house, paintings or pictures on the walls to complete the illusion. For other operational uses, a long-term safe house should be located in an area that is not subject to massive police presence, is not likely to be broken into by common criminals and provides functionality and conforms as well to cover. There are many different options for a spy or a team to live in during a long-term operation.

Buying or Leasing a Home or Condo

Nothing is more normal than a person moving to a new city, particularly someone of a certain economic class, and leasing or buying a home, condo, apartment or flat. The advantages include instant acceptance within nearly any neighborhood and a solid veneer of normalcy. This holds true in multi-ethnic America, but is not the case in most overseas locations, save those areas specifically set aside for expatriate foreign residents. Purchasing a residence is a remarkable event for anyone from another country and can instantly put them on the radar of local officialdom. This may be the only viable option if the spy has to move into a suburban neighborhood or other specific location to conduct the operation. If the spy needs the space of a farm or the respectability of the right address in the right neighborhood, buying versus renting may be the best cover option.

The cost difference between buying and renting is lower than one might think. The process can be extended over a significant period of time, since buying a home rarely requires more than a down payment and access to legitimate credit. The down sides are the implied permanence of residence and the need to interact with other residents on a more personal basis. This increases the potential for nosy neighbors cluing onto what activities are taking place. Having to juggle operational work and dealing with neighbors who expect certain patterns of social behavior can be tricky.

Renting/Leasing

The most common way to acquire a safe house is to rent it. Operating within a city offers a wide selection of properties available. The spy can pick up a place with little fuss in exactly the right location as needed. An efficient way to rent a property or several properties is to use a dummy corporation to sign the lease. Setting up a front company is easy. Dumping some money in a dummy account from offshore leaves little paper trail and provides a fire break from operational identities. It is common procedure for a company to rent apartments for extended periods of time for employees, particularly overseas. Using a company leased residence while working longer term assignments, rarely causes notice. Renting through a front company can eliminate the need to meet the leasing agent or realtor, because transactions of this kind are often handled over the phone and online. Rental agents will even overnight ship keys and alarm codes to the spy before they arrive. Setting up utilities can also be done in advance by the agent or remotely over the phone or internet. This extra degree of anonymity makes renting an apartment, flat or even a home that much safer for the spy.

Apartments or flats can be used as a primary safe house/residence for the spy while in theater or can be used as fronts for operational purposes. Holding multiple apartments under different identities is a very common maneuver employed to increase operational security.

Loft Space and Warehouses

Recent trends in urban housing include renting and renovation of old loft and warehouse space. While not universally available, renting large industrial-type spaces does not raise eyebrows anymore and can be accomplished through the same processes as renting an apartment or home. More working space proves ideal if a spy requires a secure location to house props, cars or other large equipment for an operation. The added bonus is few or no neighbors and scant area security to interfere with or record a spy's comings and goings. Renting loft or warehouse space is a good option for teams and operations that requires extra privacy or additional room for materials.

Another solution if secure storage space is required is the acquisition of a commercial storage shed or locker. In America, it is common to stash possessions away in metal storage units, instead of getting rid of them. Storage unit locations can be extremely useful for warehousing materials that might compromise an agent or are too large or out of place to keep at their home. Renting requires a bit of cash up front and a photo ID; obviously use a cover ID. If feasible, renting a unit in a smaller town near the target city provides additional operational security.

For teams involved in a long-term operation, it may be advisable for each member to rent their own individual residence. Separate lodgings decrease the risk of personal friction developing between team members and can serve to isolate various aspects of an operation in different physical locations. If the team is kept in a single location, arrange the cover so it does not raise suspicions among the neighbors or the authorities. If the team is young enough, good cover for a communal housing arraignment is living near a college campus where shared houses among undergrads or grad students are common. Another option is to tell the neighbors that the members of the team are all part of a missionary religious group which will almost certainly keep everyone at bay.

When operating overseas, housing options may be constrained by local norms and government policy. It is possible to rent or buy property in most nations, particularly if the spy uses local assets or front company cutouts. However, unless the intelligence agent can pass for a native any housing option they choose outside of the norm will be remarked on and may draw the attention of the authorities. For an operational house to remain safe, it needs to go unnoticed. This can be difficult if the team is the only six man group of white people in Calcutta living in their own warehouse or is an African American agent trying to live on a house boat on a jetty in Shanghai. Being unremarkable and blending in are the keys to effective undercover work and the foundation of tradecraft. Finding the proper location for a spy to live unnoticed is vitally important in determining the best way to maintain this most important aspect of cover.

Clandestine Operational Materials

Once the spy has sorted out their living arraignments, it is time to gather the necessary tools needed to conduct the mission. Extremely advanced spy gear, as well as high powered weaponry, is readily available in the United States, with little or no identity checking at the point of purchase. Like buying high-powered assault weapons to hunt, the American attitude towards advanced surveillance, computer and other specialized gear is extremely open. When operating in other countries, it may be necessary to import some questionable gear. However, since business mail is rarely checked and most espionage operations require little in the way of overtly identifiable gear, it is common for the materials simply to be FedEx-ed to a cutout in country.

In the past, a spy required easily identifiable espionage tools to get the job done, which made the occupation of spying open to discovery. Prior operations utilizing then-advanced equipment such as compact radio transmission gear and microfilm cameras which stood out making detection by customs and internal security forces that much easier. Items such as burst radio transmitters, microdot readers, onetime pads, special inks and cameras had no other daily or business use other than in the realm of espionage. In modern intelligence operations, however, such readily identifiable spy-specific equipment is more or less a thing of the past.

Unfortunately for gear heads, average corporate espionage operations require nothing more advanced than a decent laptop and a cheap flash drive from Best Buy. Certain types of operations do call for highly specialized gear, but virtually anything that a spy might need is almost always commonly available for purchase either online or at the local spy shop.

Mission-specific equipment for spies fall into the realm of surveillance, counter surveillance, tracking, infiltration tools, bugs and advanced computer equipment. If the mission calls for a bent technical to operate advanced communications intercept gear or other technical devices they will often require some extremely specialized kit. Hackers are the worst bunch, prone to whine if they do not have the most bleeding edge equipment, often personalized or homemade, which may not be available on site. If possible physically locate any hacker elements in an off-site area that they are familiar with so their acquisition of advanced computer hardware will go unnoticed.

For other mission specific tools, direct purchase in country, offsite purchase or fabrication and transport are generally easily accomplished. Keep any materials or gear which can compromise an agent's cover off site and away from where they live. If such gear is located in a separate area, choose such locations specifically for ease of counter surveillance. If a room filled with high-tech surveillance gear or other questionable materials is uncovered by the authorities, they will first put eyes on it to see who comes to use it. If the spy has chosen the location correctly, they can spot surveillance before they reenter a compromised holding location. A highly effective precaution to take with all safe locations is to install covert motion sensitive net-connected video surveillance units inside. With such units in place, a spy is notified via their phone if someone enters a safe location and can monitor the interior of their hideouts via the web at any time. Video surveillance significantly reduces the risk of ambush or covert police penetration of a safe location.

Rarely will a corporate espionage mission call for materials which cannot be obtained locally, cannot be purchased or fabricated elsewhere and shipped to the target area or would be easily identifiable as espionage equipment. Direct non intelligence gathering actions can call for such kinds of gear, particularly weapons and explosives, but if this is the case the operation is likely to be very different overall from an intelligence gathering mission and thus different parameters apply. In such cases, it may be necessary to use less than legal means of bringing in the required materials, which means smuggling. The means and methodology of smuggling covert or proscribed materials are as varied and arcane as the art of espionage itself. Smuggling regularly takes place into virtually every country, particularly into the USA thanks to the booming drug and illegal labor market. Smuggling in covert materials is less difficult and costly than many believe thanks again to the nature and extent of the unsecured borders and massive black market in America.

Additional items required during an operation fall into much more mundane categories than laser microphones and GPS tracking units. These operational necessities may include cars, clothes, luxury presents for the asset, phones, computers, prepaid credit and calling cards, special foods and a myriad of things that people use every day.

Cars can be leased, but to break a potential trail in the US, it is best to purchase an automobile from an individual out-of-state seller (think Craigslist) and drive it to the target location. States, for the most part, do not share registration records and personal sellers are not bound by the same degree of reporting duties as car dealerships. Individual transactions add another layer of security for the spy and can even be conducted in cash. Another means of acquiring a car is to steal it. The theft of modern automobiles is more demanding and technically intensive than in the past, but is still a relatively easy task. Theft statistics around the nation reveal that with a bit of training and the right tools, all legal or easily acquired, anyone can procure a vehicle. The down side is that a spy might get picked up for the crime of car theft, when they could just as easily have bought a workable car for cash one state over and driven it back in an afternoon. Motorcycles are wonderful tools in the espionage trade. Not only are they easier to operate in a city, more difficult to plant a tracer or explosive charge on, but they provide a faster and more flexible getaway in the event of trouble. Motorcycles are commonly sold online by individuals for cash, making them a safer bet than cars as the amounts are lower and reporting requirements are even less strict than for cars. Finally, a motorcycle is easier to steal and hideaway than a car when not in use.

The most common equipment used in an espionage operation is just that, common. Like a normal citizen, a spy buys clothes at the mall, food at the supermarket, and luxury goods at stores located downtown. For electronics and phones, there are huge super stores with part time stoned out employees who couldn't remember a particular face to save their lives. If there is a security concern or the agent simply wants to add yet another layer of tradecraft to their purchasing pattern, using a third party to buy things for them is as easy as going to a large box store and picking up a migrant helper for a few dollars. Using others to make purchases provides the unique advantages of not appearing on any store surveillance tapes. Hired help can pick up almost anything, including illicit substances or materials with little or no direct risk to the spy. There is no penalty if the sub asset is caught out as they have no connection to the spy and are singularly disposable. Another advantage of this step is that using a third party purchaser, undocumented labor, means that the individual is more likely to be unwilling to talk to authorities and capable of disappearing back into a marginal group quickly and totally. At most stores, even for larger purchases, if the cash is in hand, they do not care to question the customer.

Money

The most crucial element of an espionage operation is not some exotic piece of equipment or even mundane day-to-day goods, but quite simply money. How an operation is funded varies greatly based on the nature of the act, the natural preferences and experience of the operator and on the orders and abilities of the funding party. Moving money from one place to another can be a simple task. By licit means, trillions of dollars are moved around the globe legally every day, and then there are illicit means, by which billions are moved everyday as well. For a covert operation, the ways to move money from the funding party to the actual operator conducting the task are limited only by the human imagination. An interesting example of unusual methods of transfer was the use of carrier pigeons to move fake bills from North Africa into Italy. Time consuming and fantastically low tech, but none the less a clever operational solution which went undetected for years.

The most common means of funding an operation is to move money from the source through a series of off shore cut outs and front companies until it is virtually untraceable and then into a local bank account opened under a cover ID. The agent in the field is rarely given direct access to the offshore black fund which holds the allotted amount for the operation. Such precautions exist for operational security as well as simple trust reasons. The client will deposit and move the money part of the way and the intelligence firm then transfers the money to a black holding account located overseas and from there onto their agents in the field. Funds are cycled to the agent as needed. This gauntlet keeps an agent honest and allows the managing intelligence firm a degree of control and oversight of the operation. Operational funds are moved from the black holding account to a local bank, generally via a series of semi-legitimate cut outs, and from there the agent withdraws funds from any ATM or convenient bank location.

Funding can also be provided in the form of portable, easily exchangeable and untraceable commodities such as diamonds, drugs or precious metals. Once obtained through legal or not so legal channels, the agent moves these valuable commodities into the area of operation and converts them into cash. Valuables turned into cash are a more discreet method than a paper trail generating series of wire transfers. Straight up cash can be delivered to a cutout to hand it over or place it in a dead drop for the field agent to retrieve. The down side is the extra effort required by the agent in the field to convert such commodities as well as the need to access the black or grey markets to make the exchange of goods for cash.

Even more exotic means have been employed to fund covert operations. Examples of unusual methods of transferring money include using the agent as a middle man in a normal transaction between secondary companies or hiring them as a "consultant" for a front company. Fake lotteries, prizes, bonuses and give-aways from the sponsoring corporation have been used as devices for delivering funding covertly. Overbidding on EBay items and payment for bogus web design, security contracts and fake inheritances are additional secretive methods to fund covert operations which have all seen use in the past. The Chinese and Arab communities have their own systems of underground banking which utilizes family connections to move vast sums across borders entirely without a paper trail. Human, drug and arms smugglers can also be used to move sums of untraceable cash from one location to another via their own covert systems.

Self Defense

Keeping in shape, running and walking about a target locale are very common pastimes for a spy. Physical fitness helps the spy stay on top of their game and provides an outlet for stress relief. Walking and running are advantageous means of maintaining physical fitness and scouting out a city from the streets. Driving all of the time from place to place does not give the spy a solid grasp of the terrain. To get a feel for the layout of an area, the people who inhabit it and the patterns and flows of its daily life, one must experience a location by foot.

Thanks in large part to Hollywood's portrayal of spies, a common misperception is that all intelligence operators posses super human ninja skills, run about with guns shooting people and kicking in doors. For a spy the judicious use of physical violence, or as is much more common the perception of capability of violence, can serve a useful purpose. However, unless the mission specifically calls for violence, intimidation, kidnapping, assassination or terror, spies rarely resort to physical violence or crime during the course of their operations. The hiring party is better off going with a team of former Special Forces guys if such direct measures are called for. While many national spy agencies do train their spies in at least the rudiments of self defense and a number come out of the military in most cases if there is a call for violence the spy has seriously botched their mission. The key to effective espionage action is stealth. Covert operations work because they are clandestine by nature and are not supposed to ever draw attention to the operator. In very few cases is corporate espionage ever the normal focus of counter intelligence or law enforcement agencies. Violence acts as a powerful magnet for attention no matter how discreetly conducted. The fastest way to bring authorities to an operation is to do anything outside of strictly espionage related activity which is illegal. Authorities will always look into violence, especially against high profile or wealthy individuals. In other words, a covert operator seeking to penetrate a company who carries a gun, gets in fights or kills people is likely to quickly get cops involved and nothing gets the attention of the press and thus the security services like a body count. If the spy is forced to hurt anyone, especially members of the security forces, the risks of discovery increase exponentially.

Intelligence agents do prize self-defense training for the physical conditioning and confidence building that it provides to the practitioner. Rare or occasional utility of martial arts, combat skills or self-defense knowledge occurs only in the most extreme circumstances during an espionage assignment. A spy's best form of defense is a well developed cover. Being invisible and operating undetected are the keys to success in covert intelligence. No spy should try to match the resources or violence of the security forces or criminal elements in their area of operation. Spies go to great lengths to avoid fights or resort to violence of any kind. Once a spy has lost the protection of cover, there is often little choice but to abort the mission and flee.

On a side note, fitness is a component to physical attractiveness which, like for James Bond, acts as a force multiplier for a clandestine operative. It was once a commonly held assumption that the more ordinary and mundane the appearance of a spy, the more effective they would be in the field. While many people in the world of covert operations still hold to this belief, a growing body of evidence suggests otherwise. The more physically attractive an individual man or woman is the more they may stand out in a crowd. However, such positive features act as a powerful psychological tool of control when dealing with sources during and after recruitment. People are more likely to get along with and fall more easily under the sway of a physically beautiful person. This is as true in clandestine intelligence as it is in any other field of human activity. For corporate espionage agents who specialize in developing human sources, a high level of physical attractiveness, aided by a fit body, can prove to be a powerful tool in their arsenal.

Counter surveillance

As an operational spy one of the keys to not getting caught is to know when you are under surveillance. Security services in the democratic first world require some form of proof of wrong doing, generally, before they tromp up to your door in the middle of the night. By far the most common means of acquiring that proof is to place the suspected spy under surveillance. By watching what the spy does every day the opposition hopes to catch them out doing something illegal and then to implicate others. Spies are purpose trained to detect, evade and counter attack surveillance operations staged against them. It is this ability which highlights the difference and advantage of using a trained spy versus a common criminal to conduct intelligence operations.

Detecting surveillance depends on two main factors. The primary factor is the level of competence and resources of the opposition conducting the surveillance. The second factor is the preparation of the spy and their capacity to conduct counter surveillance. If a state counter intelligence organization throws significant resources at a spy the likelihood is that they are done for. It is just too difficult to detect massive and skilled surveillance conducted by professional state organs. Most state counter intelligence groups keep teams of highly skilled people, of many different body types, ages and backgrounds to track spies. Luckily for corporate spies these teams of state sponsored watchers are almost never assigned to work against corporate espionage cases. If anyone places a suspected spy under surveillance it is most likely internal corporate counter intelligence (limited resources and predictable) or the local police (again limited resources, and poorly trained). This places many advantages in the hands of a corporate spook. They are highly trained to detect and evade hostile surveillance, particularly when it is conducted by amateur hour local police or ham fisted corporate security personnel. Police may know the local area better than any spy and the internal corporate security forces may be former FBI but it all comes down to resources. They will not be able to muster the dozens of trained watchers needed to really pin down an operational corporate spy with any reasonable expectation of success.

This brings us to preparation. If a spy skimps on the tradecraft or has very poor operational security in place then it is entirely possible that even the most amateur surveillance operation can catch them out. A prepared spy, however, is virtually immune to low resource surveillance. Police are simply not trained nor have experience dealing with criminals (or spies) who are massively security conscious and invest in counter surveillance. Prepared spies place passive electronic/video surveillance tools all around and inside of their safe houses and common areas of operation. They remember faces and cars and will ping if they show up repeatedly. Trained spies conduct surveillance detection runs (SDRs) as a matter of course, not just when operational. They move against traffic, take blind alley and one way streets to flush followers. They use shopping centers and deserted areas to bottle neck and slip surveillance. They check their transportation for surveillance and tracking devices. They change phones and disable the internal GPS tracking functions before meeting sources. They set up meets and exchanges with assets in areas where they can control entry or watch for surveillance. They have help from others (either other spies or guy/girl Fridays they hire locally) to help spot surveillance. They operate drones to provide aerial counter surveillance in urban areas. They take buses and trains, mopeds and bicycles. Anything, to ensure that they are free from surveillance before they engage in clandestine activity. All of these things give the corporate spy a huge advantage when operating against even provoked and numerous opposition forces.

One further aspect of counter surveillance which spies use regularly is a preemptive approach to dealing with security forces. They have been known to bug police stations, bribe officers and internal security personnel, hack into opposition computer systems and many other covert acts all to detect investigation of their activities before they even get close. Most internal corporate security forces and certainly police have never been exposed to this kind of counter attack from their query. They are simply unprepared to confront a trained intelligence agent who is willing and capable of taking them on directly, if covertly. How often do you think local police stations in California are swept for listening devices? When was the last time your company checked personal financial records to see if any of its security staff was being bribed? Raise your hand if you honestly think that the SEC computers and email accounts of its top investigators have never ever been hacked. For corporate espionage agents, particularly ones on long term penetration projects, these steps are elementary. An interesting fact is that today there is a growing market for private intelligence operators to work directly for criminal groups in the US and abroad whose sole task is to conduct just this kind of counter surveillance operation on law enforcement. The skilled operators who make up the covert private intelligence industry pose a massive threat, not just to companies, but to law enforcement groups trying to penetrate transnational criminal enterprises as well. And yet countermeasures and positive enforcement by police and other security forces remains minimal to nonexistent throughout the United States.

Living Under Cover

Once an agent is in place, covert infrastructure established, safe houses and equipment acquired, the intelligence officer is ready to begin the assignment. If that assignment is the recruitment of a human intelligence source within a company, the process can be a long one. Not just the initial recruitment, but the running of an agent in place can span years. An intelligence agent in place living under deep cover for a very long time can experience sever stress and disassociation with reality.

Everyone lies to different degrees daily. People constantly tell lies to their coworkers, friends, family, loved ones and even priests. These prevarications are usually little lies about things of no real consequence should the truth ever come out. "Sure I went to the gym yesterday", "Yes, I sent the report to you an hour ago", "No baby, your butt looks great in that dress", and so on and so forth. Yet ordinary people break down under the weight of these lies all of the time. They care about the feelings of others and for the most part would prefer to tell the truth, it is how most people are wired and brought up.

For a spy under deep cover during an operation, the lying is constant and covers basically everything about the real person, not just the little stuff. They have to lie about who they are, what they do, where they are from, where they live, and their favorite color, everything in order to maintain operational security. Continued over the space of weeks, months or even years, maintaining a false front can erode the sanity of even the most seasoned undercover veteran. Very few people have it inside of them to live total lies for extended periods of time. In fact when someone is too comfortable with this degree of deception or gets to enjoying it too much, people classify that as a mental illness. Sociopaths have no place in intelligence work. Sociopathic liars are just too untrustworthy to employ. One expects the spy to lie to people while operational, not to their bosses and clients.

Spies undercover walk a razor edge between sanity and becoming the lie. For most it becomes a trial of compartmentalization.

While a source may have to lie about certain aspects of what they are doing to protect themselves from discovery, a spy has to lie about everything that they are doing to protect themselves, their team and the operation from being compromised. A source can go home to a wife and kids at night, play golf with their work buddies and not get questioned about anything else they do. A spy, however, takes every question from anyone and first runs it through their opposition detection radar and the lens of operational security. When trained and practiced in the art of deception, familiar with the ease with which whole life stories and entire mind sets can be created and feigned, it is only natural to become suspicious of everyone. It is one of the many occupational hazards of working in the wilderness of mirrors that a spy quickly learns to never really trust anyone. Think about how much normal people take the existence and assumption of simple trust for granted. When you live a life in which the cashier at the super market could really be a counter intelligence agent, where your life and freedom hinges on a constantly tended garden of fear and paranoia, how quickly do you think that begins to bleed over to the rest of life? An operation may only take days or a few weeks, but even the most case hardened spies find it difficult to switch off the radar after awhile. They allow their paranoia, tame psychosis and tradecraft to begin to seep into the rest of their lives and are forever marked by what they know. Like Adam and Eve in the garden, once a spy tastes this particular fruit of knowledge, the substrata realities of distrust, paranoia and fear are pressurized under the high keyed up state of operational activity. It becomes very difficult for an agent to shut their altered perception of the world down. The intelligence agent operates under a constant mixed state of stress, fear and hyper-sharp observational awareness.

Many in the national intelligence world would ridicule the concept of stress in covert corporate intelligence operators by saying it is never life or death and that at worst, detection and apprehension result in a few years in a cushy American prison for corporate spooks. What they fail to realize is that corporate espionage has its own unique brand of demons. The most stressful aspect of conducting corporate intelligence in the Western world, particularly in America, is the surrealistic nature of it all. In state intelligence agencies, you spy on someone else in their, usually backward and culturally different, country for god and country. But in corporate espionage you are spying on apple pie eating Americans in their hometowns, for strictly mercenary reasons. It is easy to let your guard down and let your tradecraft slip because it all feels so familiar and safe. Training keeps snapping the spy back into full operational awareness with the abruptness of a rubber band snapped against the skin. The constant low key ebb and flow of comfort and caution can take a much greater toll than the rush and boil of overseas operations. The strangeness of seeing everyone in your home country as a potential informer, a danger to you and the mission and the need to constantly break the law is a difficult and surreal way to live one's life. This push-pull lends itself to producing a gross distortion of a spy's view of the world and human nature in general. Alice may return from Wonderland to the normal one day, but that brief and horrifying appearance of the Cheshire cat along the paths and trees of home carries with it its very own brand of terror.

The Approach

Recruiting a source to commit espionage is much like talking a woman into bed. In many ways the two actions are quite similar. Sex, like espionage, is more easily accomplished when the target thinks it is their own idea. A spy uses the same methods to get clothes off of a woman as he uses to convert a target. Both require tailoring the approach to fit the needs of the target. By emphasizing the positive and minimizing the negative, the agent can usually overcome resistance to the concept of compromise. In some ways, convincing an individual to commit espionage is easier than talking them into bed. A potential source can be converted by being told that they are doing something positive for themselves, their country or their family. Plus they can get paid for doing a service which they may find exciting and rewarding. The singular moment when a spy approaches the target with their covert operation proposition can be very exciting and nerve racking, but is extremely rewarding when it works. If the persuasive approach is right, then the source will fall into the spy's arms like it was the most natural thing in the world. If the approach is flawed or rushed, then the source could run screaming straight to the opposition. It comes down to that single moment in time when the pretense is dropped and the target is asked outright to become a spy.

Judging the Best Approach to Source Recruitment

Determining the best conversion approach to take with any individual target is absolutely crucial. One of the main reasons that operations can take time to get started is the need for deep research into potential targets in order to best determine the proper approach to bring the source on board. A spy must have a very good understanding, sixth-sense of human needs and the ability to bring flexibility to their handling of sources during all stages of an operation. Even after all of the research that may have gone into the back ground of a target, there is always the unknown element, which makes flexibility during the approach of crucial importance. Having worked out in advance one approach, it is always advisable to have secondary and even tertiary lines of appeal in the event that the first move does not work or the source remains obstinate. If you ever watch a used car salesman or a dedicated pick up artist at the club work, you get a good idea how approach patterns work.

The key factor behind any move the spy makes when recruiting a source is confidence. Confident behavior has been the subject of innumerable books for business people and people intent on positive living for years but nowhere is it more vital than to the black arts of espionage. As a spy pitching a potential source you are asking them to conduct illicit or illegal acts against their coworkers on behalf of someone they do not really know. In this situation, the source is placing a tremendous amount of faith in the intelligence agent to take care of them. Recruiting an individual to be an intelligence asset creates a very personal, dependant relationship. People are deeply instinctual creatures and can detect insincerity and fear in another. Confidence exuded by the intelligence operator can mask uncertainty and present the target with a strong front on which to lean in times of doubt. Thus the level of trust, which will flavor the relationship between spy and source from the start, is intimately linked to the confidence that the agent shows during the recruitment process.

Cold Approach versus the Gradual Approach

There are two main plans of attack when it comes to an approach, the cold approach and the more gradual approach. Both have advantages and drawbacks and both have their place in the arsenal of a competent espionage agent.

Cold Approach

This is basically walking up to a person and asking them if they are willing to provide you with information or services which they really should not. It is not too much more complex that saying to someone, "Hello, I need this and am willing to offer that. Will you do it?" This direct approach is generally used against low level sources or for one time actions. There is often no need to spend time and resources building up a relationship with the guy who works nights at the printers to get them to turn over copies of otherwise unavailable plans. Knowing who they are, approaching them on neutral territory like at a bar, and straight offering cash works perfectly well. Most of the time. The cold approach is also used when coercion is the main line of attack against a target source. When someone the source knows personally conducts blackmail the added sense of betrayal is often enough to poison the target against recruitment regardless of the consequences.

Issues of betrayal are an important one which recommends the cold approach in most circumstances where coercion is used. In order to discover a solid approach to a potential source, it is often necessary for the spy to get close personally by insinuation into their lives. If that same individual turns around and pulls off their false mask of friendship to recruit the source, it can lead to a very deep sense of betrayal. This is the reason that a cold approach using the knowledge developed about a person, is often employed by an individual not directly involved in the life of a target, when there is a team of agents working the mission. Assuming such information shows that a cold approach will work, this second agent making the offer can be very desirable and effective.

Gradual Approach

For many potential sources the idea of some unknown random person coming up to them and pitching them to turn spy would produce a terrible reaction. But on the other hand, if the approach came from someone they already knew, particularly if that person was from the same social circles, they would be more likely to listen and respond favorably. The gradual approach is commonly used when recruiting a source based on ideological or egotistical grounds. If a spy is going to appeal to a potential source based on patriotism, it is often necessary to show the target beforehand that the agent is a patriot like themselves. When appealing to a person's sense of anger or betrayal at the hands of their company, it is productive to get to know that person, listen to their tales of woe and frustration and build up a sense of camaraderie before making the pitch. Highly placed sources in rarified positions of true power and authority are apt to view lower echelon individuals with a great deal of contempt, but when approached by someone viewed as a social equal, they may entertain the proposals put forth by that person.

Any approach made against a potential target should be meticulously planned and covered in case of rejection. By approaching a target, the spy is placing themselves in a very compromising position. They are now revealed to a potential source for what they are, a spy, and if handled poorly it is entirely possible that the target can contact the authorities after being pitched. Occasionally this risk is mitigated by the target fear that they will either not be believed, or even if believed, under suspicion, or considered a security risk by their employer and their career will be damaged. Just because a spy is turned down by one or two potential sources does not necessarily mean that the entire mission needs to be scrubbed. Of course a long list of rejections may indicate that the spy in charge of the mission is not very competent either. In any event careful evaluation of success or failure in the approach needs to be made each time.

Limiting Personal Exposure

A spy will act to limit the potential damage from an approach gone wrong by limiting their own personal exposure. In the case of a gradual approach against a target, if the known agent's cover persona is blown, it should be discarded immediately. A new identity needs to be assumed in order to continue operations, break the trail and throw off potential opposition moves.

A cold approached target has certain built-in buffers against discovery. The target will not know anything about the spy making the proposition and will not be able to provide the opposition with enough information relevant to the agent's identity that can be used to discover them later. Approaching a potential target with certain closely-held personal information about them can also serve to dissuade the target from going to the authorities in the event of rejection. Threatening to expose them by providing a veiled, or not so veiled, threat against their welfare keeps them from telling anyone that they were ever approached. Another form of insurance in the event of rejection is to run surveillance against the target for a period of time after the rejection to see if they do contact any authorities.

Dealing with Rejection

If a potential asset rejects the approach made by the spy, an immediate damage assessment should be conducted to determine the level of exposure and take step to minimize potential blow back against the operation as a whole. If the level of damage is severe or if the potential source gets the authorities involved, it may be necessary to withdraw the agent who botched the approach and possibly to scrub the entire mission. An alert opposition can complicate any operation and may even take active steps to root out other sources or discover and destroy the agents acting against the company.

If the level of potential exposure is low, then it is a good idea to tighten up the tradecraft of the team just to be safe. Continue to keep an eye on the rejecting party to ensure that they cannot do any damage to the operational integrity of the mission and move on.

Timing and Location

Setting the stage for the approach is a very important step in the process of recruiting an intelligence asset. Choosing the right time and location can make or break an approach.

Timing

As with many things in life, timing in turning a source can be everything. The approach should be made when the source is at his or her most vulnerable. This does not mean most incoherent with drink or drugs, but when they are most psychologically vulnerable. Some examples of good timing are late in the month when money is starting to get short, during a national holiday for foreigners, during a rough personal patch or after the source has been passed over for promotion or suffered some other perceived slight by the company or their coworkers. Depending on the method of approach chosen, judging the most opportune moment is an art and is helped greatly by developing personal information about the source.

Location

An approach to turn a source should optimally be made in a location where the spy has the psychological advantage. An approach should not be made in the source's office, for example, where they are used to feeling in control or feel they are being observed. Approaches are commonly made at the home of the potential source or at a safe location chosen by the spy. The reason for trying an approach at a source's home is purely psychological. The home may be a place of strength or considered safe by the source but the very act of invasion and the boldness of taking the initiative in such a place can turn the tables and place the source at a distinct mental disadvantage. The reason approaches are commonly used at home and not in an office is that within the lion's den of the company, the source has recourse to internal security elements directly at hand and will more tempted to reject an appeal. A spy getting caught out within the target corporate headquarters can have obvious negative repercussions. A safe house can also be used to pitch the client because the agent can control many of the variables and they hold a psychological advantage over the potential source as it is considered their domain. Recruitment pitches can be made outdoors or in restaurants and bars, but a guiding star for the agent is to always try and maintain a sense of domination and control over the source and to limit as many risk factors as possible.

The Psychology of the Pitch

There are as many ways to pitch a potential agent as there are waves in the ocean. The main objective of the agent should be developing a sense of mental control and psychological dominance from the very start. The best way to achieve dominance over a potential source is to appear all knowing and act confidently. Many assets will be overawed with the smallest bit of inside information that the agent can bring to bear which can help set the tone immediately. Once an asset is convinced that the agent knows more about a personal subject or the situation within a company than they should, the target begins a process of convincing themselves subconsciously that the agent has a much better understanding and insight (thus power) than may actually be the case.

Confidence is the key. It cannot be overstated just how important it is that the agent appear confident and in control when they pitch a potential asset. When you ask someone to conduct secretive and illegal acts on your behalf, there is an initial mental tug of war that goes on in the potential asset's mind as to who will have dominance in this unprecedented social situation. Winning that mental battle is the key to winning over the source. This objective is achieved through leading with confident and bold action.

There is, however, a difference between confidence and arrogance. The goal of any recruitment is to get the source solidly onto the spy's side. Even when using coercion to bring a source on board, remember that the mental gymnastics the sources goes through should bring them to believe that the handler is the only one who really understands their situation and can help them. Mentally manipulating the asset to the side of the spy makes for a more stable and willing coconspirator compelled on their own to work with the spy to achieve the intelligence objectives. By acting overbearing and arrogant when recruiting a source, the spy places a source immediately on the defensive and builds an unnecessary patina of resentment. Cocky arrogance creates unnecessary boundaries between the sources feeling of being abused and used by the spy and where they need to be mentally. A small dose of empathy and understanding goes a very long way when it comes to bringing a source on board. Approaches that emphasize the positive aspects of operating for the spy, as opposed to focusing solely on the negative, have a much higher rate of stability and success.

Successful Recruitment

Regardless of the means used to obtain consent, once the targeted asset crosses the magic line and agrees to provide the spy with information or other services, the relationship changes totally. It is a strange mental concept for most assets to accept that they are now working against their own company and coworkers for a purpose. People often lack real direction in life, so it can be both a liberating and a frightening thing for someone to cross the Rubicon and accept their new direction and role as an intelligence asset. Even if an asset appears willing, indeed eager, to act as a source of information for the spy, there are still a number of dramatic mental shifts that are taking place just beneath the surface. An important part of recruitment training for new intelligence officers is learning how to spot these changes in attitude and guide them properly. Observing the new source and helping to guide their mental battles towards positive outcomes is necessary in order to make a source stable and operationally viable.

Even if a source joyfully leaps at the chance to spy for an agent, certain precautions should be taken to ensure that their conversion is real and that they do not go out and place themselves or the mission in jeopardy. The first lesson a spy must drill into their new source is the absolute necessity for secrecy. Explain and warn that they cannot tell anyone at all about what they are doing. Every person that knows the secret is one link weakening the chain of operational security. The further removed that person is from the consequences of discovery, the weaker still they make the chain. A new source must be told candidly and truthfully that to reveal what they are doing risks their own freedom and livelihood and not just the spy's.

A degree of post recruitment surveillance should be conducted in order to assess the validity of the conversion, the asset's actual state of mind and realistic possibility of succeeding in their assigned mission. For operational security a new source should be told as little of the dimensions of the total intelligence gathering plan as possible beyond their own personal tasks. The less information a source knows about what is going on, the less they can betray. Under no circumstances should separate sources be aware of each other or mingled unless it is absolutely necessary. Operational security often comes down to little more than compartmentalizing information.

False Flag Recruitment

In covert operations against companies and private organizations, intelligence assets are almost always recruited under a "false flag". A false flag operation means that the spy presents himself or herself to the asset as something other than what they actually are. Few corporate intelligence agents will recruit their assets by straight out telling them that they are a mercenary spook for a business competitor. One item of note here is that often the spy themselves will not know exactly who they are working for. The benefits of recruiting under a false flag are twofold. First, there is operational security. If the source does not know the nature of the operation or the true identity of the recruiting agent, then neither does the opposition in the event the asset is discovered. Secondly, recruiting under a false flag can give the asset a sense that what they are doing is for a good cause and thus alleviate much of their concerns about the righteousness of their acts. Below are examples of common false flag cover identities that are used to recruit sources in corporate espionage. These false flags include, but are not limited to government agent, media, home country intelligence agent, business recruiter and much more. Corporate spies can, and do, claim to be working for any number of different groups in order to more easily convert a source.

Government Agent

If the source believes that they are conducting an act of espionage under the auspicious of their own government, they are much more likely to cooperate. Especially if they are informed of the potential legal penalties for resisting. A latent sense of patriotism is strong in most Americans, as with other peoples around the world, and is very commonly tapped into in order to conduct corporate espionage. In most cases, one's nation will trump the company when it comes to loyalty. For the source, helping the agent offers a chance for them to live out their deepest James Bond fantasies under the sanction of their own government. There are few Americans who have not fantasized about being asked by the CIA or FBI to work on some secret mission. It is for these reasons that this approach is so commonly employed today.

The potential down side of approaching a recruit as a government agent is that impersonating a federal or local officer can carry significant penalties if the intelligence agent is caught. The source may be tempted to search for the agent by contacting them at the agency they claim to work for. There are also groups of people who are anti-government and would be loath to work with any agency of the despised regime. Such sentiments are rarely held in and can be observed by monitoring the source's lifestyle and online posts. Always tailor the cover, approach and recruitment to the source and never assume anything when it comes to human beings.

Media

Americans have a love-hate relationship with the media, but few can resist the temptation for potential fame as an informant and are more than willing to talk to a "reporter" if given the chance. People feel flattered by the attention and will do almost anything to get into the spot light. An intelligence agent posing as a reporter doing a story on their company, is an effective approach, particularly if you can convince the asset that they are trying to uncover some terrible misdeed that the company has committed. This reporter-informant play has been and continues to be a highly successful way of obtaining insider information. A down side to this is that after a long enough period of time goes by without anything in print or on the news, the asset can easily become suspicious. It is also very easy to search via the internet to confirm the identity of a person claiming to be a reporter. If the intelligence agent posing as a reporter begins to ask for information with no place in the storyline they pitched to the asset, starts asking for secret designs or classified documents for example, the source is likely to become suspicious and report the agent to the authorities.

Intelligence Agent from their Home Country

This home country contact approach works wonders with potential assets from overseas. If the appeal to patriotism fails, there is probably family still living in the home country that can be held in jeopardy to convince the foreign national to work for a spy claiming to be a member of the secret state police. Many foreign nationals have an almost mystical belief in the all powerful control and omniscience of their domestic secret services. Another benefit of this approach is that there is almost no possibility of the source checking the credentials of the supposed spy from home. The one drawback to this approach is that the agent recruiting them has to actually be from their home country or at the least able to impersonate someone from that country well enough to fool a native. This means that the candidate pool for spies gets very narrow in the US as few actual foreign nationals are ever recruited and trained there.

An offshoot of this approach is to pose as a member of a local, or home country, organized crime group. This is the literal "offer they can't refuse" pitch. This line can work wonders since most people can be easily cowed by the threat of violence and hold some really quaint illusions about the power of criminals. The main benefits here are that sources will be held by fear from approaching the authorities and would have no means of checking the credentials of a self proclaimed gangster. The down side is that the source may be tempted to contact the authorities if they do not believe the performance of the spy or have faith in the ability of the police to protect them.

Business Recruiter

Cover as a head hunter gives the spy a number of significant advantages. There is no penalty if caught acting as a head hunter. Simply set up a web site and anyone can legitimately claim to be a business recruiter. By asking an individual to show good faith by passing along certain advance information to their "new employer" in exchange for a better position or other perks it does not come off sounding like too treasonous a proposition to most sources. The target asset is lead to believe that by helping their new company, not only do they give a final screw you to their old company, but are promised superior treatment and a hero's welcome at the new position. Business recruiting works best against midlevel and dead end career path individuals. The down side here is time. A recruit can only be expected to stay at the old job and provide information for so long before they start demanding the fantasy position come true.

Internal Corporate Security

If a potential source can be convinced that what they are doing is part of an exciting game of spy versus spy conducted to root out a mole in the company, or any other Hollywood type nonsensical mission, most will jump at the chance for some excitement in their lives. They will believe what they are doing has full sanction of the corporation and after overcoming initial suspicions, the spy can get an asset to do almost anything to help. Posing as internal corporate security is a very bold strategy to use and a difficult one to pull off effectively. It is also one of the rare occasions when a spy would make a direct pitch within the potential asset's office. This approach has been known to work primarily because of two factors. First most employees are completely divorced from the activities and staff of internal corporate security elements. And second if staged right the employee will do most of the convincing and internal justification themselves.

Honey Trap

The classic honey trap involves suborning the asset directly based on compromising information about their indiscretions. In this recruitment scenario, the spy will use a woman, or man, who is part of the team or under their control to ensnare the source. Then the agent threatens disclosure of the indiscretion or blackmail, usually of the lover not the actual target, if the source does not provide information to the spy. This tactic was used extensively and quite successfully by the KGB during the

Cold War and is still highly effective today. The benefits of this approach are twofold. First, by maintaining positive control over the lover, the spy has a direct line into the mental state and moves of the source. They can also subtly guide the actions of their source through the third party. Second, by threatening a third party, the source often feels it is their duty to protect that other person and will play ball, where a direct threat against them would go nowhere. This method requires detailed preparation and can be difficult to pull off. But love is a very powerful and strange emotional state, so when successful, this method can yield remarkable results over an extended period of time. The key to success in this approach is ensuring that the spy chooses the right lure and always maintains positive control over the lover during the course of the operation. Love, after all, can work both ways.

False Flag Direct

If a spy is working on behalf of company A and wants to recruit a source within company B, it is prudent to have the source actually believe the operation is being carried out on behalf of company C. Any source should know better than to believe someone trying to recruit them to conduct illegal acts, but many do not. If they are convinced, the more subtle the presentation of the evidence the more likely they are to believe it, they will hold this knowledge to themselves and thus expose the wrong party if caught out. The main benefit here is that if the spy is caught out or the subject reveals the operation, suspicion will immediately fall on the wrong perpetrator. This can also be used as an effective black propaganda tool to smear a target company, which will be discussed later. The only potential for trouble here is when there are numerous cutouts between the spy on the ground and the company that has hired him. It is entirely possible that the spy may use the flag of the actual client company by mistake. This has happened before and is one reason that the approach is used almost exclusively by in-house corporate espionage teams.

Ensuring Source Loyalty

There are many methods to help build source loyalty. Each source should be built up by the intelligence agent to help prevent mental instability and to develop a more dependant relationship. The most common and effective means of building loyalty is simply to listen to the asset and help with their day-to-day problems. Few people ever feel truly listened to or taken care of. When anyone, even a spy, provides this comfort it can quickly become a treasure in their lives to be defended and held onto at all cost. Other means of building loyalty include giving gifts, remembering important dates and birthdays, taking them out occasionally to show them a good time and any other ego boosting action the spy can think of. While there is less risk to a spy engaging directly with a source socially while conducting corporate espionage than with state-sponsored espionage, it is always necessary to maintain tight tradecraft during such interactions. If the spy does take a source out, they should do it in such a way as to prevent accidental meetings with friends or coworkers and not leave a wide trail.

Reaction to Initial Operations

Sources are human beings first and intelligence assets second and at the very least should be treated this way. Their reaction to the first action on behalf of their handler will set the tone for the rest of their operational careers. Sources may be excited by the initial espionage act and this sentiment should be encouraged, within limits. Do not pump a source up to think that they are James Bond for the first outing, lest they try to do too much too quickly without adequate preparation and get caught. It is a common first step for an intelligence agent to test their new source by giving them a small assignment, perhaps to provide information that the agent already possesses, in order to soft ball them into the espionage game. This is a very wise move because it introduces the asset to the reality of covert operations and also gives the agent an opportunity to test the veracity of the source by comparing the information that they bring in to that which they already have. An intelligence agent should also be prepared for negative reactions from a source upon their first assignment. Mentally weak sources will likely show signs of breakdown on their very first outing. Sources should be monitored closely to look for signs of stress before, during and after the first assignment.

Running an Agent

Assessing the Opposition

When a spy begins to run a brand new asset inside of a company the first thing that they should do is have the source provide an overview of internal security measures and the strength of the counter intelligence opposition within the target company. Most sources know a great deal about how a company works, what steps are taken internally to control the flow and access to information, and what security arrangements are in place to prevent data theft. They know this without even thinking about it because they have always been on the legitimate side of data access and have probably received innumerable emails, memos and possibly training on this subject. Now that they are a source for the intelligence agent, his or her first priority should be to assess, from the inside, what security infrastructure exists which may pose a threat to the source and the operation. Grilling a new source about internal security, or better yet having them bring out all of the memos and other information that they have on the subject, will provide the agent with a better understanding of the threat to their source and the operation as a whole from corporate security elements. With this information the spy can better tailor the approach to data collection or other mission objectives with far greater precision. This may sound overly dramatic when one considers that within most US companies nearly the entire security apparatus is geared towards technical and computer systems security. However, there is a trend in some companies towards instituting at least nominal counter intelligence programs and these potential hazards need to be tracked accordingly by the spy. For the most part, what the spy will receive is likely to be nothing more substantial than a few notes on not forgetting your key card and reminders to change your password on a regular basis, but it never hurts to check.

Establishing Covert Infrastructure

Once an asset is in play, the spy should make sure that the necessary covert infrastructure exists and is secured to handle asset meetings, information transfer, payments and other actions.

Because employees are almost never, except in certain very secure firms, subject to outside surveillance by the company, meetings do not necessarily have to be held covertly. If, as part of the spy's cover, there exists a legitimate reason for the spy and the source to run into each other or socialize, then it is acceptable to meet at restaurants, bars, on the golf course or anywhere else. Proper tradecraft dictates that public meetings with assets are held in locations with multiple exits and under strict cover, but this can be tailored to the specific needs of the operation and geared to the individual source. For more private meetings, a safe house set up by the agent ahead of time is the ordinary practice. Running counter surveillance during operational meetings with sources is a common practice to ensure that the source was not followed and that meetings stay covert as needed.

Operational communication with an asset should be handled covertly as well. There are many means to accomplish private communications, including using prepaid cell phones, dead drops, and, of course, the internet. The internet is a powerful tool that has changed the face of the legitimate business world, but it is also perfectly tailored to act as a tool for covert communications and other espionage practices. The key to keeping communications covert and useful is to make them simple. One very effective means of modern covert communications is to employ single use VOIP communications. Set up a disposable Skype account and have the asset do the same. Give the source the new account name and a time to contact the spy and you now have a virtually unhackable and untraceable communications tool that is not monitored routinely by security services and can be employed from anywhere in the world. Skype, and similar online tools, can be a wonderful modern dodge, especially because it can be made to appear to originate anywhere. If the FBI somehow is monitoring the source's VOIP communications and traced back the conversation between the asset and the spy to, say, an allied country, then it becomes a state department matter and most investigations get shut down after a few quiet diplomatic conversations. Communications between source and spy must be safe, but also easy to use. Sources are not trained intelligence officers and to expect them to master arcane methods of secret communication just means that no matter how secure the communications might be they will quickly break down.

Training

There is no need to overburden a new source with elaborate methods of secret communication or teach them to use invisible ink, when if all they really need is a pair of cheap prepaid cell phones and a free evening to meet at the club to drop off information. Teaching a source esoteric espionage tradecraft, while likely to puff up their ego, is not strictly necessary in the real world of corporate espionage. The absolute basics are more than enough. Teach a new source to keep their mouths shut and the spy has given them 90% of what they need to know. A good minimum standard to use in training is to teach the new source basic communications security, simple signals to indicate trouble and most importantly the value of silence. Other than that, the spy should arrange the secure meeting places and simply inform the asset of where and when they are to meet. This can be done in person, but these days, is most commonly conducted via the internet. If the spy feels that the source would really benefit from a dose of fantasy training as a "real spy" and from using Hollywood-esque spy gimmicks then by all means indulge them.

Codes can be a bit redundant in communications with corporate espionage agents, but are highly effective in making the source feel like they are special and what they are doing is real spy work. If a code is used it should be very simple and easy to remember. An example is subtracting two days and two hours from a set time to determine the actual date and time of a covert meeting. Another issue to consider is that sending encrypted or intentionally cryptic communications can be seen as a red flag by the opposition if the source is ever placed under actual surveillance. In corporate espionage the less the spy can get their sources to act like spies, the lower the likelihood that they will be caught.

One thing to remember when providing a source with espionage training is that, aside from the real usefulness of basic tradecraft and communications protocols, there is little need for an asset to be trained at all. Stealing secrets from Intel is not like running Red Army majors in Moscow. The level of tradecraft taught to sources should always reflect the degree of opposition onsite. That being said, it is shocking the number of assets who really get into their roles as spies in the company and are insatiable when it comes to being taught gimmicks and cheesy spy tricks. One intelligence agent operating in

Seattle ordered a series of kids spy toys and other goods from the DC Spy Museum online store and after buffing off the labels presented them to one of his assets as real CIA issue gear. The source was ecstatic and treasured these gifts over all of the expensive watches and gold knickknacks that the spy had presented to him before. There is often that bit of Bond trying to peek out from a source and indulging them, within reason, when it comes to fostering their fantasies can be a useful stress release tool. Additionally, sources tend to feel safer if they are given some form of intelligence training. Keeping it simple and using lots of cheesy gear and jargon to impress the source is an easy means of fantasy fulfillment. Making espionage fun for the source can also act as a calming force and help build a bond between asset and handler.

Receiving Illicitly Obtained Information

After the process of recruiting an asset, the means of extracting the information that the asset provides to the spy is the next great hurdle. Transmitting information can be an extremely complex task involving smuggling out terabits of data via the internet, on storage devices or the actual documents through multiple layer of internal security. But more often, transferring illicitly obtained data requires little more than a few blind servers and a single use email account. Unlike the dramatic movie version, in real life most data is exfiltrated from a company in nothing more elaborate than a ten dollar flash drive purchased from the local electronics store or attached to a regular old email. In this day and age, even the smallest iPod can be used to move out enough information to cost a company billions. Electronic means of shifting information from one place to another today have grown exponentially every year since the inception of the internet and the advent of cheap consumer electronics.

In the past, if one wanted to remove information from a company, it would involve the photographing, copying or theft of a huge amount of paper. As offices move to a paperless work environment, that mountain of paper now can be slipped out in a solid state data chip no larger than a penny. This, of course, is the physical removal of data. By far the most common means of transferring important secrets out of a company is simply via email or by direct file transfer protocol (ftp). The increased ease of transfer of confidential data has been offset by mounting attempts on the part of companies to electronically secure their information with encryption and digital rights management (DRM). However, for all of the electronic data protection protocols and intrusion countermeasures electronic (ICE) in place around important information, there always exists the human factor. People have to be able to access data and put it to productive use. The practical balance struck is access restrictions to different classes of sensitive data. All of this is neatly overcome when a spy recruits a legitimate user to access and remove data for them. Below are some of the most common means by which sensitive information is taken from companies and delivered to corporate spies today.

Email

Employees at various levels send out scores of emails everyday as part of their normal business practice. It is not cost effective to screen emails and most companies don't even try. Using email to send information is today's preferred means of covert data transmission in the corporate world. Attaching a file to an email and sending it to the spy is as simple as sending any other email, except on the agent's end. An espionage agent invariably takes steps to minimize the possibility of back tracking and tracing via email by using a number of dummy accounts and multiple anonymous remailer services. All or most of these sinister sounding tools are available to anyone with internet access and most cost nothing to put in place. If there is a greater threat of detection, a spy may employee a hacker to place still further complex digital cutouts between them and the source. It is an amazing fact that today an intelligence operative, once they recruit a source and get them sending information, can be anywhere in the world or across the street receiving the stolen data. It would take a massive effort by the white hat IT security people to even begin to track them down. By that time, the spy has finished their espresso and moved on.

Memory Stick

Available at any retailer, these marvels of modern technology are extremely cheap, come in a wide variety of innocuous shapes, colors, sizes and are capable of holding vast quantities of data. If emailing data out of an organization proves to be too dangerous or problematic, the next logical option is transferring the data to the humble solid state memory stick. When attached to a computer it because an instant external drive capable of holding gigabits of data. Actual external hard drives, used to hold larger scales of data, can hold terabits of information. The total research and development effort to produce a new product can often be held on a single commercially available memory stick. These little data hordes are very convenient for the spy because they are so small and common. Once a source has exfiltrated the requested data on their memory stick, they can either physically pass it straight to the spy or better still send it via email of ftp from their unmonitored home system. The need for spies to actually meet their sources to exchange packets of classified documents in exchange for a bundle of unmarked bills is long past.

Third Party Access

A method which is growing in popularity among the corporate espionage community is one which allows the spy to keep their source away from the data theft and transfer process entirely. By receiving the passwords and operational protocols to a protected corporate system that the employee possesses, the spy can access the data from the safety and security of their own systems located anywhere in the world, preferably somewhere warm. The company's system will believe that it is a legitimate request from an authorized user because the user info and passwords are all real (provided as they are from the source, a real authorized user). Removing the need for an on-site spy is something new and will continue to grow in popularity as demand increases among legitimate users for data access from home and via increasingly powerful mobile devices. Additionally, this method allows the spy to target much lower-level personnel for recruitment, making it safer, easier and cheaper than going after the top-level people who used to hold the only keys to the information kingdom. After all, why go to the trouble and expense of turning a senior executive, when for an inch or so of cash a spy can buy the access codes to that same executive's system from their underappreciated assistant or some temporary IT room flunky.

Personal Electronic Devices and Purpose Built Storage Media

As companies come to grips with the problem of securing data internally and begin to prohibit the use or removal of memory sticks from the office (as the US military is trying to do) an increasing number of corporate spooks are turning to innocent seeming personal electronic devices and purpose built storage media to covertly smuggle data out. Security cannot prohibit or possibly go through everyone's iPods, laptops, wristwatches or cell phones every day. Personal electronic devices have built in features which allow them to act as storage for legitimate data such as photos, music and personal files. This can also be used, with zero conversion, to store raw data from company servers as easily as it can to hold Britney Spears latest album or an employee's movie collection.

If a spy wants to get extra devious, there are programs to format common devices like iPods so that data can be hidden from casual examination. Another still more devious means of extracting physical data from a firm is to use purpose built storage media. A digital storage device is solid state memory which can be shaped into nearly any form the user may desire. Commercially available flash drives are shaped like everything from Yoda dolls to earrings. Building a memory device into an everyday item is easier than ever. Within the next few years as even more malleable and powerful memory medium comes out, expect to see a slew of creative covert memory devices built into every conceivable object. A purpose built covert memory device also makes a wonderful present for even the most jaded intelligence source. Functional and covert all at the same time, the little Bond that lives inside of every intelligence asset will go wild. After all, not even Q had such wonderfully miniature and fantastically powerful toys.

Paper

If the company is very old school, or smart as the case may be, and only keeps their most important information on paper, then a spy will have to return to the ways of the past for inspiration. Removing something bulky like paper, depending on the level of exit controls from a company can be a daunting task. The best method is to infiltrate a high speed document scanner into the company and transfer the dead weight of paper into a more easily transferable digital medium. If the source only has a limited window to access the paper materials and cannot scan them, then using the built in camera on their phone to take high resolution images of the paperwork will often suffice. Every modern phone comes with a digital camera built in and most companies do not even see these phones as a security threat. It is not possible to get high-end smart phones without cameras anymore, unless you are tied into the defense or intelligence communities and those models are classified and expensive. If all of the above proves impossible, then go back to old school spy techniques and use a false bottom in the brief case or have the source carry it out hidden in their clothes. Bribe one of the security guards that work in the exit controls to let the asset pass with their secrets. Filling a box with copies of documents and mailing it from inside of the office has also worked well. Get creative and solutions to even the most difficult document exfiltration problems will present themselves.

Physically Receiving Information from a Source

An entire arcane art surrounds covertly passing physical storage media from source to spy. Back in the day, it was microfilm and today it is digital memory sticks, but the process and methodology remains the same. Covert transfer of goods is part of every spy's repertoire. If the infinitely safer, faster and more efficient method of online transmission is unavailable, for whatever reason, then it is time to dust off some classic espionage tradecraft. The means have been proven effective against the most difficult opposition forces in the world and work well for the much softer operational environment of corporate skullduggery. Below are some of the most useful and effective covert means of passing physical data between people.

Meeting

Setting up a covert meeting with a source is filled with potential risks, but does provide the perfect venue for the physical passing of information. Getting caught receiving illicitly obtained corporate materials from a source is about as damning as evidence gets for a spy. This is a favorite set up tactic used by counter intelligence, state security and police forces because it makes their job much easier when they can catch a spy red handed with the goods. As long as the spy controls the environment and timing of the meet, they can also control the risks involved. If a team is available, other members can run counter surveillance and can potentially detect opposition action in time for the spy and source to flee or at the least to allow for the destruction of the illegal materials without which prosecution becomes much more problematic. If the spy is operating alone, choosing the time and place for a meeting becomes very important so that they can select a venue where they can maintain a look out for potential opposition forces before and after meeting.

For the source, one-on-one meetings are often necessary, even if no information is to be passed. Most sources need to feel that the spy is taking care of them and is in control. Physical meetings can play a crucial part in maintaining the loyalty and mental stability of sources. Modern communication, VOIP, cell, text, and such can replace face-to-face meetings to salve the mental needs of a source for the most part, but without occasional physical contact it becomes difficult to build that personal bond with a source that can prove critical in the event of stress.

Brush Pass

A classic spy move used in antiquity and recycled today to pass digital storage media is called the "brush pass." This entails the source and spy, or a third party courier, walking by each other feigning ignorance of each other's identity and passing the physical media between them as they innocently walk past. Doing this right takes a certain amount of choreography and practice, but when done correctly is virtually undetectable to outside observers. This technique is favored because it minimizes the contact between the two parties and can be done anywhere, preferably where there are numerous people around further obscuring the potential for detection, and is easy to teach to the source. It is another recommended move for intelligence officers to teach their sources because it feels like something from a spy movie, which as mentioned before assets love to learn. This is only useful for small items, unless you want to get really clever and trade exact replica bags at the gym or something similar. One very interesting modern twist on the brush pass has come with the use by corporate spooks of urban camouflage to further hide a pass off of data. Timing the brush pass encounter to coincide with a flash mob (groups who coordinate via the internet to all meet up in a public place and engage in some form of strange/entertaining behavior) gives the covert operator and their source a readymade distraction for any would be surveillance team and can act as the perfect cover for the exchange. In today's espionage world, where vast amounts of data are held in tiny storage devices, this classic move has found a new lease on life and is a valuable tool in the arsenal of the modern spy.

Dead Drop

Another classic espionage move is to use a "dead drop" to exchange information between source and spy. A dead drop is a chosen location, usually out of the way and secluded, where a source can go to secret physical materials for later retrieval by the espionage agent. It is highly effective because, if done correctly, the opposition never sees the spy and the source in the same place at the same time.

Choosing locations for dead drops around a city is another reason why spy services have their agents out walking or running around outside during their down time. A dead drop should be located in an out of the way spot that will not be disturbed and most importantly, the source has a legitimate reason to go. Senior executives do not normally hang around the ghetto for no reason or walk their dogs at a park located half way across town. Making an asset use a dead drop location outside of their normal routine is an obvious tip off to any opposition surveillance team that something is going on. It is important to tailor each dead drop to the lifestyle of the specific source at play.

Taping a memory stick to the back of a toilet at the source's favorite café or restaurant will arouse zero suspicion if that source is under surveillance. If the spy wants to take further precautions, they can always use a third party to retrieve the media and run counter surveillance to detect any opposition presence.

Communicating that a dead drop is full and ready to be serviced can be done in any number of innocent seeming ways. Once again, the internet provides the perfect tool to covertly communicate short messages between a source and their handler. Having the asset post on a prearranged web site with a short code phrase or use a burner cell phone provided by the spy to call another number to leave a message are all potential means of quick and easy clandestine communications. A very popular method for covert communication (though one that has been publically exposed and is more actively monitored now by the security services) is to open a Gmail or similar email account and then type out the message to be communicated but not send it. Saved as a draft it does not go out over the internet (thus is supposedly immune to intercept) and is only held on the email provider's sever. The source has the log in information for the same account and will simply open the draft, read it and respond, and that is that, covert communications.

Dead drops can be any size and are very useful for exchanging large volumes of information or objects. They come in handy when the intelligence agent wants to give the source something like an encrypted drive with instructions, cash or special tools. One thing to remember is that dead drops today do not necessarily have to exist in the real world. Cyber dead drops, as made famous by Wikileaks, are extremely useful and can provide a great deal of security for all parties. Have the source upload a file to a pre-selected server, usually located overseas to prevent easy access by state security forces. Then the source instantly contacts the spy to let him or her know that the file is in place, allowing the spy to remove the file and purge the server at their leisure. This provides a simple, yet highly effect, buffer between source and spy in cyber space and can be set up in minutes anonymously.

Couriers

Having a third party operate as a cut out between the source and the spy can be convenient and increases operational security. The spy can use the services of commercial shipping companies or regular mail to move sensitive information covertly. An interesting fact here is that today in America it takes many times more legal paperwork for security services to intercept and open an individual's physical mail than it does to tap into their email. It is also possible to use trained or anonymous people to do the deed. If a bit more discretion than that provided by known express package companies is required, then the use of bonded private couriers is popular. When one uses a private courier it is always best to do so off the books. In large cities it is easy to find the hang out for the local bike couriers and by slipping one of these free spirited guys or girls some quick cash, the spy now has a private messenger who can go into any building in the city without raising suspicion and receive covert materials to deliver at a prearranged and discreet location for pick up by the spy. All carried out via an almost impossible to track/follow bicycle.

I would like to digress here for a moment and talk a bit about the utility in corporate espionage of the spiky haired urban bike messenger. These tribes of wild young kids are present in nearly every major metropolitan center in America and in many cities overseas as well. They know their cities inside and out are almost universally young, intelligent, creative, driven, often poor and have a natural aversion to authority. Add to this that as a low level service kid, the bike messenger is invisible to almost everyone, including security personnel, and is a common fixture in most corporate environments. Their profession allows them the ability to regularly pass with little or no notice through even the heaviest corporate security. This makes for the perfect combination of traits for use as a guy or girl Friday in corporate intelligence operations. Recruiting a messenger from among the spandex clad throng in front of the local cheap espresso stand in down town America just requires cash and a bit of brass on the part of the spy. The utility of such people to act as couriers, go betweens, errand runners, surveillance assets, and generally useful sources cannot be overstated. They can perform many of the same tasks as would be handled by other trained intelligence agents for a fraction of the price. It is not just bike messengers who can fill these roles, cleaning staff, strippers, taxi drivers, day laborers, college students and many other resources are easy to find and can provide instant, cheap and disposable talent for a small stack of bills. Of the lot, bike messengers do provide certain significant advantages and form a very convenient pool of high-end talent just waiting, overly strong espresso in hand, for a corporate spook to come and put them to work.

Unorthodox Solutions

There was once a corporate spy who was passionately involved in the remote controlled model aircraft world. He developed an ingenious means of covert communications with his source in a high-end pharmaceutical company. Since operating overseas as a racially different foreigner, it had proven problematic for him to move about town and meet covertly with his source as freely as he would have liked. This led him to look for more unorthodox solutions. What he ended up doing, appropriately enough given his personal hobby, was to kit built a two meter long radio controlled dirigible. He painted it matte black, fitted it with an adjustable IR camera and long range controls. He would fly this dirigible to the back yard of his source at night and the asset would place the data he had collected into a receiving tray built into the airship. Once the data was on board, the spy would fly the ship back to his safe house and take possession of the illicit data. The airship was virtually silent, had the same radar cross section as a bird and could operate for hours on a single battery charge. Because the spy flew the dirigible low and crossed the street grid, it would have been nearly impossible to track even if the opposition had clued onto it. They didn't find the airship, but they did discover the leak at the company and had the spy's source under surveillance. Occasionally the spy would take his black airship out to run serendipitous counter surveillance on his various sources around town. This guy was really into his drones. A good background to have these days as they become a very common adjunct to modern corporate espionage operations. On one such occasion he spotted the stake out at the source's house two days before they were due to have a semi-annual face to face meeting. Needless to say, he immediately contacted the source to alert him to the fact that he had fallen under suspicion and to go underground for a time. The source was never brought in. The dirigible loving spy was last known to be working on an improved model airship with radio intercept capabilities, a fuel cell for extended operation and onboard wireless for easy direct upload and relay of data without even the need for landing.

As the above story shows there are all kinds of different ways of getting data from one place to another covertly. Even the venerable carrier pigeon is still in use and can carry enough digital data tied to its leg to fill a bookshelf. The only limit to what can be done in the twilight world of covert operations and communications is the human imagination. With so many clever people working in this field, it is no wonder that some of the solutions reached have been both bizarre and brilliant.

Paying the Source

Once the source starts delivering the goods, a spy has to start paying up. Often a covert relationship will begin with payment of one kind of another, but in order to maintain that relationship and build leverage over a source through addiction to money, the spy has to deliver on his side of the bargain. Payment to assets can take many forms, but obviously the most common is cold hard cash. Delivery of money to a source covertly can present more challenges than receiving the intelligence from them.

Delivering payment to a source can take one of three main forms: cash, commodities or credit. Cash is convenient because, for the most part, it is untraceable and is a universally accepted form of currency. The disadvantages of cash are that it is bulky in large amounts and the source must somehow account for suddenly making large cash deposits to their bank, the authorities and others. Laundering large amounts of cash is a major problem for people involved in all forms organized illegal activity. Thanks to the never ending "war on drugs", operating covertly using large volumes of cash has become problematic for upstanding citizens such as a covert intelligence source within a major company.

The best solution to the cash problem is to come up with other forms of payment. Paying a source in easily exchangeable commodities like art, gold or diamonds is one option, although a majority of common employees have no idea how to convert such assets into cash and are often reluctant to take such forms of payment. Another option is to pay in kind. Making payment to a source by giving them jewelry, a boat or buying them a new house is a very effective way to compensate an asset for their work. An advantage to this method is that people feel a tangible "gift" such a car has an even greater value than a corresponding amount in cash would. Paying in kind provides the agent with the double psychological bonus of both delivering on their promise of payment and doing so in such a way that the source feels that they are getting even more than they expected. Such gift-like payments are more difficult for authorities to detect, if setup correctly, than large deposits of currency into the accounts of a person with a set salary.

The most common modern solution to the payment problem is to use the grey market banking sector to establish an offshore account structure and directly depositing payments to the source into this account. One immediate benefit of this form of payment is that by using an offshore haven the spy is given an amount of built in security from scrutiny by the banks themselves. It is also convenient that large amounts of money discreetly deposited into an offshore haven come with little or no state scrutiny. Not so if that same amount was transferred into a personal checking account at Bank of America Wichita branch. The drug cartels have both made the process of covert money transfer more problematic and at the same time set up a number of easily accessible illicit money transfer and holding services that are already covert in nature and thus very secure and user friendly.

It is not just in Switzerland and the Cayman Islands that such havens exist. In fact, using a well known haven like Switzerland has become extremely dangerous these days as these one secure countries open up their records under intense US pressure. The solution to this problem has come through diversification in the grey and black banking sectors. Highly secret and effective illicit money transfer points now exist in such exotic locales as Macau, Moscow, Shanghai, Kuwait, the UAE, Brazil and Indonesia among many other places. Another perennial favorite for well connected covert operations funding is through Japan. The yakuza organized crime groups in Japan operate a very successful, if somewhat difficult to access for non- Japanese, money laundering and clandestine transfer service. For a very competitive percentage of the deposit, money is held in total secrecy behind a wall of legal and national protections in a country that can easily be accessed and in banks that are as legitimate and solid as any in the world.

Much of the illicit money transfers occurring around the world have absolutely nothing to do with drugs, guns or crime as most people conceive of it. Instead it is corporations and high value individuals that use these systems to move vast amounts of cash from one investment project to the next in order to dodge taxes and maximize returns. In many cases, where a covert operation is run out of a company, they already have access to long established grey and black banks and money transfer routes overseas. There have even been cases where a company runs all of its covert operations through a single bank or particular shelter and comes to be identified with it to such a degree that covert operations agents can tell exactly who they are working for simply by seeing checks from that particular shadow bank.

One significant challenge that a spy faces is how to keep the source from giving themselves away through ostentatious displays of unaccountable wealth once they start to receive payment. This lack of discretion is famous among organized crime groups and is one that the authorities are already keyed to looking for. This was the key to detecting the long serving Russian source in the CIA, Aldrich Ames. Here was a man who became head of Soviet counter intelligence at the CIA, ran operations to penetrate Soviet and later Russian intelligence for the US. For reasons of greed and ego, Ames sold out every operation he could get his hands on to the people he was supposed to be helping his country spy on. Indirectly killing a lot of people along the way and blinding American intelligence in Russia for years. What finally gave him away was the ostentatious lifestyle he adopted once the Russians began to pay him. He went from chronic debt to paying cash for a big house in one of the posh areas near DC. His wife was spending thousands of dollars a month on phone calls to Columbia to talk to her parents, in the 1980's when thousands of dollars for a phone bill was something remarkable. His case is also instructive because it took authorities years to detect, build a case against and finally arrest Ames. It also goes to show that if the spy can provide an asset with a valid reason for increased wealth, the likelihood of suspicion goes down. However, any obvious break from normal behavior of the source can be considered suspicious and should be mitigated against or avoided all together.

Building Up a Source

Nurturing both the mental health and position of an asset once they are in play becomes a vital role for the intelligence agent. Once they have employed an asset that person becomes the responsibility of the spy and their position within the target company is of critical importance to the agent.

Building the Position within the Company of a Source

Improving the asset's position within the target company is a useful tool when operating a source over a long period in the field. If the spy is engaged in a long-term assignment to penetrate a company, sometimes the people who have direct access to the materials they seek cannot be easily compromised. One solution to this barrier is to recruit a competent lower level source and then remove the higher level employees above them so that the spy's source then takes over the now vacant elevated position giving them access to secrets. This does not necessarily have to involve any violence on the part of the spy, although that can be a quick solution. More commonly, spies will employee covert means to gather compromising information on the superior and use it to remove the person from their position through exposure. Another option is to use black propaganda methods to discredit the superior and have the company remove them of its own accord. Upward mobility of a source can be a delicate and time consuming process, but has proven to be highly effective.

Another means of building up an asset is through gifts and information. By providing the source with covertly or overtly obtained intelligence about business deals and strategy, they can give the asset a major advantage over his rivals within a company which can lead to natural promotion and further enhanced access. Advice from the spy on how to operate within the corporate world or on life issues in general can aid the source to become a better business person and more socially adept which will further aid their rise. Tasteful gifts and bribes provided by the spy on behalf of the source to superiors can also help speed their promotion within the company.

Helping a source to develop within the target company and take on a better position with greater fields of access can often be done quietly and is a highly effective, if longer term, approach to building up a deep penetration within an organization. It serves to boost the morale of the source and build their dependence on the spy, which is beneficial to both mental stability and source loyalty. A spy who becomes the fountain of plenty in the life of the source will quickly become a treasured resource to be served and protected.

Mental Health of the Source

Maintenance of the mental health of a source during the course of an operation can be one of the most problematic aspects of running a human intelligence asset against a company. People are fragile creatures, who for the most part are neither conditioned nor capable of dealing with the extreme stresses of covert employment. Every source, no matter how gung-ho they may seem, feels the stress of covert operations to one degree or another. How they react to this stress can dictate the dimensions of success or failure for an intelligence operation.

Reassuring a Source

It may seem counter intuitive and certainly not very sexy, but a great deal of what a spy does is hand holding assets once they are in play. People under operational stress require constant reassurance that they are special, that what they are doing is safe and that the spy cares and will protect them in case anything goes wrong. Generally, all that is required of the spy is a kind word or two, to really listen and tangibly address the concerns of their sources. In many ways, running a covert source is similar to conducting an illicit love affair. The egos and worries of both lovers and assets should be addressed concretely by both word and deed. Often it takes very little to reassure an asset, but as in love, it is the smallest of gestures that make all of the difference.

Gifts

If flowers for no reason make a person's wife smile, then image what little gifts to an asset who has a much more complex, dependant and emotionally uneven relationship with a spy can do. The power of gifts is understood and deeply ingrained in many cultures for good reason. In America, where people are conditioned to only expecting gifts on special occasions, they hold a powerful magic in the minds of sources.

Gifts do not have to be elaborate or costly, just thoughtful. A careful balance must be struck so that the agent is not over gifting, which can lead to the source becoming jaded. Typical gifts that spies give to their sources to boost them up are watches, jewelry for their wives or girlfriends, cash bonuses, rare books, items the source collects, alcohol and drugs. Gifts do not necessarily need to be things either. Taking an asset out for a good time on the town, paying for flying lessons, providing school fees for their children or arranging that dream vacation have all been used by spies to buy loyalty and reward assets.

Developing Long-Term Leverage

The process of building up an asset often involves indulging their vices and becoming the provider of covert services. Supplying goods and services can be a very useful role for a spy to take in the life of an asset because it allow them to take control of the asset's outlets for pleasure and to build up long-term leverage over the source to better keep them in line. It also keeps the source out of the black market where they are more likely to be stumbled upon by police and other security services.

Becoming the panderer for an asset can be as simple as supplying them with lap dances at the strip club or bags of cocaine on the weekends. It can easily be built into an elaborate system of services which are only limited by the depths of depravity of the source. It all depends on what the source is into and how willing the spy is to provide these services. One bonus for the spy in becoming the source for these services is that with their covert training and illicit resources they are better equipped to supply the source with illegal goods and services than are the sources themselves. This can keep the source from being arrested for other illegal activities, which is one of the main avenues that the authorities have for detecting covert operations. A source arrested in a whorehouse or drug sting can be counted on to try to buy their way out of trouble by offering up their connection with a spy every time. Thus by putting a buffer between the source and the underworld, where virtually all law enforcement efforts are targeted, the spy can add an additional layer of operational security and simultaneously build a deeper dependence on the part of the source.

Cultural and Social Differences

When an asset is in play and the spy turns into their minder, it is important for the intelligence agent to remember to be culturally sensitive and operate with full awareness of the individual needs of the asset. A spy, at all times, must keep themselves from coming between a source and their religion, sense of national pride or other culturally significant practices. In this way, they appear as more of a friend and prevent unnecessary friction from developing within the source-handler relationship. Being cultural and socially sensitive can be achieved by observing the little things. Don't take an observant Muslim source out to for pork ribs; don't offer cocaine and hookers to a Mormon source;

don't demand a meeting with a Chinese source during Chinese New Years and so on. If the spy has never dealt with a person from the source's background, there are books, websites and any number of resources and people available to help them get a grasp on the cultural issues that may emerge, as well as generate a useful list of do's and don'ts.

Managing Psychological Reactions

Over the long term, a spy must keep a close eye on their sources in order to prevent psychological breakdown, which is an unfortunately common occurrence among all participants in the espionage game. The operation may hinge on detecting an imminent breakdown in a source early and treating it effectively.

A very good method of shoring up a source psychologically is to change the MICE equation running the overall relationship and broaden the vectors of justification that a source can use internally to come to terms with their actions. If a source starts out spying for money a clever spy will attempt to engage their ego or create a sense of national duty to broaden the justification base for the source. Changing the MICE equation with the source is especially valuable if a source was recruited under duress or by coercion. Shifting the source's self justification vector onto something more positive and less mentally corrosive can make or break the level of cooperation that a spy can expect to receive from them over a long period of time. Engaging in illegal and covert acts is especially emotionally taxing to anyone not trained or hardened against the wear and tear of continued stress. The stress can be counteracted best through self justification and placing a positive spin on the actions of the asset in their own minds. The best stress medicine, after all, comes from within.

A frequent symptom of emotional stress in an asset is self destructive behavior. Sloppiness at work, careless grooming habits, cheating on a wife, drinking too much, doing drugs too often, and emotionally abusing loved ones are all common symptoms of stress among assets. Unfortunately, there is little that a spy can do during an operation to counteract these symptoms except act as a support to their source and try to encourage the source to engage in more constructive behaviors. Using the leverage that a spy may hold over their source to force overt changes in behavior can work over the short term, but is rarely effective over extended periods of time. Getting the source into new hobbies, getting them laid and controlling the amount of illegal substances that they consume are sometimes effective stop gap solutions to self destructive behavior. If possible providing them with a bent psychologist or spiritual advisor, one who is under positive control by the spy, can be extremely useful. In the event the asset will not seek or accept help, then the spy must prepare contingency plans for the occurrence of final self destruction on the part of their source. In this phase of the relationship, constant monitoring of the asset, if possible, is desirable. Burning links and potential areas of exposure in the event of the asset turning is also advisable. Tearing down the infrastructure for a long-term operation can take time and may require significant resources. This dismantling should be started when the signs begin to point to terminal breakdown of a key source. Being prepared by staying on top of the mental condition of the source can make all of the difference.

There is a brilliant line in the movie Spy Games between Robert Redford's character the veteran spy and Brad Pitt's young agent in training, "If it ever comes down to you or your source, send flowers". If a source self destructs, it is time to burn the links between the spy and their source and move on or flee. It is a very common occurrence between spies and their assets that during the process of recruitment and running the source the intelligence agent develops a very deep attachment to their Joe. This can be a good thing when the source is safe and operating well because it can deepen the sense of dependence and loyalty felt by the asset. When things go wrong, however, more than one professional espionage agent has gone to their grave or to prison because they went too far out on a limb trying to save their source.

Corporate espionage is not state intelligence. There is no amorphous reputation of the nation at stake if the private intelligence agent burns their sources or allows them to self destruct. This is one of the main areas of difference between private and state-based intelligence. In the CIA they teach new officers that the safety and security of the source is all important. This is proper because if the CIA gets a reputation for letting their sources twist in the wind when things get bad, fewer people out there in the world will agree to work with them in the future. For private intelligence organizations, potential sources have no way of checking an agent's pedigree or the reliability of the organization that runs them. Thus, there is no reputation to protect and for corporate spooks the needs and safety of the asset always come after the needs and safety of the agent. This may seem cold, but for mercenary spooks, if it comes down to their freedom or that of their source, most send flowers.

In corporate espionage the risks for both assets and agent rarely include death. However, prison or personal law suits are never a pleasant experience and are the reasons that intelligence gathering measures are kept covert. Private intelligence practices that cross the grey line are illegal after all. If a source gets caught out doing something illegal and flips or succumbs to the stress and guilt of living a covert life and confesses and the agent does not detect this, the result is often jail or worse for the unwary spy.

Constant vigilance and good tradecraft can help to protect an agent against their sources and the opposition, but nothing beats having a solid cover and a good lawyer, just in case. The US is not Soviet Russia and the means available to law enforcement agencies in America to prove espionage charges are few, time consuming and cumbersome.

Because the corporate intelligence agent is not involved in a violent crime and many jurisdictions hold the elements that make up corporate espionage activities to be misdemeanors or minor felonies, a decent lawyer can often have an agent out even before the State Department steps in to release them. Corporate espionage is a tricky subject for many law enforcement agencies because it often involves potential conflict with national interests and security and is so difficult to prove, that they devote little or no resources to policing it on a regular basis. State opposition forces can be extremely uninterested in developing effective prosecution, so even if caught, if an intelligence agent keeps their head, they are at low risk of ever serving jail time. Another aspect is that in order to develop the kind of volume of solid evidence that a prosecutor would demand of federal agents or local law enforcement to take a corporate espionage case to trial, they would have to place the agent under surveillance for extended periods of time, penetrate their safe houses and tip their hand through investigation. If the spy does not detect this kind of surveillance and does not use basic tradecraft to detect counter intelligence activities against them, then they almost deserve to get caught. The targets of corporate intelligence may be soft, but that is no excuse for the intelligence operators to skimp on their basic tradecraft. After all, much of the core work in intelligence training is targeted on teaching spies to detect and evade opposition investigation and surveillance. Covert operation is what makes corporate espionage cases so difficult to prove and hard to investigate for authorities. In case after case, where the local authorities have come close to a corporate spy, they were detected and the spy went further underground until the mission was completed or just fled.

If opposition action is discovered working against the agent, it is time to either finish the mission quickly or get out all together. Few spies will risk their freedom to complete a corporate espionage operation in the face of real opposition pressure, but there are always a few who are reckless or skilled enough to pull it off. If the spy feels that they have been detected, then going underground, assuming a back up identity and pushing the assets for quick and dirty completion of a mission is the order of the day. If the spy does continue to operate after being detected a good tactical move is to start their own system of surveillance on the watchers. Planting a bug in the offices of the task force looking into the case can be done as can turning one of the members of the opposition forces to feed the spy information from inside of the investigation. Police, counter intelligence and other opposition forces will rarely feel threatened by the prey they hunt. Counter-intelligence can work to the advantage of a clever spy, since it means that if they take steps to penetrate an active investigation into their activities there will generally be few obstacles and little internal security in their way. Once penetrated, the spy can thus learn exactly what the investigation has uncovered about their operation and perhaps deploy counter measures to give them enough time to complete their assignment. Running an intelligence operation against the police itself is a tactic being employed by criminal cartels around the world, so it is not surprising that this is also a favored tactic among trained private intelligence agents as well. As a further option, if there are numerous assets in place and the operation is only lightly penetrated, bring in a replacement intelligence agent to take over and have the spy visibly flee so that the opposition focuses on looking for them and eventually on closing the case with what they have in hand.

Occasionally an operation is exposed by internal corporate security. Often this is due to a source confessing to their employers, but occasionally a company stumbles upon a penetration or wrongdoing on their own. In this event, a company's first act to isolate the leak, determine the degree of internal security breach, deal with the offender and bury the issue before they would ever consider taking the matter to the police. One of the main reasons that corporate espionage is rarely reported to authorities is that no reporting requirement exists, certainly not one that is enforced, and the repercussions if news got out that the company was effectively penetrated can be devastating. Just look at the case of the Sony network. Their systems were penetrated by "rogue hackers" and they are actively trying to pin down blame with the help of the FBI and other counter intelligence services. Even if they manage to catch those responsible how could that in any way make up for the billions of dollars in loss that the company has already suffered directly in addition to the damage to their reputation and peripheral services. Penalties for companies, if a penetration is made public, include a drop in share holder confidence and stock price, which in turn means that senior executives get fired. In a nut shell fear within the upper echelons of the company itself of exposure of lax security to the investing public is what makes corporate espionage such an easy and relatively risk free option for companies in America and elsewhere. Corporate America has not gone out and demanded effective policing, government action or sanction against countries, companies or individuals that conduct such corporate intelligence actions, despite the estimated losses to American businesses annually of hundreds of billions of dollars, because if there ever was effective action taken against espionage agents it would mean detailing their targets and the penetrations which took place among these companies. In the real world, that means virtually every CEO of every Fortune 500 company would be vulnerable, because all of these companies have been targeted and many have been penetrated repeatedly. Self interest and self preservation keep companies silent on the damage inflicted by corporate espionage and thus keeps agents safe, even when discovered.

Backup Plans and Exfiltration

When an agent is at risk, they are most likely to flee, with or without the mission being completed. To run away is actually encouraged by the employers of a spies because, while losing a source is one thing, a spy is likely running multiple assets in a company and has a great deal of information with which to trade with law enforcement and counter intelligence in return for immunity or a lighter sentence. Just as there exists little loyalty of sources to the target company, private spies are mercenary and more likely to flip on their corporate employers if caught, than those who work for state intelligence services. So the extraction of an agent from a dangerous situation becomes a priority, not just for the agents themselves but for those sponsoring them as well.

Trained intelligence agents universally keep what is called a "bug out kit". The kit contains alternative identity documents, cash and other tools of escape in a safe location in the event of an emergency situation, particularly if an agent is operating overseas or against more draconian counter intelligence services. These kits help an agent make a quick getaway and are often emplaced as the first act upon arriving in a target area. By secreting a bug out kit in an area that is secure, easy to get to at any hour, has multiple exits and from which they have access to multiple means of transport, an agent can make a quick get away with little or no notice.

Fleeing the area of operations is not always necessary at the first hint of trouble. If an agent goes to ground in a prearranged safe house that has been kept sterile, they can often weather the initial search and leave at a later date when the heat is down. If no such facility exists or there is the potential that it is burned, then running is often the only option. The goal is to get away from pursuit and go somewhere safe. Safe can mean many things, but usually consists of a foreign locale or home country. To get from point A to point B, the spy can choose from a range of travel options, some more covert than others. Even the most massive manhunts rarely close major freeways in the United States. For example, if a spy needs to flee from Dallas, they just get in their car, usually a sterile car that has not been used operationally, get on the freeway and drive to the nearest major city and fly out from there. Spies often take a moment during the course of their flight to stop and change their appearance. A good backup cover identity has a completely different look than the identity under which a spy was primarily operating. More casual or more sever, older or younger, facial hair or no facial hair, citizen of the country or foreigner, a great many changes can be made quickly and easily to alter the appearance and demeanor of a spy seeking to escape detection.

The spy has a major advantage, particularly in a country like the US, over the pursuing forces ranged against him or her. One just has to look at how difficult it is for police to find murderers and other violent offenders, who are generally not the most clever people to roam the earth, to consider how a high degree of training improves a person's chances of avoiding capture long enough to get on an international flight or serendipitously cross an unsecured border. A spy typically has resources behind them, false identity documents and money to aid in their flight as well. It is important to note that most spies will not attempt to fight it out with authorities if cornered during the escape. There is little in the covert intelligence collection process that stands as a major crime and unless the agent has committed a felonious act, it is better to let a lawyer get them out of trouble than a 9mm.

Once a spy is abroad, they will be debriefed by their organization to determine what went wrong, then perhaps a bit of rest and then off to another city and another assignment.

Completing the Intelligence Gathering Cycle

Most missions have a set series of goals and operational parameters. The spy is given a specific target to penetrate and a set of instructions on what the individual or corporation hiring them is interested in learning. Once these goals are met and the client satisfied the mission is over. If the client chooses to continue the operation and keep a turned source in place spying for them, then that is their decision and mission parameters can be adjusted accordingly. In most cases, corporate espionage is in and out. Clients are interested in a single set of data and once this is received they want the agent out and the covert operation shut down, primarily for cost and security reasons. What does this mean for the sources that have been recruited and are busy turning over those juicy company secrets?

In most cases, the agent explains to their inside assets that since the mission is completed, their services are no longer required, but another mission may arise and they will be called on again. If the agent has recruited under a false flag or is using coercion, the source may be relieved that their term of service is at an end. If the asset is doing it for the money, or more egotistical reasons, the end of an assignment may not be a happy day. This closure and departure can test the resourcefulness of the agent and their bond with the source to the limit.

Espionage relationships end once the spy has what they came for. Shutting down an operation may be the result of asset collapse, but if the source is chosen carefully and managed well, the most likely outcome is that they continue to operate until the agent has no further need for them. Termination may be emotionally painful, and put an end to the asset's new found money tap, but there is little that they can do. The resource is placed on an intelligence agent's list of open sources that may be used again in the event that the agent is sent back to target that company or any other company the source eventually moves to. A few agents do keep private sources running, but this is the rare exception rather than the rule.

In some instances, the agent is required to burn their agents. This sounds sinister, but it basically means that they inform the company or the authorities, that the source has been spying on them and let them sort it all out. There are several reasons why this action is taken. The most common motivation is money. Known as double dipping an operation, a spy will recruit a source within an organization and once they have received all of the target information or the usefulness of the source is exhausted, they sell the identity of the source back to the target company for a fee. Generally, spies are opposed to burning sources to make a quick extra buck and agents do get emotionally attached to the source to one degree or another. As well as being seen as wasteful, it is difficult to hang people you work with and care for out to dry. But a job is a job, and often the decision is made higher up the cut out chain. There is also the mercenary aspect of private intelligence that holds to getting what you can while you can regardless of what the outcome is for individual assets. Double dipping is one of the primary sources of discovery of corporate espionage assets by companies. Another reason for burning a source is to place suspicion for the act of espionage on another competitor company. This can be a highly effective way to get more bang for your buck from an asset. Burning targets the anger and repercussions from the act away from the actual company engaged in espionage, and is also useful to burn particularly effective members of a rival firm's team by laying the onus directly on the door of a sharp rival employee.

Leaving Presents

When an intelligence operation is at an end it is always nice to leave a few "presents" behind in the target company. If the spy has access to the necessary technical tools like computer virus programs and other trap door utilities, they can always try to get the source, even if it was not part of the intelligence tasking, to lay in some covert programming onto the company systems. These presents can be personal for the individual spy or as part of a general program that the private intelligence firm has to maintain latent access to already penetrated systems. As a last act this is a very good way for an agent to generate some additional benefit from their already turned source. Even if the source is caught emplacing these backdoors, it doesn't matter to the spy because the main operation is complete and the source was disposable anyway.

Some sources are just too valuable to burn or leave behind. For these individuals, maintaining an active relationship can be difficult, but is generally worth the effort. Modern technology helps to keep a spy in touch with his or her flock via email, VOIP, cell calls, etc. One regularly employed option is to leave a junior member of a corporate intelligence firm on station to service the important assets in place after the senior spy leaves to take another assignment. This is a cost effective method which allows the more junior members of an espionage team to get field experience while under minimal threat and with little possibility for error. A further option is to turn the source into a sleeper. Creating sleeper cells within a company by using already recruited and confirmed sources is a very common practice. As long as the source is kept in positive stasis, this option allows the spy to keep a ready source of assets within a certain company (perhaps one that they are regularly tasked with penetrating) with little risk of being discovered since they are inactive and thus almost invisible to counter intelligence agents. After all, kinetic action on the part of assets and spies is what most often leads to discovery. If a source is to be kept in play or turned into a sleeper, it is most commonly the intelligence firm, not the individual spy which takes the lead. They have resources which the individual spy does not and run groups of corporate spooks whose efforts can thus act to mutual benefit.

Sanitizing the Operational Area

The last act of an espionage agent when a mission is concluded, is to dismantle the covert infrastructure that was laid in at the beginning and to move on. Taking apart the infrastructure of an operation means destroying any files or other evidence that remain in the hands of the asset, sanitizing the safe houses and cars, purging as much as possible of the record of the time that the agent was in theater and any number of other housekeeping chores that might be needed to break the trail in the event of later discovery of the espionage actions by the opposition.

Getting rid of cars is as easy as dropping them in a bad part of town with the keys in the ignition and walking away. A spy can drop computers and other technical equipment, once their hard drives have been thoroughly purged of information, directly at the local dump or just leave it in a coffee shop anywhere in the local university district to affect magical disappearance. For papers and other materials nothing beats a good bonfire. If fire is not an option a shredder or a box of hefty plastic bags and a trip to the dump or the nearest large body of water will do. Any storage medium including computer hard drives, memory sticks, servers, printers and copiers that have been used operationally should be completely purged and their hard drives overwritten multiple times if not destroyed outright before they are disposed of. There are numbers of different freeware programs available online that do a terrific job of writing over hard drives thousands of times so that the contents becomes irrecoverable.

Once the spy has sanitized the operational areas it is time to leave. Larger organizations often have specialists who fly in to handle only the post operational cleanup which frees the operational spy from such chores. Even still many spies prefer to do this work themselves to make sure everything is taken care of. After all it is their life and freedom on the line if traces are left for the opposition. It is always a good idea to move spies around after a period of operational endeavor, even if just for a short period of time, in order to better break any potential trail between the spy and local wrong doing. A spy should never work where they actually live because there are just too many potential risk factors, even in a large city.

Now that the mission is complete, assets sorted, operation shut down and the trail broken, it is time for a vacation. Going somewhere sunny that has quality red wine and a good library is recommended.

Technical Collection

Introduction

The collection of information via technical or non-human means plays a prominent, if not dominant, role in the modern covert intelligence collection process. The infancy of technical intelligence gathering techniques such as radio intercepts, aerial photography and direction finding has given way, as advanced technologies for communication and data storage become more prevalent in business, to a golden age of information espionage. As the information revolution continues to evolve, spies all over the world are coming to absolutely rely on advanced technology to help them develop and gather intelligence. The utility of technical intelligence collection is increasing as greater amounts of valuable commercial data is stored externally and communicated digitally, much of it minimally protected against intelligence gathering.

In today's world, most information is held on computer systems and digital communications rule the air. Single source human intelligence within a corporation may be able to provide the spy with a limited amount of insider knowledge about company operations, personnel and individual secrets, but virtually every piece of valuable information generated by a company is held on its internal computer systems. If a spy can access these same systems, they can obtain total information awareness and bleed a company dry in minutes. Recognizing this vulnerability, companies have spent fortunes on securing their internal networks and corporate computer systems. Systems security today receives the lion's share of total corporate security spending and computer systems are becoming better protected all of the time. For the corporate spy this enhanced security means that such systems are often difficult to penetrate directly. Spies must resort ect measures to covertly gain access to secured company tems.

ɘarch for data access, more often than not, leads to the sources to provide access to systems and not as individual data sources. Unfortunately for most companies, the disproportionately large share of security spending on information technology has left glaring weaknesses on the human side while giving a false sense of safety from attack. Time and again supposedly secure systems are penetrated by intelligence agents and malicious hackers. Given the level of resources that accompany major corporate intelligence efforts, it is shocking how complacent leaders in the business world have been on this critical security issue. Corporate spies contract with extremely adept world class hackers who spend their lives discovering weaknesses in computer systems. The more complex a system is the greater the likelihood of a security weakness existing. For corporations, that makes nearly every system on Earth hackable if the proper resources are deployed against it. Corporate spies also have the distinct advantage of their ability to recruit human sources within the company itself. Protecting company secrets with powerful external penetration barriers and ICE (intrusion countermeasures electronic) has never been wholly sufficient to protect important data. With the recent boom in computer and device integration, online and cloud computing and other advances new loop holes in even the most hardened systems are discovered with disturbing regularity.

Not just heavily guarded corporate computer networks are at risk from technical penetration. Communications intercepts, bugging, laser mic surveillance, digital surveillance, GPS tracking and other vectors can all yield massive amounts of commercially valuable data to the corporate spy and those who employ them.

Technical intelligence provides vectors of attack that hold significant advantages over a pure human intelligence gathering approach. Intercepting communications and corrupting computer systems can be done covertly without the need for turned em and the penetration can remain undiscovered for a long time the mess and drama of human recruitment and source running. I persistence and operational security of technical intelligence collection that are its biggest assets. Once a computer penetration is opened, the likelihood of detection is relatively low. As with human intelligence, the greatest threat of detection exists when the operation is in motion. Kinetic penetration activity leaves more traces to detect than does passive monitoring or occasional data dumping from a compromised system. A further benefit to this form of espionage penetration is the fact that few people are aware that the majority of esoteric measures used to gather technical intelligence even exist. Due to the very exotic and technical nature of these actions, they are hard for non specialists such as senior management to really understand and thus to allocate the resources needed to defend against.

The internet, while developed as a legitimate communications tool, has proven to be the most revolutionary development in intelligence gathering since the first whisper spoken by man. The vast amount of information available to a spy online and the lack of effective security provide a perfect medium for intelligence gathering. The internet also gives the spy an entirely new means of conducting non-technical operations covertly. The net has proven to be a true revolution in the intelligence world. It provides information, surveillance options, vast fields of raw data held externally and open to penetration, as well as secure communications options undreamed of even a generation ago. The internet has supplanted entire fields of tradecraft and taken the art of state and corporate intelligence into a new digital golden age.

Technical intelligence can be conducted by a sophisticated spy or by specialized members of their team as a standalone method for generating intelligence or more effectively in conjunction with a human intelligence program. As a standalone operation, technical intelligence gathering is often focused on computer hacking, communications interception and bugging to directly generate commercially valuable information. The increased sophistication of computer and communications systems, while opening new vistas in the intelligence world, has also made such actions more difficult and technically demanding to carry out. This barrier is where a human intelligence program can aid the technical side of intelligence gathering. An authorized user, once recruited, inside of the protected circle of legitimate users can provide the spy unfettered access to otherwise virtually impervious systems. A turned employee at the cell phone provider can give records and potentially covert access to a target's smart phone. A source inside of the IT or security staff can give the spy, and their hackers, a complete run down on the type and level of defense in place and help them devise effective penetration vectors. A turned employ can implant bugs and other monitoring equipment onsite at the target company. The utility of the human source in the aid of technical intelligence operations can be many. While technical intelligence on its own can be highly effective, few spies seek to employ it without also considering a parallel human intelligence program.

Technology has come to dominate the modern business and social world. It is only logical that spies and their backers rely more and more on that same technology to develop new avenues of intelligence gathering against their targets. The internet and advanced communications tools have placed nearly all commercially valuable information at risk of compromise from a growing worldwide cadre of highly skilled hackers. These hackers, acting freelance or as part of an in-house team, have access to some of the most advanced cyber crime tools in the world and little compunction to using them. Providing a hacker or team of hackers with corporate grade ICE breaking software and advanced cyber weapons systems and paying them to use these tools to operate against other firms has revolutionized the capability of companies to gather intelligence on or actively attack their rivals.

Digital communications are vulnerable and easily intercepted. The degree of vulnerability of communications is something that few business people realize as they discuss sensitive company affairs on their phones all day. Other technical means of intelligence gathering, such as bugging and covert monitoring, have become increasingly easy to carry out and the tools needed to do so are constantly shrinking in size and price.

Many companies have placed significant barriers around their most critical computer systems, but ignore the myriad other penetration vectors that are available to the modern corporate intelligence agent, let alone the teams of sophisticated technicals that such spies may employ. In this section we will examine what a corporate spook looks for when they use technical intelligence gathering measures to operate against a target. Many of these areas will seem better suited to the realm of fiction, but all continue to be used by increasingly tech savvy spies around the world against unsuspecting firms and they are all very real.

Identifying Personnel and Equipment Needs

When an operation is being planned the spy will look for the most efficient means of acquiring the data required to fulfill their tasking. In many cases, penetration and acquisition will require a technical intelligence gathering capability of one variety or another. Determining what might be needed, both in terms of specialist personnel and equipment, is very important so that resources can be sought out and installed before they are required and not scrapped together at the last minute.

The majority of technical intelligence can only be gathered using specialized equipment and by individuals with advanced technical knowledge. The average corporate spy is not capable of operating the high-tech intercept and computer penetration resources needed to conduct technical intelligence operations, and often requires a team of specialists to help them. Needing a team is a significant drawback to technical intelligence gathering operations because it may require several highly skilled individuals operating covertly. There is always an increased risk when bringing more people into a covert operation, particularly if they are techs and not trained intelligence agents. The need for expanded technical staff makes an operation easier to detect and more difficult to set up and run. Technical capability included in an operation can provide many benefits, but if not strictly required to complete the set objectives is often better left off of the table. A balance should be struck to suit the conditions on the ground with each individual mission.

Coming up with a balanced approach to intelligence collection is critical to success. If there is limited appeal in extracting information via a human source, but the target company leaves its R&D section conference room unprotected or the company is using compromised ICE to protect its core systems, then a more technical approach presents a superior option. The goal is efficiency and knowing what tool to use for each job.

In some instances, no matter how desirable it would be to have a first class hacker on hand, such a resource is not available or would be difficult to recruit quickly to the task. If resources are unavailable, the spy will just have to do the task themselves or chose another approach. A quick search online often yields many of the tools and training required to conduct even highly specialized technical intelligence operations. Corporate spies spend time training themselves in technical fields to improve their individual capabilities between and during operations. Yet, few are true masters of the more esoteric technical aspects of intelligence gathering and will require assistance if the task is too complex.

Corporate intelligence teams run in-house often maintain a stable of bent technical specialists and black hat hackers who can run technical operations as needed. Recourse to powerful technical assistance is another reason that in-house and larger intelligence firms hold the advantage in the corporate espionage world over freelance operators.

Building a Team

Assuming that the spy has access to the bent specialists needed during in operation, the first step is to recruit them to the mission. This recruitment is usually handled separately by the agency or firm running the intelligence agent in the field. The need for cutouts is greater with bent technical specialists than with most other players on the darker side of the grey line. Given their skill sets and the vulnerability of most communications medium, even those used by spies, keeping the techs away from the originating source of an operation can be critical. Hackers and technical types tend to be info-fetishists, so extra precautions are taken to keep critical information walled off from these types even while they are directly involved in an ongoing operation.

Larger private intelligence firms, in-house intelligence and state run corporate espionage organizations all keep personnel with advanced technical intelligence collection skills available and on call to deploy to the field in support of their espionage operations. Once a technical intelligence objective has been worked out, staff with the right skill sets are chosen and sent to the area of operations to set up and run technical penetration equipment. For net-based technical operations, where physical proximity to the target is not required, the hacker generally conducts the required tasks from their base, wherever that may be. It is always advisable to limit the number of people sent out to the field in support of technical operations as much as possible. If a task can be carried out remotely, then it should be. If a bent technical goes into the field in support of operations, they become the responsibility of the intelligence agent in place. The main reason not to send bent technical operations staff into the field is that most do not possess adequate tradecraft training to operate solo and must be monitored by the espionage agent running the operation in theater. Have to keep some hacker or communications specialist safe and secure in country complicates the job of the spy and makes the operation itself more vulnerable to detection and compromise.

Individual intelligence agents tend to develop relationships with their own group of bent technicians and black hat hackers. They prefer to work with proven resources that are trustworthy in the field. If possible it is usually better to let the lead agent select their own personnel rather than to send a group of unknowns to them. Occasionally, spies recruit personnel from legitimate business circles and use them for covert jobs. This method provides an excellent cover where many technical specialists and hackers work freelance anyway.

It is something of a cliché, but bent technicians are some of the strangest individuals around. Hackers in particular, because of their youth and prowess, tend to be arrogant and eccentric to the extreme. Such individualistic personalities have trouble working undercover and require extra care and handling by the agents in the field. Coordinating techies in the field is an art and requires the agent to keep a tight rein on their teams at all times. This can easily lead to a significant level of distraction for the spy in theater and is one reason that a number of agents actually prefer to do without if possible rather than run the additional risks that untrained techs present during a critical mission.

Maintaining operational security, while babysitting a team of bent techies, can be a challenge. One benefit to working with hackers is that they rarely appear in theater and are very protective of their own individual security by nature. Keeping a hacker safe from opposition detection is something they are much better at doing themselves than any intelligence agent. Keeping the technical team located in separate safe houses and physically disconnected from human sources is an operational security priority. Technical experts are often an integral part of the recruiting and asset running process, but given their generally limited skills at trade craft, it is advisable that they be removed from daily operations as much as possible.

Technical staff almost certainly will require specialized equipment to operate effectively. The need to acquire and operate such equipment is one of the main drawbacks to using advanced technical intelligence techniques. Within the realm of corporate intelligence with its lower level of defensive countermeasures, the need for highly specialized and powerful equipment is reduced. That being said, computer hacking, communications interception, wifi cracking, bugging, technical surveillance and sabotage can still require some sophisticated gear which may be difficult to acquire locally. In the US, a staggering amount of highly potent technical intelligence gear is readily available commercially. Overseas, much of this same gear can be imported legally, purchased locally or assembled by the technical personnel themselves. Anything over-specialized that is solely and recognizably used for espionage should be avoided.

Embedding a technical team on-site means providing cover, a safe operating environment and exfiltration infrastructure for them to use. Although extra work on the ground is required of the spy, the benefits of a technical intelligence collection apparatus can be dramatic. When feasible, it is included in every operation that can support it.

Identifying Technical Targets

Similar to human intelligence targeting, just because a person can be turned, a network penetrated or communications intercepted, does not necessarily mean that they should be. An experienced spy knows how to custom tailor all aspects of an operation to meet specific mission goals. The more kinetic operations are, the greater the possibility of detection and compromise. But spies are, by definition, information junkies. It is the rare operator who will not want to read every email or tap every phone they can get away with. Thus, it is very important that clear targets and penetration options be selected as carefully as possible.

The most common technical targets are computer systems. As a rule, corporate core systems are highly protected and require sophisticated techniques and highly skilled hackers to penetrate directly. Obviously, this is not always the case. Many times a lone spy probes a company that spends millions annually on network security, only to find that a lazy administrator didn't change the preset passwords or used one that took mere minutes to crack. An experienced spy will always discretely probe a bit, just in case, before calling in the class A hacker teams. Home systems tend to be much easier to penetrate than core corporate systems, making them obvious next in line targets for the spy when the corporate main systems are tightly held. Third on the list are systems that handle valuable information but are not part of the corporate network. Off site service firms, suppliers, lawyers and offsite backups are all part of this list of tertiary target systems.

After computer systems, the next common technical intelligence collection points are communications. Targeting cell phones and land lines, fax systems and wifi networks requires specific gear and advanced technical training, but can yield exceptional amounts of information. Because the majority of modern communication is wireless, collection nodes can be placed at a distance from the targeted company or individual's home. Not being right on-site provides the spy with an extra degree of operational security.

The third most common technical means of penetrating a company is to bug it with visual and/or audio listening devices. Placing a bug in the CEO's office or secret R&D group's meeting room requires physical access to the location, which the spy must work out before the device can be emplaced. Currently, there are "work around" options and even remote controlled surveillance drones available which can remove the need to physically implant a bug onsite. Cell phones and other devices can be converted into clandestine listening devices with simple programs available online. Laser microphones can reflect light off of a window to receive sound from inside. Drones can be tasked with loitering above an office complex to soak up wireless signals and cell calls or to utilize the duck system to emplace discreet bugs. All of these devices eliminate the need for actual physical penetration on the part of the spy, but do require other degrees of preparation. If physical penetration and placement is called for, the use of a source to emplace the clandestine listening device is generally preferred over the spies themselves breaking in. Because bugs have become so small and self-sustaining, the implant process has become much easier than it used to be and the need for maintenance or replacement much lower.

Target Selection Criteria

When mounting a technical intelligence gathering operation, the first criteria for target selection is access. There are many different avenues of technical intelligence attack available to the modern spy, but some are more difficult to emplace than others. Looking for open or accessible systems is the first task to determine which technical intelligence assets are to be used. Once an information goal is determined and access tested, the next criteria question is who and what to utilize. This comes back to the idea that less is often more when it comes to intelligence operations. The fewer components in any operation, the more secure it is going to be.

Net Based Intelligence

In the information age, the majority of technical intelligence collection is done online. Breaching corporate systems, hacking online identities, gathering basic intelligence and direct attacks can all be accomplished via the internet. The very openness of information and communications that have allowed companies to grow over the past decades and become more productive has also placed their most sensitive data within relatively easy reach of corporate intelligence agents.

Net based attacks on computers and other systems are the preserve of the hackers. While most of the corporate intelligence gathering operations today do not strictly require the services of high grade hackers, they are becoming an ever more common fixture. The need for high grade hackers will only grow as the utility and reach of information systems increases. Thankfully, there exists a glut of extremely talented hackers out there for covert intelligence agents to employ. Hackers used by corporate intelligence tend to be solo operators and located off-site. This privacy is for security and personal reasons. Hackers are universally loath to reveal their identities or physical locations to spies. They consider it something of a challenge and show of prowess to remain as anonymous as possible. Although recruited from all over the world, the operational spy on the ground will rarely know exactly who it is they are dealing with or where a hacker is actually physically located. Even in-house corporate intelligence teams and larger private firms tend to keep their hackers separate from the field intelligence agents. Hackers and high grade programmers are kept apart because there is rarely a need to bring them out into the field and giving hackers more inside knowledge of an operation than they strictly need can prove to be extremely problematic from a security stand point. It is safer for all involved that the hackers and spies never actually meet. When nearly everything that a hacker can do is done from the safety of overseas, it makes sense to keep them there and out of the field spy's way. Larger intelligence firms keep their hackers busy between assignments developing new penetration techniques and tools or devising special mission specific viruses. Progressive in-house intelligence arms have entire information tech campuses stuffed with computer programmers and hackers working on covert penetration software, tailored viruses and other advanced cyber weapons. These nests operate under legitimate auspices as computer security or research companies and are capable of producing some extremely powerful attack software. This is a very high growth industry and one that is sure to play a pivotal role in the covert corporate wars of tomorrow.

Much has been written and even more speculated about the covert cyber warfare development and operations arm of various state militaries and intelligence services in the US and abroad. The US government today employs thousands of skilled computer programmers and other techs to build up the nation's cyber war arsenal. Not far behind the US in the development of advanced cyber warfare capabilities are the Chinese, Russians, Israelis, Germans and virtually every other industrialized state. Such new technological weapons are seen as vital to future warfare and great asymmetrical weapons. What is always missing in the media hype surrounding this topic is the fact that a growing number of private companies are doing the exact same thing. Two insightful items are of interest here. First, private industry pays better than governments. Why work for the Russian government for a few rubles when a high grade hacker can make a private sector level salary of hundreds of thousands working for a corporate espionage group? Private intelligence groups are also able to recruit class A hackers from Germany, Scandinavia, the US, Canada, Russia, Korea and Japan without requiring a potential recruit to pass through an overly protective security clearance system. This is a huge advantage over domestic state run intelligence services and military cyber weapons development programs. Second, a number of the best hackers in the world would not work for the National Security Agency or any other government agencies even if asked. Hackers with criminal records (black hat hacking is a crime) may also find it difficult to get employment commensurate with their talents in the legitimate private sector, making them prime recruiting material for covert corporate operations groups.

The attack and penetration programs that in-house groups of hackers are producing for corporate espionage agents are easily on par, and often exceed the capabilities of the best government cyber weapons programs. It is not unheard of either for military grade cyber weapons to take a walk off base and right into the hands of private sector intelligence groups. A growing number of countries find it expedient for private firms to field test cyber weapons for them against corporate targets which use similar defenses as rival government or high value private sector systems. This allows them to study the effectiveness of their cyber weapons systems without any possibility of blow back if the operation is exposed.

Privately developed cyber weapons target "zero day" as well as known vulnerabilities in corporate systems. Zero day vulnerability is one not yet exploited by hackers and thus discovered and patched by IT security. Vulnerabilities like these can be extremely valuable because there is no defense against them. If no one knows there is a problem, then nobody is going to be able to close the loophole. Hackers can still exploit many previously discovered security bugs as well, because in all too many cases the target company IT security has yet to actually get around to fixing the problem. Vulnerable systems are common in smaller companies and those who are so big that they get overconfident or IT security becomes overstretched. The deployment and use of high yield cyber weapons by private industry in their attacks on competitors is a rapidly growing danger. If deployed by trained intelligence agents and their private teams of corporate hackers, there is little risk in utilizing advanced cyber weapons that are nearly impossible to trace back on rival companies. This is a newly emerging but extremely significant threat to companies around the world and will play a very important role in coming corporate conflicts in the future. One has only to open a newspaper today to get a taste of what private/corporate use of cyber weapons looks like.

Open Source Digital Intelligence

Gathering information about a target company or individual using open sources available online has never been simpler. The sheer amount of personal information available, indeed provided by an individual, is staggering. The internet has made it easier to stay in touch with friends, make business connections and share information socially, but it also provides spies with an open window into the lives of potential human intelligence sources and vast amounts of data about the company they are targeting. This is a significant and growing field for corporate intelligence (both above and below the grey line) due to the sheer amount of data that can be collected legally. For companies that wish to keep their secrets, open source research presents a major problem since it is legal and extremely difficult to monitor and control.

Social Networking

Observed through the eyes of an intelligence agent, personal web sites, blogs and social networking sites are a veritable goldmine of personal information. From sites like LinkedIn, Twitter, Match.com and Facebook, extremely personal data can be obtained about almost anyone of value to a spy with a few strokes of the keyboard. Everything from a complete professional history, views on politics, taste in women, to an individual's favorite brand of scotch is there for the taking, legally. Information obtained through social networking sites can be more in-depth than purely background. Profiles often provide personal details that are used to crack passwords, provide travel patterns and spending habits, as well as an individual's opinions and thoughts on a range of topics. As a basic means of researching, a company website or an individual target's freely provided social networking data is difficult to beat and takes much of the long-term research and guess work out of source recruitment. If someone thinks that they are immune to this just because they do not have a twitter account or Facebook page think again. People around you talk about you all of the time online and it is the rare individual anymore who has zero data about them or provided by them online. Personal and business data available online is a glaring weakness in every company's security profile which will only get more valuable to spies as ever greater amounts of information is shared by employees, family members, friends and others.

Company Data

Companies give out a tremendous amount of information about their operations and personnel online. From corporate web pages, online industry publications to annual reports, the internet contains a wide array of data on just about every company in the world. Digging through published and broadcast material can give the spy a rather complete picture of a company's operations and staff, as well as potential security weaknesses. Secondary publications and information sources concerning a company are so plentiful online they are often used to fine tune operations, select source targets, and generate useful intelligence about a specific corporate intelligence topic remotely before an operation is even begun. Few companies monitor the information available about them online and fewer still know how or even attempt to censor sensitive online data. Open source data gathering about a target company is a key ingredient in virtually every intelligence operation mounted today and as such has a very important role to play on the defensive side of the espionage equation.

Covert Online Intelligence Gathering

Going a single layer of penetration deeper increases the amount of data an intelligence agent can collect online about companies and individuals exponentially. People spend so much of their lives working and communicating online that penetrating the simple s surrounds most people's net centric lives can provide the the data a spy could ever need.

Email Hacking

Email hacking is a very common espionage tool used to gather personal information about an individual's life and even to directly breach secured corporate systems. Despite being told over and over how venerable it makes them, most people still use the same single password for all of their online functions. This means that if a spy can break one password, usually through email hacking, they can gain access to everything that person does online, including bank accounts, medical history, net viewing habits and secure corporate systems login. Email hacking is considered the easiest approach to cracking a person's single personal password, because email providers have password recovery services that are not digitally tied to a personal computer address, among other reasons. So if a spy can guess, or through research, gather a few bits of personal information such as a mother's maiden name or the name of a favorite pet, they can own that person's email and all other accounts which use the same password (which for most people is all of them). Another aspect to consider here is that many people use their email as a kind of post-it board to help them remember things such as passwords for other sites, security keys for their home and office, important dates and even company projects. In any number of cases all the spy has had to do is break the simple lock on a target's personal email account and they gained access to every piece of data that they were after. There are brute force methods to cracking an email password which use programs to crunch passwords through advanced algorithms, but even these require very little in the way of technical expertise or time. More subtle methods such as targeted phishing scams or the use of social engineering to have the user divulge the information themselves also exist and have proven highly effective. As we see in the media again and again email accounts of very important people are regularly targeted by governments, paparazzi and espionage groups the world over. If a foreign government's intelligence program can crack senior US officials' Gmail accounts by the hundreds then less high profile individual corporate targets must be aware that they are even more vulnerable and take steps to mitigate this danger. For corporate spies opening access to a target's email is an almost reflexive first step in any espionage operation. Because of the ease of entry into an individual's email account and the vast fields of information held there, not to mention potential for secondary access, email hacking is universal in corporate intelligence.

Systems Hacking

Covert attacks against corporate systems take place all of the time. The difficulty of breaking into a corporate system depends entirely on the level of defenses in place. No system in the world is immune to covert penetration. Most corporate computer systems are geared towards stopping so called nuisance attacks mounted by unskilled hackers. While higher levels of security may place significant hurdles in front of a skilled hacker, such an individual has access to a myriad range of sophisticated tools to penetrate even the most robust security. There has been much discussion recently in the media about state-sponsored cyber warfare and the many vulnerabilities to attacks that exist within both public and private systems. One of the things that tends to be overlooked is that a large number of corporate espionage groups targeting American companies are run by the self same national intelligence and military agencies that serve as a source for highly advanced cyber penetration tools. The use of cyber weapons by nation states to breach and own foreign corporate systems are an off shoot of their overall efforts to penetrate secure state and military systems. Remember that corporate espionage teams, funded and operated by large corporate groups, have the resources and access to expertise to develop and employ cyber weapons just as potent as anything found in the arsenals of a nation state. Indeed, corporations pay better than national intelligence organizations and are not at all loath to employ the top talent regardless of their ethnic or national background giving them a significant edge in weapons development over the state. Corporate espionage groups also focus solely on targeting commercial systems and do not dilute their efforts working against government or military targets. Non-state actors face far fewer hurdles to the development and actual employment of these new kinds of weapons. Where a country may balk at the potential for sanctions if they were ever found using cyber weapons against their strategic adversaries, private intelligence groups often have no such compunction. Particularly since such actions, even if detected, tend to be the assumed responsibility of a state and not an individual group.

The ways and means of hackers targeting secure systems are beyond the scope of this book, but suffice it to say that a well funded private corporate espionage team is capable of bringing to bear a wide variety of extremely potent cyber weapons and advanced penetration techniques to breach the defenses of complacent corporations anywhere in the world. In addition to the direct cyber vector of attack, there is the possibility of recruiting human sources within a company to circumvent the external security of a system entirely. Hackers are also adept at finding secondary, less secured systems which have access to core corporate systems and can be used to dodge much of the main line defenses in place. The reality is that despite devoting massive amounts of funding and worry to cyber security, most corporation systems are in fact wide open. The most potent cyber weapon a spy possesses is the complacency of their target.

Benefits of Net Based Intelligence

There are two main benefits to using net or computer based intelligence penetration to obtain information. The first is operational security. Net based attacks can be run from anywhere in the world and conducted at the speed of light. There is no need for the messier aspects of human intelligence to open windows of potential compromise when penetrating a system from the outside. A further advantage is the ability to run an operation, or make it seem as though an operation originates, from any point on the globe. Being able to mask a cyber attack or covert penetration as coming from an allied nation, or even China which is everyone's favorite cyber boogeyman right now, provides the corporate espionage team with a very powerful layer of protection even in the event of discovery. The US government has continuously shown itself more than willing to sweep corporate espionage cases under the rug, in favor of not embarrassing their allies or further antagonizing strategic competitors. The operation does not even have to be physically located in a country like China to make it appear as though the attack originated from there.

The second advantage to net based technical attacks is their rate of success, breadth of data that can obtained and the persistence of system corruption. Attacking a system from the outside to obtain access to information has worked in the past, continues to work extremely well in the present and is only going to get harder to stop in the future. Attacks against computer systems work so efficiently that nations and companies across the globe invest tens of billions of dollars each year in the development and deployment of cyber defenses to protect themselves.

Even as cyber security systems advance most companies are just not able to keep abreast of the latest developments or are loath to take the actions or spend the resources necessary to secure their systems adequately. This reluctance has opened the door to cyber attack for profit. Companies keep so much important and potentially lucrative data on their systems that even narrowly focused attacks and human source penetrations targeting specific data will, as a matter of course, penetrate a corporate system to bleed out all potentially profitable information.

Last but not least, during a successful penetration of a corporate system, hackers always leave behind a series of backdoors so intelligence agents can return into the company system anytime that they wish, without having to re-compromise the system. Backdoor openings give the agent unfettered access to all future development within that company. Additionally, an open backdoor allows direct action later to damage or destroy the data and other parts of a compromised company's computer network. Sabotaging a rival's system untraceably is an increasingly common, and destructive, practice in corporate intelligence.

Other Technical Information Gathering

Traditional technical intelligence gathering is still extremely useful for an intelligence agent and has not gone away just because everyone has an iphone and a laptop. On the contrary, because companies pay so much attention to securing their computer systems, basic precautions are often not taken to secure their facilities against more traditional technical intelligence gathering vectors. Such vectors include bugging, surveillance, tracking, physically compromising systems and communication intercepts.

Bugging

Covert audio and video bugging has been around since the technology has existed to make it feasible. As the technology improved and the size of bugs decreased, the ease and utility of placing hidden listening devices has increased dramatically. Bugs can be extremely tiny, run covertly for long periods of time and transmit their data in real time either via radio waves or the internet. Their size and simplicity make them perfect for covert use to gather intelligence. Imagine the potential damage to a company if there were bugs in the boardroom, CEO's office and a few other key locations. All that is required is a person with a limited amount of training, but with access to sensitive locations, to install an audio or visual bug.

A recent form of bugging coming into its own is the use of laser microphones to detect vibration in glass, which are converted into an audio feed from the target location. Laser mike systems have a significant range and can be emplaced and operated remotely. Such systems are often used to target secured offices and meeting rooms in major companies across the globe. The advantage of an offsite system like the laser mike is that it is undetectable, even if an office is swept regularly for listening devices.

An intriguing modern twist on the old bug is the ability to convert nearly any electronic device with a built in microphone into a bug. Modern cell phones are extremely vulnerable to a number of highly effective programs which can be manually input or sent via the web to convert them into covert listening devices. By turning a phone into a bug, not only can the spy eavesdrop on telephone conversations, but also on anything taking place within pickup distance of the built in mic. Anyone who has ever had a friend accidently dial out to them on their cell phone knows how potent a tool this can be. Add in advanced computer programs which can scrub the audio feed and make it clearer, and you now have a device which the victim caries everywhere they go, recharges for you and is as good, if not better, than most purpose built bugs on the market today.

Built-in video cameras are standard in many modern electronic devices. These can be turned or their feeds intercepted by intelligence agents. Turning on a built-in web cam in a target's home or office system makes that same computer that you use everyday a high-powered listening device and video surveillance tool. Everything from web cams, building surveillance systems, baby monitors to ipads are all vulnerable. Purpose built video surveillance bugs are also commercially available and can be emplaced by anyone in seconds. Undetected surveillance devices can be used to obtain compromising material on a potential source, visually monitor a key board to obtain passwords, record business meetings or as a means to track the actions of an individual.

The art of emplacing a bug in a secure location is tried and true. Turning an employee to plant the bug is the most common method, but there are a number of other covert means to install clandestine surveillance equipment serendipitously. Old school penetration techniques should never be overlooked when a company adopts a serious security plan. Regularly sweeping critical meeting rooms and offices is an increasingly necessary part of maintaining basic corporate site security.

Surveillance

Surveillance of a target used to mean long days and nights in uncomfortable vans trying to stay unobserved as the spy tracked the movements and interactions of a target person. While this is still a method employed by many operations, much of traditional surveillance can now be conducted remotely. Technology has changed radically the art of surveillance. Remote cameras are tiny and can be implanted anywhere in seconds. They are so cheap now that a spy, or counter intelligence team, can easily afford to use dozens if not hundreds during a single operation. Their feed can be extremely covert and run in real time through the internet. Using cameras means that the subject can be observed without fear of them detecting the surveillance. Computer programs using facial recognition and other biometrics can alert the observer when the target enters the picture and even provide data on who they are with. Keeping tabs on an individual can reveal much about them. Actually seeing where someone goes, who they meet, what they do and how they do it is a vital part of the espionage arsenal.

Keeping eyes on a surveillance target formerly meant just that, using the mark 1 eyeball to watch a person go about their daily life. In the modern technological era, personal surveillance is increasingly being replaced with remote video monitoring and GPS tracking. Instead of keeping teams in vans outside of a target's house or office, today most spies simply affix remote cameras to send feeds over the internet directly to the spy in the comfort of their safe house or even to their phone. Remote video can be an extremely efficient system allowing a single spy to maintain constant surveillance of multiple targets all in real time. Remote surveillance is also used when monitoring a source after recruitment to ensure loyalty. The spy can also emplace video surveillance inside of a company to generate intelligence directly. Spies regularly use hidden video cameras to monitor their safe houses and the surrounding neighborhoods to watch for the opposition and ambushes.

A great deal of surveillance is tracking, knowing where the target is at all times. Tracking a target is most commonly done today through electronic means. Why chase the target around in an easy to spot/avoid car when almost everyone worth being followed has a smart phone with built in GPS which can be hacked inside of 3 minutes? A quick hack allows the spy to keep real time tabs on the movements of that phone, as well as checking on where they have been before. For tracking a car, it is possible to buy miniature GPS tracers online or at any decent spy shop. Car mounted GPS trackers can be emplaced discretely in seconds and followed online. A spy can also tap into an onboard GPS system and obtain the tracking data from it as well as a complete travel history. GPS tracking units are also small enough today for them to be inserted covertly into a target's clothing or other personal effects. This is one reason that a number of operational spies will keep multiple gym memberships open so that they can duck into a changing room during their pre meeting SDR (surveillance detection run) and unobtrusively change into a set of new clothing before they meet with a critical source. Many parents know all about this kind of technology since tiny covert GPS tracking devices are most often marketed to concerned adults who want to know where their children are at all times. Indeed, a great many spies do their surveillance/tracking equipment shopping from the same online stores that provide next day shipping of hyper advanced tools to tech savvy but neurotic adults with teenagers. Electronic and technical methods have not totally replaced old-fashioned foot work, but they make the act of tracking a target much easier and safer for a solo spy or small team of agents.

The difference between following a soft corporate target and a trained intelligence officer is that the corporate target will have virtually zero security consciousness. The very reason that corporate surveillance targets are considered soft is because they have no training and zero situational awareness. Security consciousness is simply a heightened awareness of one's surroundings and the people and objects that make it up. A critical part of this awareness is the absolute knowledge, not just the abstract thought, that one is a target. Conducting surveillance on soft targets and tracking them is not nearly the chore or challenge it could be. In fact, an indicator to look for if you are a civilian spotting a spy, is their consistent situational awareness and the basic tradecraft precautions that come second-nature to them. Spies like to keep their eyes on entrances and exits when inside. They like to take multiple forms of transportation along different routes each time they move. They like to mask these behaviors to make them seem "normal".

The art of surveillance is the art of blending in while paying close attention to a target. There is a scene from the Hong Kong movie "Infernal Affairs" which illustrates this perfectly. In this scene, there are two criminals keeping watch outside of the safe house prior to a big drug deal. One looks around at the many people milling on the busy Hong Kong street and sees nothing out of the ordinary. The other says "you know how you spot an undercover cop? You look for anyone who is doing one thing, but is really watching you". The other glances around the street again, his gaze alighting on a number of people going about their business and yet every once in a while glancing his way. He dismisses the paranoia of his friend, but low and behold every person he looked at was indeed an undercover cop keeping the building under surveillance. When it comes to conducting surveillance and counter surveillance, it is necessary to maintain a certain degree of awareness and tame paranoia about your surroundings. Surveillance conducted by a large and well trained team is virtually impossible to spot or evade. In the world of corporate espionage, the likelihood of ever encountering a trained team of watchers is close to nil, but that does not mean that it is impossible. Efficient spies listen to their guts and constantly look out for signs of operational breach. For normal people who may be targets of covert intelligence surveillance the best defense is to get some training in counter surveillance and develop a degree of situational awareness. Who knows it may even be possible to catch a corporate spy out one day. They certainly don't expect the civilians they target to have any kind of security consciousness and may just get sloppy.

Communication Intercepts

Throughout history and from the first uses of courier, telegraph and radio in wartimes, it has been understood that one of the best means to acquire intelligence on the actions of others is to read their messages. This holds equally true today as the personal use of communication devices has increased the number and value of communications exponentially. The technology to intercept communications has lagged a bit as novel and powerful communications tools have come to common usage, but it is still entirely possible to cover virtually every means of communication that a target may employ, particularly a soft target that does not use any additional encryption tools or communications countermeasures.

Telephones

Tapping a telephone line has historically been a very powerful tool to gain intelligence from a target. Just ask the Mob how much can be learned from listening into telephonic communications. For law enforcement, tapping a telephone line requires warrants and seemingly endless paperwork regarding probable cause, but for the spy it is as simple as splicing a land line, cloning a phone or setting up an intercept post to catch cell or other wireless signals.

Efficient tools to intercept telephone signals, especially for wireless phones or cell phones, exist and are commercially available. With the growing use of Bluetooth headsets a further avenue of signals intercepts is available to a spy with a minimum of technical knowledge. A highly advanced system for call interception can be assembled in the field from commercially available components. Ironically, the possession of such a set up is not itself illegal, just the use of it (go figure). Purpose built equipment can do the job, but is significantly harder to obtain outside of the state sponsored intelligence world. A homemade set up is more than adequate for all but heavily encrypted communications or frequency jumping phones. If the spy runs into these kinds of counter measures, then there is always the physical emplacement of a listening device within the device itself or in the area where it is used.

Intercepting digital communications can be useful for voice calls, but also for data and text messages. People keep a massive amount of data in their smart phone. If the spy can see what they see when they use their phone to surf the web or send emails and messages, a good deal of intelligence can be obtained. By far the most useful data intercept tool is wifi hacking. People do not like it when their neighbor piggybacks on their home network, so they think that by encrypting their signal they are perfectly safe. All they are doing is erecting a single barrier at the router, the signal itself is perfectly coherent and easily picked up by a technically proficient spy. Hijacking a router and using it to send virus programs directly to a home system is a tried and true means of infecting unsecured computers. A further option is to intercept the signals generated by a wireless keyboard and mouse. This can quickly gain the spy passwords and other useful data and these signals are completely unprotected. Corporate systems are generally insulated against this basic form of wireless attack, but it never hurts to check at the target office. Sometimes a spy can catch IT security asleep at the wheel and use wifi hacking to quickly take over a system through the back door. Home systems are rarely secured to the level found at corporate locations and are therefore much more vulnerable to penetration.

Since intercept equipment has a relatively limited range, if it is not possible to physically be on or near the target location to intercept communications, one can build a monitoring post near the target's home or office. When the desired signals are intercepted, the equipment will retransmit them to wherever the spy may wish to set up. Monitoring stations can be configured to retransmit via the internet, in some cases using the very same network connection they are hijacking, making it possible to remotely monitor intercepted signals from anywhere in the world. A covert monitoring post can be disguised as almost anything and emplaced in minutes. When required, even more exotic solutions to the problem of remotely intercepting signals are available. Esoteric radio gear and microwave interceptors can pluck the most secure signal right out of the air if placed correctly. Drones can be used to remotely intercept signals and to maintain surveillance. Creative covert operators find solutions to even the most challenging problems.

Drones

Using drones to conduct surveillance, intercept signals or even conduct direct action against targets is all the rage with state military and intelligence elements these days. Private intelligence drone use is starting to take off as well. Remote control drones offer an outstanding platform for all manner of missions. Drones can be constructed relatively cheaply, are easy to operate, are increasingly common in the skies over major cities and can be customized to be extremely covert. This method of electronic surveillance is a field to watch as more advanced drone technology enters private hands and the ability to mount highly capable electronic intercept and surveillance technologies increase. The main use, however, to which drones are put today in intelligence gathering, is surveillance. Just like the CIA in Afghanistan private drones can be used to watch targets from afar for extended periods of time totally covertly. Most private spooks will not have access to a predator drone like systems but the smaller kit systems they do employ are more than capable of the simple urban based tasks that they are used for. The use of drones to conduct pervasive covert surveillance is already an issue in Hollywood where early adaptor paparazzi have been using these systems for some time to spy on media stars for money. Drones have already been used to engage in sabotage, private military, terror and other malicious actions against companies. They are discreet, easy to destroy after use, difficult to trace and increasingly common. This makes them the perfect platform to carry out all manner of direct actions. The use of drones will increase in the corporate intelligence world as they become more common, cheaper and better able to carry out missions.

Technical Direct Actions

Not all technical intelligence actions have to do with information gathering. The same capabilities that can give a spy access to a system can also be used to sabotage that system, implant false or misleading data, or hijack it to attack other systems. Hijacking one system to use as a cover to attack another is a classic hacker trick. Hijacking is commonly used on less secure systems to spoof any attempt to deny access or locate the true origins of an attack. Once a system is penetrated, it is at the mercy of the spy or hacker who has breached it. If the mission calls for the spy or hacker to corrupt files, create false or misleading data or delete specific important files all they have to do is find a door past security. Planting misleading or false data into a corporate system can prove to be anywhere from annoying to downright catastrophic for a company. Another commonly employed tactic is to hack into an email, bank, trading or other account and use it to send out false instructions. This can be highly destructive for an individual and can sow untold confusion if used on a larger scale within a company. Fixing the damage from such a target specific attack can take months of work and require millions of dollars.

Disruption tactics to directly damage the operations of a rival firm are becoming more prevalent. A prime example of technical disruption is the 2011 attack against Sony networks. It demonstrates how an outside attack to penetrate a system, ostensibly to steal credit card data, could additionally destroy corporate credibility, cost the company vast sums of money and even remove them from entire industries. Another option available to the hacker once they have access to a system is the simple theft of customer data, internal emails or other sensitive files for external distribution or sale. This may not directly damage the operations of a company, but can prove to be deeply embarrassing and cost the company in lost revenues and image degradation. Blackmail of the company itself in exchange for illicitly obtained information from a compromised system is another disturbingly common occurrence.

The final and most destructive act that an intelligence agent with computer access can perform on a compromised system is sabotage. Recently, the Stuxnet virus targeted centrifuges in Iran which were used to process nuclear material. The virus was specifically design to infect the control system for these machines and cause them to go out of control. This single invasive program destroyed hundreds of expensive and difficult to build machines in a matter of days, putting back the Iranian nuclear program by years. Imagine this kind of a tailored virus attacking the production line for an auto manufacturer like Ford or computer chip maker such as Intel. By reprogramming the assembly machines to go crazy and self-destruct, the target company will be out vast amounts of money to replace the assembly machines themselves and the destroyed merchandise, and also to debug their entire system and erect new security measures. Throw in lost production time, damage to corporate image and the drop in stock value, and see how a single tailored virus could conceivably ruin a company.

For smaller companies with tighter bottom lines, computer hacking is a tremendous threat. If the sabotage does not target physical production, but rather the computer systems themselves, the results can prove to be apocalyptic. A single easily built program can turn off the cooling fans or spoof the thermostat in a corporate server farm causing the machines to literally melt with no one the wiser until the entire system goes down irreparably. Any modern company would take massive losses from the destruction of its entire computer and network infrastructure. These are examples of the threats that companies face in a world where restraints on corporate intelligence and direct action against competitors are eroding quickly.

Other Means of Intelligence Gathering

Several means of intelligence gathering do not fall under the rubric of human or technical intelligence. These methods generally involve direct acts against the target to develop or steal information. While subtlety may be the holy grail of most intelligence operations, there are times when it is desirable for the spy to simply take what they need rather than gaining access to it through an employee or sly technical penetration.

Legal

One form of intelligence collection action that defies easy classification is by using the legal system or via green mail. This is considered an intelligence action because the goal is to retrieve secret information and the means fall into the very murky grey realm of covert and overt intelligence operations. Forcing a company to reveal sensitive information by filing a legal action is an effective tactic, if the basis, time and resources are there to make it work. A company can be compelled in discovery to reveal their secrets through above board legal coercion. Many companies are somewhat unwilling to have their names attached to such obvious frivolous law suit ploys and will often employ third party shells to handle the litigation for them. In order to ensure that the action is not traced back to the original company, these third party corporate creatures are set up by intelligence agents using semi-covert means.

Intelligence gathering procedures can also be used for greenmail actions. Greenmail is the practice of purchasing enough shares in a firm to threaten a takeover and thereby forcing the target firm to buy those shares back at a premium in order to stop the bid. As part of this action the green mailer can quite easily gain access to secret internal company data, under the guise of legitimate due diligence.

Stock manipulation by corporate raiders has been used to leverage information out of a company or to affect their stock value and distract their senior management at a crucial point before and will be again. These operations are sometimes carried out using covertly generated front companies set up by intelligence agents in order to create deniability and a legal buffer.

Coercion

This action is different from coercing cooperation from a source by threatening exposure of marginal acts, because certain coercion tactics involve a direct threat to the physical wellbeing of an individual or their loved ones. While coercion is a highly effective strategy employed in the grey and black economies of the world, it is seldom used by professional intelligence agents against legitimate business concerns. The reluctance to use physical coercion is more for the sheer inelegance of the act than for any overriding tactical or operational concerns. Various forms of coercion practice may well become more common as the restraints on corporate espionage agents weaken and the need for quick results increases. Corporate spooks have been known to resort to collusion with organized crime groups, who have little compunction about such matters, in order to get what they want.

Physical Theft

Another somewhat inelegant solution to information gathering, occasionally employed by a professional intelligence agent, is the outright physical theft of data or materials. This method is rarely employed because it is almost always unnecessary for a clever spy to break the law in such an obvious and easily traceable way to get what they want. Personal involvement in the theft of data or goods brings with it increased risks of capture and the penalties are almost always more sever if they are caught than they would be for other methods of covert intelligence gathering. Breaking into secure locations is illegal and penalties are more stringent than for receiving the same goods from an active source. Physical corporate locations are also guarded against such direct attacks, most of the time effectively. However, if the need should arise during an operation to physically penetrate a facility or home, intelligence agents' training often includes the know how to defeat security systems and act directly against such targets. A growing number of specially trained second-story men are also coming out of the state intelligence apparatus who are quite experienced in such work. If direct theft of materials or goods is called for, a spy can also contract out the job to a local organized crime group or a specifically trained asset. These groups regularly take on such assignments if the price is right and generally employee professionals who may be more capable and are certainly safer for the spy to use.

Part II

Intelligence Analysis

"Facts mean nothing when they are preempted by appearance. Do not underestimate the power of impression over reality."
Crown Prince Raphael Corrino

Once the specific intelligence requested by the contracting company is received by the spy and sent back through covert channels to the company, the analysis of this information generally takes place in-house or via a third party group. For freelance intelligence agents working without specific instructions, it is important to know what kinds of information are marketable and how they can be sold once obtained. The fascinating and relatively new practice of data laundering also falls under the ambit of private intelligence analysis.

Types of Marketable Information

A common assumption is that anything secret that can be learned about the operations of a target company has value to its competitors. This is simply not the case. Companies that purchase intelligence, particularly illicitly obtained intelligence about other firms, do so based on specific needs. There is a great deal of information about companies, especially large companies, available through overt means of collection, and even more that is held secret. Numerous legitimate corporate intelligence firms operate out of the shadows and focus on gathering publically available information to process and sell within the industry. For the solo intelligence agent, legitimate corporate intelligence companies are the main competition because their reach is quite broad, even without recourse to covert operations.

Information that has commercial value and can only be obtained covertly must be identified by the freelance intelligence operative before being sought. A careful analysis of a target company's public information and the needs of its competitors should take place before an agent dashes in to steal data. A fishing expedition is much more likely to generate worthless data, which is freely available online or at a trade show, versus any secret and marketable intelligence.

The most common intelligence targets for corporate spies relates to future actions. Competitors have a relatively thorough understanding of where their rivals are and what they are doing at the present time. But like any good fighter, a company will try to conceal its future moves as carefully as it can. Intelligence about what products are about to be released, specs and costs, marketing plans, future acquisitions, internal issues a company faces, problems that a company is trying to cover up, and staff changes are all generally considered marketable pieces of intelligence. Proprietary technology items such as pre-patent product designs and specific technical innovations are also considered to be prime targets.

While most corporate espionage tasking serves a specific need for targeted information, freelance spies have to include a serious study of their potential targets and most importantly their potential buyers, before they undertake the risk and expense of mounting an operation. In-depth knowledge of the targets and the potential buyers is critical. In general, covertly obtained information is much easier to sell outside of the United States than to American companies. Unless the agent intends to steal and then resell critical information back to the target company, it is usually prudent to search overseas for a buyer before they go knocking on the doors of an American firm, who is more likely to send them to the nearest FBI office than offer a big check and a smile.

Middle Men and Data Brokers

Most of the world is made up of middle men who tend to get upset when you try to cut them out of the loop. This extra layer in the black market for information plays a critical role in corporate espionage, particularly for the freelancer. Data brokers can be found in the darker corners of the legitimate information markets around the world in abundance. Their job is to take a piece of stolen information and shop it to different potential buyers until there is a bite. They take their percentage and that is that, everyone is satisfied. Finding the right middle man, though, can be more difficult than the actual acquisition of the illicit data. Intelligence brokers do not generally have a shingle or a web site. For as many "honest" grey and black market brokers as there are in the world, there exist several times as many who will rob an unprepared spy blind. Because the world of corporate espionage is a somewhat small one and people do not tend to just stumble their way into becoming corporate spooks, a freelance spy often comes from the same ranks as those who work in-house for a specific company or are part of a larger private team. Using personal connections to receive assignments, fence data or find a reliable intelligence broker is what most freelancers end up doing. In the murky world of global corporate espionage, word of mouth and reputation is the key to moving information around for profit.

After the spy has found an intelligence broker and he, they are almost all men, has found a buyer for the stolen data, the matter now comes down to price. Just how valuable is corporate intelligence? Conservative estimates place the costs to American companies each year from corporate espionage at over one hundred billion dollars. Include the rest of the world, as much as companies spy on their US rivals they do so against their domestic ones as well, and you can safely double that figure. Firm numbers on this enterprise are difficult to pin down because there are so few public prosecutions and black market rumors are difficult to trust fully. The industry is, by its nature, jealous of its secrets, but there is little doubt about the massive scale of modern corporate intelligence. The above figures, with all their zeros, should give an idea of the scale of the activity and value of corporate espionage. The metric used here is the cost to the targeted companies, not the actual street value of the data itself. In the case of secret data wholesale, a good rule is to divide the potential amount gained by the buyer from the intelligence by ten to one hundred. It all comes down to how badly the company wants the data and how difficult it would be for them to acquire it on their own. Supply and demand play a part in these kinds of transactions, in addition to bluff and bluster.

A successful corporate freelance spy can expect to gross between one to two million dollars per year if they operate continuously. This may sound like quite a bit of money, but a freelancer also has to cover their own expenses. Unless a covert agent can get his hands on a very valuable piece of information or can run penetrations on the cheap, the actual take home is more in the range of half a million US dollars. For corporate spooks on retainer, whose operational costs are covered by the contracting company, they can expect to make around one million dollars per annum operating continuously. A certain amount of side work comes from corporate intelligence and there are always ways to make a bit of extra cash on a job well done.

In-house spooks, as opposed to freelance and private group operators, tend to make less, but the up side is that they have more down time and operational support in the form of black funds, specialized personnel, advanced computer penetration programs and high-end technical gear from their company. They also target the same competitor companies repeatedly so generally have a better idea of the defense and structure of their targets. Their operations tend to be much safer and easier. In some cases in-house teams even get medical and dental coverage like other employees. In all cases they will receive access to high end legal assistance in the event of trouble paid for out of the black operating budget. A number of seasoned spies, after leaving the national espionage services of their respective countries, have been known to put in a few years as a corporate spook and then retired in a much better financial position. Since the market for trained and experienced spies is growing, especially in the US and Asia, there is always more work than spies to go around.

Former spies have been known to parlay their experience into corporate security positions but these are rarely if ever as well paid as those who play for the other side. It is not unheard of for spies to run a long con on a corporation by coming in to manage their security and counter espionage programs, only to get quickly disenchanted and switch teams.

Data Laundering

The concept behind data laundering is almost identical to money laundering. You have data that could only have come from an illegal source, you move this dirty information around and wash it so that it seems to come from a legitimate source and then you sell it to the client company. The purchasing company may know where and how the information was actually obtained, but as long as the data itself can pass legal muster and the company is protected, the laundering process is considered successful. The process of transforming dirty data into clean data is one that typically involves stripping out the specifics and turning it into a long, seemingly legitimately obtained, analytical report.

A very successful recent variation of data laundering takes illicit data and pours it into an extremely complex looking computer algorithm, which then comes back with a super complex data set showing that the information (the initial piece of stolen data) was just out there in cyber space waiting for this super data mining program to pluck it out of the ether. Looks legit and so far everyone who has ever questioned the process has come out awed at the magical piece of software and that is where it has stopped.

For the most part, data laundering is merely smoke and mirrors to prevent any potential for legal blow back from the use of covertly obtained information on the part of the purchasing company. In real life, the company gets the raw data straight from the spy, uses its own people to analyze it and then just waits for the laundered data to be returned from a third party laundering service to satisfy the lawyers. So basically it is spy steals data, submits the raw take to the client and turns it over to a data laundering service, the laundering service comes back with a legally clean data set to cover client actions which use the data and that's it. This obscure trail keeps the purchaser of illicit information covered and the lawyers happy. Legal immunity in corporate espionage for the client comes from plausible deniability.

Receiving the Information

If you think that the president of Sony, CEO of Microsoft or Ford Motor Company ever comes within a mile of raw data generated by corporate spooks or is directly involved in covert attacks against rivals, you are sorely mistaken. Like the President of the United States, senior executives at corporations are intentionally kept in a state of plausible deniability. They demand accurate, quick and total intelligence from their staff but it is up to the middle level, most commonly junior VP, people to actually develop the intelligence resources to provide that data. Foreign companies take the need and regular use of covert intelligence for granted and most have highly delineated responsibility trees and entire in-house intelligence arms. However, In America the use of high-grade intelligence that can only realistically come from covert sources has not really taken hold except at a few firms. You can usually spot these companies, because they are smaller, highly mobile, ambitious, and own their competition for no immediately apparent reason.

Selling to Governments and Other Entities

Corporate intelligence does not necessarily have to go to rival companies. Often governments, non-governmental bodies, extra legal organizations or even individuals will deal in corporate intelligence. Playing with governments, especially foreign governments can be extremely hazardous for a corporate spook. Government employees in general, and universally within state intelligence organs, take the attitude that they are always on the side of the angels and that mercenary corporate spies are completely disposable. For government agents there is no downside to dealing unfairly or high-handedly with corporate espionage agents so many don't even make the effort to conceal their contempt. Rudeness is the tip of the iceberg. Government intelligence organs have been known to steal from, imprison and even kill corporate spooks who don't kowtow to them. As a rule of thumb when dealing with governments it is always best to have significant leverage and not get too close to those intelligence officials who are tasked with dealing with the private corporate spook side of business. There are cases though where countries value a specific type of corporate intelligence so highly that they literally role out the red carpet and give out big checks for a successful spy mission. These grateful and generous entities are mostly strategic competitor states and then almost exclusively for the handover of defense related technologies.

Stealing from US defense contractors is its own separate category in corporate intelligence and is almost always the preserve of state sponsored corporate espionage groups. Private corporate spooks tend not to target the defense industry because companies there are more secure, opposition is much higher, and governments will actually go after people who steal military secrets as opposed to the almost zero level of prosecution for theft of commercial data from the private sector. While there is a market for such technology with certain countries, most legitimate companies or rivals within the defense industry won't touch the stuff. The pay out for defense related secrets is also much lower than a corresponding effort to develop commercial intelligence. Factor in the added risk and it is easy to understand why defense contractors are almost exclusively targeted by state intelligence organs whose agents have no choice in the selection of targets.

Selling information to non-state and non-business actors can be even more hazardous than selling military technology to rogue nations. The vast majority of non-state actors who are willing and able to pay for corporate secrets are organized criminal groups. This is big business in many parts of the world. But dealing with criminals means that the spy has to deal with some rather ruthless people who kill sources more useful than the random spy to enhance their bottom line all of the time. If an inside connection exists with such groups and the spy can add some safety into the deal, then significant money can be made in these circles. Profits in this field have prompted trans-national criminal groups to develop their own corporate espionage capabilities to compete directly with more mundanely sponsored spies. This trend, criminals as spies, will provide some significant competition in the future as the line gets ever more blurry between trained spy and criminal freelancer. Crlminal groups around the world are hiring private intelligence personnel to work in an intelligence gathering or counter intelligence capacity as well. Highly trained spies who accept employment with a trans-national criminal organization is a growing area in private intelligence and should seriously concern law enforcement, which they are targeting, more than it seems to at this time.

There are cases where a non-governmental organization (NGO) that isn't a criminal group will pay for covertly obtained corporate intelligence, but dealing with them can be problematic. There are two main reasons for this. First, they are very cheap and will always ask the spy to hand over secret material by appealing to their sense of duty to humanity and moral obligation to whatever save the fuzzy whale cause they are promoting. Second, such groups are extremely unsecure. NGO personnel have no sense of secrecy and are easily penetrated by state security organs on a regular basis. If a spy deals with an NGO they are likely to get onto the radar of state security organs within a very short period of time. The final issue with NGOs is the attitude. They can be smug and are superficially violently opposed to the very idea of secret intelligence, unless it serves their cause. Of note, NGOs are regularly put to use by private intelligence agents to disseminate black propaganda and perform other intelligence actions, wittingly or not. Non-profit groups can be amazingly credulous when it comes to believing corporations capable of any evil. Feeding an NGO false information about a target, to embarrass the company or cost them money and market share, is a common tool of the black propagandist.

Dealing with terrorist or revolutionary group is possible, but the danger from the group itself and also from the many state intelligence agencies that invariably target them is simply too risky for all but the most desperate or foolhardy private intelligence agents.

The final option for sale of covertly obtained information is back to the company from which the spy stole it in the first place. In many instances, the company does not believe the spy has the data until they feed part of it back. That realization of infiltration is when the bluster and desperation sets in. Selling information back to a company can prove to be a highly lucrative proposition if the spy is wary of the pitfalls attached to such a transaction. Target companies are often willing to pay top dollar for their own secret information, especially if it comes with a rundown of who hired the espionage agent and how the information was obtained.

The practice of penetrating a company, stealing their secrets, selling them back and then offering your services to reinforce their corporate security dates back ages in the private intelligence world.

When it works, it is a very cozy niche to be in. However, it can be very difficult to prove to a company that (1) the spy has indeed turned over all of the data; (2) they are not double dipping by selling it back to them and their competitors at the same time; and (3) they will actually build a stronger defense and not just a back door riddled sham defense for themselves or their real employers.

Transfer of Illicit Information

For in-house and contract spies, there is always a built in means of covertly sending the information obtained to the controller and then on to the contracting company. This process, however, can get very convoluted and dangerous for freelance spies. Not physically dangerous, as spies are almost never targeted for liquidation despite how dramatic it makes movies, but rather dangerous in that people tend to not pay for things if they can get away with it in the black market. Information also has a certain expiration date and if the spy is not careful it can quickly turn from solid gold into a worthless series of 1's and 0's. The safest method for a spy sending information to a company is the old half now, half on delivery, with the added potential for more business later. This rarely works out so neatly in real life, but it is a good place to start the negotiations.

Transferring data between parties is almost exclusively done online today. The need to actually meet with the person who is paying for illegally obtained data is nearly a thing of the past. A good way for the spy to ensure that they are paid, especially if there is a lack of trust between the parties, is to send the data back but encrypt all but a taste first. Thus the agent can move the data but still hold a bargaining chip, in the form of the encryption key, until they get paid. The old days of the cloak and dagger rendezvous in some exotic port to exchange cash for secrets has fallen victim to modern technology. While the death of such adrenaline filled clandestine meetings in romantic locations across the globe may be lamented by old school spies in today's world operational security more often than not means data exchange by digital dead drop and secured wire transfer for payment. For both the spy and the customer of illicit corporate information, safety first is more than a mantra, it is a way of life.

Payment

The means of paying a spy are almost identical to those used to pay a clandestine source. Corporate espionage agents never exist on the payroll of the companies where they work. This does not mean that they do not "work" and pay taxes like everyone else, they just say and do two different things. The most common means of paying a corporate spy, assuming they are in-house or under contract, is through a front company so that they can claim legitimate income and live as normal citizens in whatever country they choose. The intelligence agent is then paid the remainder of their fee or salary into a covert overseas account, in cash or with similarly convertible assets. This method provides superior protection for the spy and by using enough cut outs and fronts it is virtually impregnable to official scrutiny.

Virtually every company in the world, even those not directly engaged in espionage, will have some form of black budget or fund they keep off of the radar. These funds get used for all manner of things which make up grey and black global operations. If anyone can find a perfectly clean international corporation out there I will show you a company that is incapable of effective competition. Keeping money off of the books to use as the various powers that be within a corporation see fit is utterly common. It is from these black budgets/funds that spies get their pay. Most companies have ready access to at least a portion of the grey banking market and can move funds from their black operations accounts around the world untraceably in seconds.

For non-aligned freelance corporate spooks, the proceeds of their sales are usually deposited into a numbered account, still the preferred means of making clandestine payments for governments, spies, drug dealers and corporations. Where there is a valid lack of trust, payment may be made in cash or kind, but as this presents obvious problems of further transport and conversion it is being phased out of use rather quickly. The majority of spies vastly prefer to use the grey and black market banking sector to safely receive and hide their money over more dramatic suitcases full of unmarked bills.

After the Mission

Once an intelligence mission is completed and payment received, most spies get right back to work. One would assume that a long vacation on a beach somewhere is the natural reward of anyone who breaks the law and gets away with it, but corporate spooks are a rather self-selecting group not generally known for their love of down time. One trait that stands out among intelligence operatives the world over is the addiction to the excitement and stresses of espionage work. When there is no work lined up or some heat prevents the spy from operating, most drink and play themselves silly. This is not to say that all spies are wrecks when not on mission, but for many the mundane world holds little interest if not viewed through the eyes of operational alertness. Spies are human, they have hobbies, profess a desire to get out of the game altogether or claim to just be doing it for the money. If that were true, one would expect that after a few solid scores they would actually leave. Most just keep coming back because the excitement and demands of the job have proven to be more than a little bit addictive. And, of course, there is the money.

Immunity through Government Connections

Corporate espionage agents coming out of the state intelligence sector will often maintain solid connections with their home government's intelligence service even after they have left. In some cases this bond is for purely personal or patriotic reasons, but for many it is an insurance policy in the event of trouble. Being able to get claimed as a state intelligence agent, even if one is operating privately, is such a huge advantage that many former intelligence officers do all that they can to ensure their connections with a home government stay fresh. For governments and private spies this is a two way street. Spies share information obtained during the course of private intelligence operations or knowledge of specific players and organizations involved so that the state might build intelligence on and leverage over target foreign companies and black market entities. From the spies' point of view, this exchange is a perfectly acceptable trade off as they can then claim a degree of protection and even receive occasional help from the home country as needed.

Government intelligence agencies like to keep their fingers on the pulse of the private intelligence world. What this arrangement amounts to is tentative immunity in exchange for low-level intelligence about a non-critical global activity in the eyes of the state. Most client companies do not mind this behavior on the part of their corporate espionage agents since they would be unable to halt it anyway. State intelligence connections can also serve as back door access for the company in the event they themselves need the services or protection of state intelligence organs in other areas. The grey world of covert intelligence connections between governments and corporations can get very intermingled and convoluted at times. The potential legal and leverage ramifications are held in check with multiple cut outs and the unspoken agreement between states and corporate entities not to engage in mutually assured destruction. As much dirt as states gather on companies these same corporate entities often carry more potent materials to hold over the heads of state organs and elected officials which at the end of the day is their insurance policy. In many cases these same companies are so deeply tied into rarefied political circles that they make themselves all but immune to state intelligence interference.

Penalties if Apprehended

For a spy getting caught is one of the worst possible events, particularly for corporate espionage agents. It is not only potentially life threatening or a threat to one's liberty, but a huge embarrassment, since it means that even against a soft corporate target, their professional skills were not enough to prevent capture. The consequences for being caught committing corporate espionage vary greatly depending on the country in which the spy is apprehended. In a number of countries around the world, commercial or state espionage, it doesn't matter, the penalties are equally sever. In these states, if the spy cannot wiggle or bribe their way free, the penalty can be death. Such draconian states tend to be the basket case economies in the world and few operations are conducted in such backwaters so this is rarely an issue. As a general rule, the more draconian the laws against espionage and sabotage a country has, the more North Korea-esque the economy is likely to be, and thus the less there is to steal there anyway.

Getting caught in the first world does carry its own risks. If one is a foreigner caught conducting corporate espionage in another nation much depends on the relationship between that state and one's home country. If the two countries are allies, the penalties are likely to be less than severe, but if they are not on good terms a spy may face a long stay in a rather small concrete room.

Most corporate espionage is conducted in the United States and the penalties for such actions depend totally on what can be proven in a court of law. If one is caught breaking the law in the US and is not under diplomatic cover or operating under the protection of an allied government, the spy can possibly face some jail time. Espionage operations being caught out in the US, especially corporate espionage action, are extremely rare and even fewer still are actually brought to trial. If one is caught red handed in the US, the corporate spy's first priority is, like anyone else, to get a good lawyer. If possible try for bail and flee. If not, do a deal with the local security forces or simply shut up, cop a plea deal and look forward to a relatively short stay. Even if convicted of the various crimes that make up corporate espionage in the US, the spy can realistically expect to get released within a few years or sooner due to prison overcrowding from low-level drug busts. There are additional secondary penalties for getting caught in the act conducting espionage. Corporate spies that are captured during an operation are unlikely to get hired again as discovery and prosecution demonstrates a tremendous lack of ability on the spy's part. There is also the ever present trust issue and the question of whether or not the spy was turned by state counter intelligence forces while in custody. Getting caught as a spy is not just bad because of the potential for jail time but is usually a death kneel to their career as well.

Part III

Other Intelligence Actions

"If you focus on the risks, they will multiply in your mind and eventually paralyze you. You want to focus on the task, instead, on what needs to be done."
Barry Eisler

Corporate spooks engage in a wide range of actions which have nothing whatsoever to do with developing commercially valuable intelligence. These tasks typically involve direct action against another corporation's assets or personnel or the state in which a company holds interests. Non-espionage related intelligence actions can be broken down into two main categories: (1) Paramilitary operations and (2) Propaganda actions.

Spies make exceptional criminals. Their training and predilection for operating covertly, their ability to blend in and resources available to them give them significant advantages over your run of the mill criminal or terrorist. While many spies do specialize in specific operational areas, some work as jacks of all trades and are more than willing to break the barrier between data theft and physical crime. Thanks in large part to the climb down with the end of the global war on terror, there also exists the option of hiring former special forces and other military trained professionals to conduct covert paramilitary actions. Spies are also known to make exceptional conduits between companies and the underworld.

There is a long history throughout the world of companies using state intelligence agencies and their own privately hired paramilitary forces to conduct operations beneficial to their interests overseas and at home. Corporations have fielded armies, hired spies, and even taken over and run whole countries. In the US, go south a bit to find a long legacy of the direct involvement of US companies with everything from covert intelligence operations to coups and civil war. In the modern era, groups like Executive Outcomes and Black Water (or Xe Services LLC as it now calls itself) serve as the legal face of private paramilitary forces. The darker side of the private military industry is found in the innumerable smaller covert operations and paramilitary capable groups that offer their services to corporations and private individuals all over the world. Such groups provide discreet services ranging from protection of strategic corporate assets to direct military action and intelligence gathering.

A quick look at the published Pentagon budget under contractors or examination of the CIA employment statistics exposes how many jobs are now held by private consultants and contractors even in the state system. Basic national security services in the United States are increasingly being carried out by private companies and their legions of contractors. It should come as no surprise that companies with direct investments and billions in assets around the world are turning to these same companies and their shadier subsidiaries for off-the-books covert actions just like their home governments have been doing for years. Not many citizens are aware of how many of their domestic corporations employ such paramilitary services overseas and given the lack of media coverage over the years apparently not many care. To imagine, however, that espionage and direct actions are limited to distant parts of the world and are never employed at home is fantasy. When paramilitary and other direct action operations are carried out in the first world they are simply run on a more covert footing.

Risks and Rewards

The risks of a paramilitary operation going wrong and coming back to bite the company who engages it are many. Not least of which is prison for the senior executives and the possibility of dissolution for the company. The risk mitigation factor is one reason that companies become very cozy with political power in their home states. An act is only illegal if it is declared to be such and judgment can be enforced. History, as well as present times, is littered with stories of private military and intelligence operations gone wrong and companies acting badly with zero consequence. The rewards for a company that can utilize violence strategically are often game changing. The truth is that covert operations are not run out of the board rooms of the corporate west. Like corporate espionage, strategic violence is managed at a much lower level in the originating organization. While a senior person at the company may, through subtle hint or gesture, indicate their desire to see such actions performed, the strictures of plausible deniability are generally maintained. There have been senior executives who like to play war lord and get elbow deep into covert operations, but when it comes to failure it is rarely the CEO that falls on his sword.

Even limited exposure is rare in cases of corporate involvement in paramilitary activities. This is because legally proving direct corporate involvement can be difficult. Even if some corporate run foreign horror show is exposed in the media, a few sacrificial lambs are generally enough to keep the wolves at bay long enough for the 24 hour media cycle to forget the story and move on. Prosecutions are even rarer since it is difficult for victims to bring cases from overseas and legally batting a multibillion dollar corporation from a farm in the third world is something of a Sisyphean task. Corporations are generally politically protected from litigation of this type and the blame can always be apportioned to an individual or very small group of people working for the company to deflect legal consequence. Even if legal recourse is successful the cost is often less than a few days operating capital anyway. This is of course assuming that any proof can be obtained from behind multiple cut outs and corporate fronts inevitably surrounding such covert activities or that political pressure is not brought to bear from the start to bury the issue.

Certain actions are difficult to bury and blow back is not unknown in the corporate world. In many cases it is not really the risk of legal sanction or jail that keeps firms, particularly in the US, from conducting covert direct actions, but the potential for embarrassment. Companies, and those who run them, can be stunningly risk adverse if the consequences for exposure include social stigmatization for the top executives or major negative publicity for the company.

If there was no or little reward to engaging in such actions then they would not happen. Despite what the anti-corporate leftist fringe might say companies are not populated with evil men bent on causing worldwide suffering just for the fun of it. Given the relatively high-level of risks involved, logically the rewards must be correspondingly great. Direct actions are used to compel others to act in a beneficial way, damage rival positions, alter government policies, remove obstinate officials and dramatically improve a corporation's power within markets across the globe. Oil concessions, mineral rights, trade advantages, removing internal restrictions on potentially objectionable corporate practices and directly attacking a rival company's holdings or personnel are all common objectives. Direct action can be incredibly effective in helping a company secure dominance within a given market. These actions work well and are relatively cheap and easy to mount given the right connections to the murky world of private spies and soldiers. Benefits to a company for strategic use of direct action can often be measured in the billions. Because these issues arise in home markets as often as they do overseas, it is surprising that many still imagine that such effective measures, which work so well elsewhere, are not being utilized domestically (albeit on a much smaller scale and under deeper cover). The following is a rundown of some of the more common direct action programs which corporate spooks and soldiers engage in on behalf of companies overseas and at home.

Assault and Intimidation

In the immortal words of Jane Cobb, "pain is scary". Threats or acts of physical violence have been used to change the minds of business people the world over since time immemorial. The reason that this tactic is so successful is that people, especially the average John Q. Citizen, generally live their lives trying to avoid physical confrontation as much as possible. Bringing such intimidating acts to their door leaves a person grasping for any way to remove the threat. This may seem like work best left to street toughs, but highly trained spies are far more adept at committing crime and getting away with it than your average criminal. They leave fewer traces and can be trusted to maintain operational security even when engaged in such low-level grunt work. Spies can also be used as conduits to crime groups in order to facilitate assaults and intimidation as needed.

Criminals, Spies and the Black Market

This is a good place to add a few words on the connection between spies and organized crime. A spy, at their most fundamental core, is an individual trained to commit crime, by the state on its behalf. Espionage and direct action are crimes everywhere. The majority of private sector spies are products of state training who now use their skills to benefit corporate interests. Virtually every act that encompasses espionage and especially direct action is illegal. Data theft, system hacking, communications interception, suborning assets within a company, theft of proprietary property, to assault and assassination are all acts that corporate espionage agents engage in and they are all illegal. Obviously some actions are more severely punished than others, but that does not mitigate the reality that spies are people who commit crimes with sanction. While working for a state a spy's criminal acts are considered justified and in the national interest, however, once a spy goes private sector they can no longer legitimately claim such a veneer of legality.

Spies inhabit and work in the same murky grey and black market world as criminals, giving them a common bond and often putting agents in touch with criminal groups, warlords, terrorists, revolutionaries and others as part of their work. It is a mutually cozy arrangement since criminals hold valuable intelligence and maintain vast covert support and operational infrastructures that a spy can use to complete a mission and stay under the radar. In some countries criminals form an almost legitimate part of the society and business world. The grey line between spy and criminal is as blurred and meaningless as that between businessman and gangster in such places. The use that spies and criminals make of each other is often a two way street. Criminals are commonly as interested in access to the rarified realms of covert state institutions and high corporate business as spies are in what criminals can provide. This degree of interoperability provides concrete benefits for both sides.

Theft

Theft can serve to disrupt rival corporate activities and directly acquire valuable materials and secrets. Stealing valuable goods or physical data can cost a company tremendous amounts of money, access to markets, and the trust of their clients. Theft of critical material from a state can be used as leverage or to damage their ability to pay and control the various groups that keep the regime in power. High value theft can also be used to covertly fund an operation. This is a common tactic with terrorists and revolutionaries as well as spies. Because spies have training, intelligence, planning capabilities, patience and daring, they often make exceptional thieves. Covert operators also have access to criminal groups who employ thieves and second story men as a matter of course.

Toe Cutters

A related activity that corporate, and other classes, of spies engage in is called "toe cutting". This extremely sinister sounding activity is basically the act of targeting criminals to steal money or illicit goods. Spies who have contact with criminal groups will often develop a significant amount of information about the players, activities and infrastructure of these organizations which can be used to steal from them. Spies may also have access, directly or covertly, to law enforcement files which provide further useful information on high value criminals. Just because the DEA needs a warrant to search a suspected drug lords stash house does not mean that a spy is not free to use that same information to their own ends.

For many spies criminals make the ultimate targets. They are generally quite lax in their operational security, at least against intelligence penetration. Criminals have no recourse to the state and legal means of seeking redress for losses. Criminals believe that they are immune because they have the ability to engage in violence against anyone who works against them. It is this last that makes criminals across the spectrum so vulnerable to direct action by spies. Normally it is true, criminals are protected from theft because they torture and kill people who cross them and this provides a rather significant deterrent to their work force. But if a spy gets information about a stash house or shipment of cash there is nothing stopping them from attacking it themselves or selling that information on to others. They are not directly linked to the criminal group. Spies can disappear beyond the reach of even major transnational criminal groups after such an act is carried out efficiently and totally. They have the training, tools and connections to take what they want from criminals almost at will. Spies often will have connections with and the ability to covertly hire very highly trained spec ops and military personnel who are willing to steal from criminals. And finally most spies are clever enough to create a false trail which plays to the expectations of the criminal group leading them back to an employee or to corrupt police forces which will effectively disguise their actions.

Criminals operate in an extremely high risk world and expect a certain amount of loss. They have many preconceived notions about where they are vulnerable and who to blame in the event of an attack. Using this, spies have repeatedly targeted and successfully stolen vast sums of money from a wide range of criminal organizations across the globe. For obvious reasons such cases are not publicized and the fall out is limited to the local grey and black market elements where such actions take place.

A number of spies will take targets of opportunity which present themselves to steal from criminals but there are others who use their covert operations training exclusively to work against criminal organizations. These are the toe cutters. They bug criminals' mansions, tap their phones, intercept their emails, hack their computers, torture their employees and liquidate anyone who gets in their way. These roving groups of former spooks and spec ops guys are completely unconstrained by law or operational directives from higher authority and they have been extremely successful. Criminals don't report these attacks and spies don't talk about these kinds of private groups but true or not the myths that are circulating about this growing side of private intelligence work can be quite alarming. As the number of highly trained and combat experienced soldiers, spec ops personnel and spies increase in the private sector this kind of activity will also certainly become more common. Organizations on both sides of the grey line are finding themselves more exposed and under threat from private spies then was ever the case before.

Kidnapping

An offshoot of the assault and intimidation genre of direct action is the act of targeted kidnapping. Any company that operates in high-risk countries knows how destabilizing, demoralizing and costly kidnapping can be to business operations. When used as a tactic to force action covertly, it can be a powerful weapon in the corporate arsenal used to attack competitors. Spies have all of the necessary training and skills, as well as resort to covert infrastructure and criminal groups, to make exceptional kidnappers. This is particularly true today when so many spies coming out of western military or intelligence organizations have received special training to conduct extraordinary rendition operations. Extraordinary rendition is, of course, little more than a euphemism for abduction. They have honed these skills against much harder targets than are likely to be found when using kidnapping on behalf of corporate interests.

Sabotage

Sabotage is a common and effective tactic used to target the vital corporate infrastructure of rivals. While useful to damage the capabilities and reputation of a rival company, this tactic can also be part of a broader campaign to destabilize governments or against specifically targeted officials. Sabotage against soft domestic targets can be done relatively easily and when conducted under a false flag can be virtually untraceable.

Sabotage does not have to involve the physical destruction of machinery, plants or important locations. In fact, the most effective form of sabotage today is digital. Using a company's computer systems against them is a very effective means of damaging their operations. Using digital sabotage also limits the risk of injuring workers or other civilians thus removing much of the potential for media coverage once the act is carried out. A further appealing aspect of digital sabotage is the unwillingness of many companies to report attacks of this kind to the authorities in the first place. If a company, using a private intelligence agent, can massively damage their competitor by mounting a digital attack which the target then covers up themselves, there is zero down side for the tasking company.

Terrorism for Money

Certain acts of sabotage, as well as acts of violence against civilian and military targets, carried out by spies all fall under the rubric of terrorism for money. Corporate attacks against the state in which they operate are not just limited to the world of fiction. If anyone believes that companies would never commit or sponsor acts of terror against civilians and states, one has to look no further than recent history in Central and South America or Africa. Revolutionary movements around the world regularly received covert funding from major corporations. Revolutionary and freedom fighters conducting terrorist acts all over the world receive support from state intelligence and military sources, mainly because their acts directly benefit domestic corporate interests. If the state proves unwilling or incapable of effectively working to further a corporation's agenda, there is little stopping that company from using its own resources to fund or commit acts of revolutionary violence and terror for its own benefit. A particularly damaging aspect of terror for money is the use by corporate intelligence agents of a front terror group to cover the tracks of their operations. This can be seen mostly today in the use of false flag digital terrorism and sabotage.

Net Based Attacks

A modern offshoot of attacking the infrastructure of a rival company covertly, either as sabotage or terrorism, is the use of information warfare and net based attacks. As Paul Atreides once so eloquently put it, "The power to destroy a thing is the absolute power over it." Corporations, through corporate intelligence sources and in-house covert action arms, have access to a wide array of high yield cyber weapons that they can use to attack a competitor or even an entire country covertly. Using corporate intelligence assets as surrogates to conduct such direct action insulates a company and is an increasingly popular and powerful tool. The damage done to a rival firm's systems and even their physical infrastructure can be catastrophic. The costs in terms of manpower and technology are minuscule when compared to the impact on the targeted firm.

It is not just states that covet and are developing destructive cyber weapons capabilities. These weapons can include such simple vectors as DDOS attacks all the way to military grade or better high yield systems destruction programs. The threat exists against smaller states as much as it does against rival companies. A corporation which through their covert direct action arm has access to deniable high yield cyber weaponry possesses a powerfully coercive tool to influence the actions of less developed nations and their leaders. Ready access by companies through corporate intelligence groups to military grade or better cyber weapons is making net based attacks a truly formidable threat against both rival companies and unprepared states. This is one area that is only going to grow as the effectiveness of such attacks, or even threat of attack, are proven through use.

Assassination

Throughout history, greater changes have been wrought on the world by little bits of metal moving very fast than almost any other cause. Assassination is the most effective means of removing problem individuals decisively and permanently. Just ask the local drug dealer or warlord about the utility of death in business.

Assassination is also the most commonly misrepresented action in fiction when it comes to intelligence. In the real world, there is no clandestine group of super assassins, ninja kicking and sniping their way around the world for vast sums of money. Militaries have cadres of Special Forces and some state intelligence organs do keep trained killers, but with the potential for international fallout if such operations are exposed, countries tend to keep their assassins on a very tight leash. State sponsored assassins exist almost exclusively in the third world and are used primarily against political opponents of their great and glorious leader. One finds real life private assassins almost exclusively in the black market and within criminal groups. Criminals retain people who have no problem shooting others, generally from the back of cheap motorcycles for $50 dollars a head, on their payroll.

Fiction runs into fact when it comes to assassination based on the simple market dynamics of supply and demand. The demand for killers exists almost solely within the black market and among criminals. They possess their own willing and disposable supply. Depending on the locale, death dealing can be an amazingly cheap commodity. It is only against hardened targets or those whose deaths need to appear accidental that there exists a real market for skilled assassins in the first world. When corporations hire assassins they do tend to prefer to go through covert intelligence groups rather than the local drug lord. The quality of the killers is higher and there exists a greater degree of built in deniability. In such cases, a company will need to find a skilled operator through an intelligence organization with paramilitary contacts.

The use of assassination as a corporate tool against rivals is not nearly as farfetched as it may first sound. The utility of death is obvious. And executives are killed all over the world each year. The likelihood that these deaths are all the result of burglaries gone wrong, car accidents or accidental bathtub drowning does not hold much water. If the potential for discovery is low and the result worthy enough, there is no reason to think that corporations, or more precisely on-site lower level executives, are any more likely to shy away from targeted killing than Israel is in the Gaza Strip or the US was with Osama Bin Laden. This is not to say that major companies all operate death squads, but as a tactic globally it is undeniably employed regularly and effectively to further state and business interests. The perceived need for companies to possess state level capabilities in arranging convenient death is real and shared by many.

Corporate Defection

An increasingly popular covert action need among companies is the assisted defection of key personnel from their rivals. Most high-level researchers or other important staff members are under very strict contract obligations to their present employers. As companies gain more leverage over their employees and contracts continue to become more draconian, the field of covert corporate recruitment and defection becomes ever more important. At present, assisted corporate defection is only rarely practiced but the numbers are rising. Using corporate spooks to talent spot and convince key employees to change jobs is something that is already done on a very regular basis across the globe. As companies harden their defenses against corporate defection activity, there will develop a corresponding need to plan and carry out snatch missions to safely extract top people covertly. This role can best be filled by corporate intelligence and paramilitary personnel.

Legal Removal

One does not have to kill a person to remove them from play. There are a number of highly effective means of legally removing an individual from their job or even society that can be employed by corporate spies. Legal removal is a favored tactic in countries like America where a highly effective police and state security force makes kinetic direct actions such as kidnapping, assault, assassination and others more problematic. The flip side of having an effective police force that cannot be easily corrupted or bribed is that these same legal enforcement agencies can be used to efficiently do the dirty work of a spy for them.

Planting false evidence of wrong doing is the most common means of removing an individual legally. The most common crimes that spies use to legally excommunicate someone from their job and society are deviant sex, drugs and child pornography. There is no legitimate reason for anyone to possess illicit materials relating to drugs or kiddie porn. If discovered by the police in someone's home or on their computer, they go to prison, period. Due to a rabid fear in America and elsewhere of certain types of crime, few questions are ever asked about individuals who are accused of such acts which make them highly suitable to covert application. After all, who believes or ever defends a secret heroin user or a closet pedophile, even if they are a highly placed corporate personality. Planting such evidence is as easy as conducting a quick break in to an individual's home or remotely accessing their personal computer and placing the compromising materials there. One little "anonymous" tip in the right ear and poof the target disappears more effectively and with far less possibility of discovery than if you dropped them into a vat of acid.

Black Propaganda

"There is no such thing as public opinion. There is only published opinion."
Winston Churchill

The pen can be mightier than the sword. In the modern business world where image is increasingly critical to success the use of black propaganda tools to covertly attack rival firms is becoming a very common fixture. Black propaganda is information, both true and false, broadcast to intentionally damage another company its products or employees. Among governments black propaganda has been used historically to paint the strategic competitor with the evil brush and damage their external relations or internal cohesion. This has taken the form over the years of everything from faked news stories (AIDS was created in a secret US bio warfare lab) to elaborate programs of misinformation (Radio Moscow). In corporate intelligence it is typically used to embarrass, misrepresent or vilify the opposing company. Associated with covert psychological operations, the fabrications, lies and deceptions are intended to cause maximum damage and to be untraceable back to the tasking rival company. Ultimately, black propaganda depends on the receiver accepting the credibility of the message and the source.

Black propaganda is the art of painting a target company, product or individual in a negative light. Image is so important in the business world that if done right a black propaganda campaign can eviscerate a company more effectively than any data theft or cyber attack. The goal of black propaganda is to cripple a target corporation's business by destroying their image. Like so many other aspects of corporate espionage, the art and ability to sell bad news has been made much easier by the advent of the internet and the information revolution. What has really opened the door to modern corporate black propaganda is the voracious appetite for scandal and lowered quality controls within the media.

Black propaganda artists tend to be something of a separate breed from standard corporate spooks, but only in that they are specialists in media manipulation and apply their training and tradecraft to the corruption of mass media sources. Black propaganda specialists tend to be more permanently based and hold solid legitimate front occupations as well.

Propaganda artists specialize in the recruitment of media people, such as journalists and more recently bloggers. Media personalities, for the most part, can prove to be even softer targets than other corporate employees. The media is insular and progress within the industry is based on perceived accomplishment and image. There are also built in source safeguards in the media that act to buffer the covert propagandist from suspicion or detection. This is mostly down to the media's own aversion to admitting exploitation and mistakes. Much of what a propagandist does is legal common practice in corporate marketing and the media itself. Like any good marketing campaign, black propaganda is only as strong as the reach and strength of its message. Propaganda has a long and proven track record, making it an effective weapon in the corporate intelligence arsenal.

Targets of Black Propaganda

Most black propaganda attacks target specific products not a company as a whole. The rational is that it is very difficult to bring down an entire company without significant resources, but the task of destruction becomes manageable when attacking discreet products or services piecemeal. Obvious deployment of vast sums of money and wide spread efforts makes larger operations easier to trace back and more problematic than limited strikes. Using a more limited approach against a specific product or service can severely disrupt sales and market share with little effort and tremendous result.

An example would be a selective black propaganda strike against a rival pharmaceutical company's new drug. By employing net based trend influencing techniques and a few turned journalists to bring the issue into mainstream news, the black propaganda artist can raise serious doubts about the safety of the target product or its efficacy. Modern media is ideally suited to this kind of an attack because much of their coverage is already geared towards generation of fear and does not have to contain actual accusations, merely insinuation. The target company, in this case, would be out billions of dollars in lost sales and additional marketing to counteract the rumor. The most common industries targeted by black propaganda are bio-medical, consumer electronics, fashion, automotive and the financial service sector.

Personal Targets

One area of black propaganda that has seen significant growth in recent years is the targeting of individuals. By placing the bulls-eye on particularly effective executives, researchers or other important staff, it has been proved possible to have the target company remove these stars from their position itself. Once an innocent employee is left twisting in the wind, the company which initiated the covert action can pick them up cheap or just leave them hanging, removed from the rival's side of the board.

There is any number of ways to destroy an individual's reputation and most of them do not even involve real scandal. The process usually goes something like this: First, an "incident" involving the target individual is concocted or a real predilection revealed; Next, a planted media report decrying the incident is published; Then, a planted group of "concerned shareholders" demand the removal of said employee, even though senior staff demurs because the individual is a valuable asset to the company; Eventually, the demands from the media and shareholders are artificially increased and the company caves. Most companies are wimps when it comes to standing up to media pressure. Even if the story has no merit or truth on its own, and the source is unknown or not credible, a degree of leverage over a reporter or editor is all that it takes to build and sustain media pressure for as long as the spy and their client company wishes.

Generating Scandal

Bent journalists are a bad joke in most national intelligence agencies and more so among the private intelligence sector. Anyone familiar with the operations of the CIA or KGB back in the day knows about the large numbers of journalist that were turned by state intelligence officers and used to push black propaganda. National intelligence agencies before, and private intelligence groups now, turn media people as a matter of course. States recognized the importance of propaganda, both black and white, early on and have been using the media to further its goals for a very long time. The KGB even went so far as to include exact counts of how many stories they were able to implant each day into Western media outlets during the briefing they gave to senior Soviet leadership. With the resources and skills of corporate intelligence agents, the number of bent journalists operating today from the pocket of black propaganda agents is significant.

Legitimate, unturned, journalists are often taken in by targeted black propaganda disinformation campaigns as well. After all, a good story is a good story and few stories have legs like those involving corporate or executive wrong doing. By feeding well crafted disinformation to a journalist posing as a source from inside of the target company or merely as a concerned citizen with access can start a fire storm most companies would give anything to avoid.

Forgery

Forgery is a classic intelligence art and has been highly successful in deceiving people across the spectrum since the time of the first clay tablet. It is not just passports and fake IDs that forgers are skilled at making. Many trained forgers in the world, using both digital and old school paper, are in fact employed primarily in the creation of black propaganda materials. Selling disinformation is much easier if there is documentary evidence to support it. Whether or not such material is capable of being proven real does not matter to the black propagandist or indeed to many journalists. Forged materials are often considered better because the propagandist can mix in grains of truth with as much disinformation as they wish. As long as the true parts of a document can be checked, the document as a whole will often be accepted. If there is one thing that the media hates, it is having to admit that they were duped, which gives well done forgeries tremendous power.

Wikileaks is a fantastic example of this process at work. Material from a number of covert sources is anonymously deposited online at a "secured" web site. Wikileaks "fact check" the secret information in conjunction with a number of newspapers and magazines and then publish it all over the world via the main stream media. There have already been instances where media outlets were fooled into publishing material supposedly from the Wikileaks documents which were in fact forgeries. Not even well made forgeries, but that didn't matter the damage was done. So far the forgeries that have been detected are all relatively poor and target local interests in countries like Pakistan. But this is just the beginning.

Spoofing sites like Wikileaks with expertly crafted forgeries of real materials perhaps obtained covertly meant to damage a target company will happen, if it hasn't already. The beauty of forgery is that it can be done easily and relatively cheaply. Even if discovered, the mainstream media will likely spend less time saying sorry and correcting it than they spend covering high school badminton. The damage, once done, cannot be undone and all most people will remember anyway is the negative message.

Profiting from Black Propaganda

It is not just the contracting company which can benefit from a disinformation campaign against its competitors. The spies themselves can double dip a black propaganda operation to reap huge profits from the inevitable drop in stock prices once the bad news is picked up by the media. If the spy knows that a very negative article will go out about company A tomorrow, it is easy for them to short sell that stock and make a tidy profit. Companies themselves have been known to engage in black propaganda operations for the express reason of generating some quick profits from the market reaction. Corporate raiders are known to use forgery and black propaganda tricks to undercut the value of a target stock before they make a takeover bid. The possibilities for profit are endless.

White Propaganda

White propaganda, covertly using bent journalists and disinformation to promote products and services, is an area that has seen huge growth recently. If the media can be duped into making negative pronouncements about target companies and products, it has proven only a bit more difficult to put the net and the news to work pushing selected products. A company that employs covert means to influence opinion about its own products or share value can reap tremendous profits from its actions. In many case, using covert media control is actually cheaper and more effective than traditional marketing campaigns.

One aspect of white propaganda is called guerilla marketing. Guerilla marketing is a new wave method of overcoming media saturation on the part of consumers by attacking them in new ways and in areas where they do not expect to see advertising. It is advertising that is not viewed by the target consumer as an advert. The net has led to an explosion of covert marketing which accounts for a growing percentage of total advertising budgets among even the most traditional brands. Give this kind of white propaganda marketing campaign a covert pressure boost and the impact will be greater still.

Individual Use of Corporate Intelligence Resources

The massive corporate intelligence apparatus that exists in the world today can and is utilized by individuals, not just corporations, to distinct advantage. Once an individual gains access to the shadow world of private intelligence operators they can utilize them to help better their position within a company, attack rivals, cover affairs and vices, launder money, evade taxes, subvert the legal process, for personal security or any other task that might bring them advantage in life as they see it.

Generally, a corporate espionage agent in the field does not know exactly who put them there or for whose benefit they are conducting an operation. This anonymous placement is important because contracting companies do not want any direct ties to the people doing dirty deeds for them and to prevent a spy from gaining leverage over the company itself. Engaging in covert intelligence operations at arm's length with numbers of cut outs means that these powerful resources are just as easily employed by an individual with the necessary money and connections as by a company.

Professional Advancement

As an ambitious employee in a major company, the easiest route to advancement is to scoop your competition and to make yourself invaluable to your superiors. What better means exist than to constantly be on top of the actions of a main business rival or even those in your company who might be internal rivals. Beating the competition at every turn and returning to the company with new products, contracts and sales would make any employee shine. Doing this legitimately can be exceptionally difficult, so why not cheat and employee your own personal intelligence team to get that inside information for you? Most intelligence operational costs are within the budget of a mid-level executive or anyone with a hundred thousand extra dollars or so. Tailoring a mission to include pervasive target coverage over an extended period means that an individual will only have to spend the high start up costs and then can coast for years on the intelligence feed that is created, either digitally through a deep systems tap or with a long term asset in place. If these expenditures gain the mid-level executive access to the rarified heights of corporate leadership and multimillion dollar annual bonuses, maintaining a personal intelligence capability can pay for itself within a very short time. In addition, the power and allure of secret information and possession of one's own personal spy can be more than a little addictive. One can understand how personal spies have become the fastest growing area of corporate intelligence right now. It may even be possible to have the company itself fund the intelligence operation if the controlling employee can get access to black budgets or come to an arrangement with whoever runs covert ops inside the company. It can even be funded semi-covertly under the rubric of legitimate business intelligence as long as steps are taken to properly launder the information received.

Using intelligence resources to help an employee to destroy their rivals within the company is another tried and true method of accelerating advancement within a corporation. It is a common practice for spies to build up their sources inside of a company by clearing the asset's way to the top through the covert removal of troublesome internal rivals. This can be done using personally targeted black propaganda, legal disappearance or other means limited only by the ruthlessness of the contracting individual. Is senior VP whoever standing in the way of your rise to ultimate power, a trophy wife and a house in the Hamptons? Easy, have a document forged showing that he is leaking information to another company, reveal the alleged sexual harassment of the secretary, hack his home computer and upload a few gigs of naked kid pictures, have an intelligence agent slip him LSD at the company Christmas party and he disappears, problem solved. If these steps don't get rid of him, well there are always other options. Private intelligence resources as a tool in a personal agenda can provide the user with untold advantages over other employees in the work place and beyond.

One very fascinating area where this type of covert action is getting employed today is in the trenches of Hollywood. Using a covert operator to target specific rivals in the media world and take them out either through black propaganda or more direct action is something behind a number of high profile headlines recently. LA based spies have been known to work for a number of firms in the industry to help promote or destroy individual media faces. This is a corporate thing. Glittery stars and starlets do not usually hire their own spies, but the companies which operate them and reap massive profits off of their fame do. What makes this aspect of personal covert action interesting is that it is happening in the full glare of a massive media presence. If spies can be employed regularly to influence media saturated LA with little or no detection profile then their effectiveness working on hyper soft corporate targets elsewhere can only be imagined.

Vices

Perhaps the private intelligence consumer wishes to use covert resources to aid him, or her, in the conduct of more personal business. Spies make for excellent panders, drug dealers and providers of all manner of vice. Their connection to the underworld and security consciousness makes them an ideal source for covert enjoyment of sinful or illegal activities. If the cash is there most spies do not care. These kinds of actions are common place when working to recruit and run a source in a target firm and can easily be provided at little extra charge to individual users as well.

Money Laundering and Tax Evasion

Perhaps the individual's need is less of the flesh, and more of the wallet. Spies and their handlers invariably have access to high-grade money laundering and tax shelter contacts as part of their job. Covertly moving money around, setting up front companies and off shore accounts is how spies and their sources get paid. An upstanding executive need not go to some underworld figure or shady money launder when they can access a private and professional intelligence organization to get the same service without having to deal with the less savory elements that make up grey and black market banking. Corporate spies, after all, are so much more genteel than most local gangsters. For a small consideration, a spy can easily arraign access to covert money laundering organizations that are more than willing to help a flush executive or anyone else with enough money, hide their spoils outside the reach of authorities.

Legal Issues

Hiring a spy to compromise a criminal prosecution, develop information about divorce proceedings, covertly alter wills and otherwise corrupt the legal process can be a very expensive, but extremely effective means of assuring victory in court. The costs are generally higher for legal arena operations because the risks of targeting the authorities directly are greater. Stealing the case files of the opposition, compromising witnesses and bribing judges or others involved in the process are actions that a spy is trained to handle but rarely engage in when operating in the first world because of the many risks.

Generally, spies are no more sinister than normal people and would be loath to take any operation that involves corruption, targeting the legitimate authorities, direct action against witnesses or other such unscrupulous deeds in their own country. But ethical compunction, especially if backed up by a really big check, can be overcome or indeed isn't even present in some. In fact, there are more than a few intelligence agents who relish the challenge of taking on the authorities directly. Perhaps it reminds them of their glory days targeting Chinese diplomats and tangling with third world security forces. In any event, if the individual has access to a broad enough pool of potential recruits, there is little doubt that they can find a spy willing and able to covertly handle any action required to skew the legal system.

Personal Security and Over Watch

Personal security is an interesting field because of the commonly held belief that spies are supermen with all kinds of ninja skills. Like hiring the A-team, it is believed that if an individual can get a former Mossad or CIA trained spook on staff, they will become invulnerable. Some spies take on well paying personal protection details and end up discovering that they are little more than another trophy and status symbol for their rich clients to show off to their friends. A spy is a highly trained individual with very unique skill sets, very few of which, despite what Burn Notice might indicate, have to do with blowing up cars or saving little old ladies in trouble. What spies do well is steal secrets and manipulate people. If the individual has need for covert theft or controlling people, then hiring a former spook makes sense; otherwise they should just buy a Ferrari and get it out of their system.

There is a growing field for certain kinds of former intelligence officers in the counter intelligence, over watch, and high value individual (HVI) security spheres. Knowing tricks from the offensive side often does make corporate spooks, with their unique skill sets and operational experience, downright ferocious when fighting for the defense.

One development in this area that has been quite interesting to see emerge recently is the over watch and vulnerability assessment for

HVI clients. It is a positive sign that more American companies and high value individuals are taking security seriously enough to hire corporate spies out of the shadows to test the vulnerabilities of their systems and personnel. Services like this can take many forms, but mostly serves as a loyalty test and a data security review. After all, if the spy on a leash can turn your senior designer or penetrate the CEO's home computer in less than 5 minutes, information about such vulnerabilities can save the company in question immense hassles and treasure.

Over watch is similar to security checks, but more persistent. This process is a periodic security review of selected senior employees and can include constant monitoring of their lives (covertly or overtly) to detect potential threats and disloyalty before they become a problem. Most companies use counter intelligence personnel for these functions but sometimes it is a good idea to test the defenses against the real thing.

Opposition Countermeasures

"Show me a completely smooth operation and I'll show you a cover up. Real boats rock."
Darwi Odrade

The Wilderness of Mirrors

Called the "wilderness of mirrors" by former counter intelligence head at the CIA, James Jesus Angleton, counter intelligence (CI) is one of the most complex and mind bending tasks a person can engage in. In a nut shell, CI is the detection, removal and debriefing of intelligence operations attempting to penetrate an organization and also consists of operations aimed at penetrating the intelligence apparatus of rival powers to compromise their organizations. It is an attempt to out spook the spooks and get inside of their intelligence collection cycle to both deceive the spies and their masters in order keep them blind to your own operations. The most existential threat that an intelligence operation faces is against the activities of counter intelligence forces both state sponsored and increasingly corporate based.

Local police and security forces may, from time to time, either stumble upon or actively seek out spies, but their mandate is generally gear towards more mundane crimes. Local police and security forces are not in the same threat category as counter intelligence. They are neither tasked, trained nor equipped to seek out acts and agents of espionage, corporate or otherwise. This, by no means, infers that local police or security forces are not an omnipresent danger to an intelligence agent or are in any way incapable of detecting espionage when they do come across it. It is not inability on the part of local forces as often as it is inattention that makes them a lower category of threat than other more dedicated services.

In-house corporate security forces, including any existing counter intelligence personnel, are also a threat to an espionage agent and their operations. Since in-house security has to work with and through properly empowered police and counter intelligence agencies to bring legal sanction against an intelligence agent, they too are often considered lower on the threat matrix than dedicated state counter intelligence agencies. Corporate counter intelligence, even if they employ former state counter intelligence personnel, have limited power to legally stop or penetrate intelligence operations once detected. There is often little love lost between state and corporate counter intelligence. This means that corporate counter intelligence can be significantly handicapped by lack of information about what is happening in other companies, let alone information about trans-national corporate intelligence activities.

In-house corporate security groups do have one thing going for them, however. The scope of their responsibilities is limited to a finite number of employees and the data systems that link them. The biggest hurdle for corporate counter intelligence is not lack of cooperation with state agencies as much as it is inattention from senior executives. Companies that employ counter intelligence assets have a major advantage over those that do not, but even in the best cases, these forces rarely sit at the big kids table within the company. Counter intelligence, where it exists, only rarely will have a say in such vital matters as the corporate structure, operation or examination of personnel, business practices or computer security. The inability of counter intelligence assets within a company to affect policy and effect operational changes to create a more secure environment is the main reason that they have so little impact on the detection and prevention of intelligence operations which target their firms.

As secure as it might be, creating a police state mentality within a company is rarely conducive to productivity and retention of high value employees. There are, of course, ways that corporate counter intelligence can dramatically increase the security of a firm with minimal impact on day-to-day operations. Suffice it to say that most corporations, particularly within the US, do not consider security threats beyond what they read in the newspapers and magazines. Thus, on-site threats such as petty theft, rampaging employees or more amorphous threats such as those posed by low grade hackers to their internal computer systems are the ones that are the focus of corporate security today.

It is the rare company that understands the value of an effective in-house counter intelligence apparatus. The costs of counter intelligence sections always seem to balloon with little tangible results. However, detection and neutralization of a single penetration of the company can generally be counted on to pay for an effective counter intelligence effort many times over. There is also the benefit of deterrence. Corporate spies pay very close attention to which company has what levels of internal security and are apt to decline contracts to penetrate the most secure organizations. This means that the more secure a company can make itself, the fewer highly skilled spies will attempt to penetrate it, the more it will cost their rivals to attempt a covert penetration and the lower the skill level is likely to be of those who do attempt to suborn their employees.

Determining the Level of Opposition

A spy seeking to penetrate a company will often begin operations by attempting to determine the level of opposition from internal corporate security as well as the local police and other forces. Companies with efficient in-house counter intelligence resources will often advertise the fact far and wide in an attempt to deter would be spies from targeting their organization. A deeper investigative read can be accomplished by the spy through examining the company organization tables and employee lists available online and via such common social networking sites as LinkedIn. Further information can be obtained readily from employees themselves. Approaching mid-level employees at any given company and steering the conversation to counter intelligence training they may or may not have received can give the spy a good picture of the effectiveness and reach of a particular organization's counter intelligence program, or the lack there of.

From time to time a state of spy mania exists. This fear will drive local police and security forces to actively seek out espionage agents, real or imagined. Only rarely will they actually catch anyone who is a real spy, but the common mind set of citizens and police forces can make corporate espionage work more difficult and increase the threat of detection significantly in such an environment. In developing countries the government regularly uses the existence of external threats to justify significant internal repression, but spy hunts have been known to pop up every once in a while in first world nations as well. The flood of calls from concerned citizens after September 11th in the US actually did uncover a number of budding corporate and state sponsored espionage operations. But a siege mentality is difficult to maintain, especially in advanced countries, and is almost never applied directly to corporate espionage activities. Governments and police simply do not rate private espionage activities which are not targeting their national defense or intelligence infrastructures very highly and thus do not expend resources trying to detect or liquidate those who engage in corporate intelligence activity or their paymasters.

A few countries maintain active special branch type police organizations to specifically target corporate espionage activity. However, these efforts tend to be rather small and, given the scale of global corporate espionage activity, have limited effect. Judging the best country and city to strike at a company is often predicated on the level of opposition force and their perceived effectiveness in that region.

The same force limitations that apply to local police and security services also apply to national counter intelligence agencies. A government defends what it considers of greatest import to its own survival. Governments in the West target those intelligence operations which seek to compromise its military, defense industrial and intelligence organs first and almost exclusively. This prioritizing has opened the door to extensive corporate intelligence operations because those with the best tools and most resources to combat them, namely state counter intelligence organizations, are rarely tasked with the discovery or destruction of corporate espionage elements.

A further impediment to corporate reliance on state security agencies for protection against corporate intelligence operations is the lack of willingness on the part of many companies to pursue legal recourse in the event of discovery. Indeed, there is a lack of significant sanctions covering many of the more easily provable acts that make up corporate espionage activities which makes drawn out prosecution even less appealing. Companies are rarely willing to take legal action against espionage agents because it would cost them too much time and money in the short term. Of more importance, damage to stock value, lost customers, damage to their image and most importantly termination of senior staff are by far the most common cause for inaction. Most known cases of successful corporate espionage invariably lead to the dismissal or resignation of the upper echelon executives within the targeted company. More often than not the self preservation instincts of those running a company will outweigh the marginal benefit to be had by making an example of some hapless corporate spook that has been caught out.

Underestimating the Opposition

It is a common view among seasoned intelligence professionals that targeting soft companies is many times easier and safer than going after government agencies and military organizations let alone terrorists and drug lords. This mind set can, however, lead to a fatal case of overconfidence and land even the most professional spy in jail or worse. Just because a given company is not locked down under state security protection does not mean that their internal security, the local police or state counter intelligence are not out there and more than capable of detecting and picking up a spy who slacks on their tradecraft. Inattention to the corporate world by no means indicates an inability on the part of security organs to step in and destroy an espionage operation if they are pushed. A spy must be aware at all times of the potential for significant counter intelligence resources to be deployed against them and their operations and employ the countermeasures necessary to stay covert and situationally aware.

Legal Limits of Counter Intelligence

Corporate espionage is a crime. Most of the acts that go into the conduct of an intelligence operation are themselves crimes and this leads to both advantages to the corporate intelligence agent and significant drawbacks. The advantage is that it forces the intelligence agent to operate clandestinely. This focuses their minds on danger and allows them to utilize extra legal means to overcome security and other obstacles when operating against a company. A further advantage to operating covertly is that in order for the opposition forces to move against an intelligence agent they must first work their way through the cover and clandestine defenses that the spy has erected to obscure their identity and purpose.

Once the opposition discovers a spy, they then have to build a solid case against them to prove their actions and put them away. Depending on the power of lawyers within the country of operation this can take anywhere from days to years. It is yet another reason that operating against American companies within the United States is such a popular approach to generating corporate intelligence. Consider America's war on organized crime and drugs syndicates. Everyone knows that these characters are hardened criminals engaged in all manner of illegal acts up to an including torture and murder. The police and a broad range of security forces in the United States spend untold billions every year investigating and prosecuting these groups. Officers know with certainty that many of the people they watch and gather evidence on are the worst of the worst. Such illegal groups often have limited or no counter surveillance or other tradecraft training to protect themselves. And yet it often takes years of painstaking work by vast teams of skilled police and federal agents to make a valid case against the known baddies. The absolute rule of law, procedures and the need to generate an overwhelming preponderance of evidence to bring such criminals to trial for significant crimes means that they have a huge advantage over the police and security forces.

Now consider corporate espionage. Rarely, if ever, would a corporate espionage case get anywhere near the resources committed regularly to a major drug or organized crime investigation. Legal limits hinder prosecutions, plus there is great reluctance on the part of most companies to cooperate or push prosecution in the first place. The typically short duration of most intelligence operations and the nomadic and clandestine nature of spies provide limited scope for security forces to create an easily prosecutable case in time. This is not to say that such cases are never brought before a jury, but the successful conduct through to conclusion of corporate intelligence cases does require many stars to line up perfectly.

Techniques Used by the Opposition

If, through poor tradecraft, asset leak, internal breach or sheer bad luck, an intelligence operation is compromised to the opposition, there are numerous techniques that they can use to entrap the spy and break their ring. Some of the more common techniques include surveillance, informants, direct contact, removal and more.

Surveillance

The greatest, indeed the only, protection that a spy has in the real world is not their Walther PPK, ninja-like combat skills or their ability to bed scores of beautiful women all while suavely drinking a martini, but their simple anonymity. Once a spy is detected and steps are taken to place them under surveillance that anonymity evaporates quickly and with it the spy's only real protection. Early detection of surveillance is where good training and active tradecraft comes into play. A major portion of the training that goes into making an intelligence agent involves teaching them how to detect when they have been discovered. Anonymity can be the only difference between safety and a cell or worse and spies are taught from day one that they either preserve this or fail. Limiting the possibility of detection and knowing what to do if one is under surveillance is the key to survival and prosperity for an intelligence agent.

Means of spotting a tail are taught to spies and most of these detection techniques fall under the rubric of situational awareness and counter surveillance. However, when enough trained manpower is deployed against a spy it can be nearly impossible to shake or even detect the web of surveillance. If a spy is placed under active surveillance in order to determine if they are involved in a case, and they then display signs of overt situational awareness or counter surveillance moves, the interest of the opposition often jumps several notches.

The trick to good tradecraft is making actions seem as normal as possible. The average Joe Q. Citizen does not conduct elaborate surveillance detection runs prior to buying their morning cup of coffee. If a spy trying to pass themselves off as a harmless civilian does engage in such behaviors, chances are, the brunt of security service focus will swing immediately over to them. This is not to say that once in the field all tradecraft is poison to a spy, but again the key is to make it look as natural as possible and fit action with the situation and necessity. If a penetration is detected, but the individual spy is not, surveillance will tend to be blanket and general until the security services discover a target. This interim is the best window for the spy to successfully detect and evade suspicion.

For the modern counter intelligence forces, following someone and keeping them under surveillance is easier than ever. Access to cell phone tracking, GPS locators, aerial drone surveillance platforms and stand alone video surveillance tools can allow a much more hands-off approach to surveillance than was ever possible before. These same advances in surveillance techniques also place the spy at a very significant disadvantage that requires even more elaborate and technical measures to be taken to detect and evade potential threats.

The best and only means for a spy to remain safe from surveillance and tracking is to stay constantly aware and on their toes. Tame paranoia is an invaluable tool for the espionage agent. Controlled fear brings focus and makes the agent take steps to minimize their risk factors. Some risks are out of an intelligence agent's control, but by maintaining a grasp of their surroundings, taking positive and preemptive steps to detect surveillance and operating in a deeply clandestine manner, they can place major obstacles in the path of opposition forces.

Informants

One of the most effective means that the security services have to flush out a spy and gather prosecutable information against them is the use of informants and dangles. These are very commonly employed techniques used every day by police forces around the world to penetrate common criminal operations and can be just as effective against spies as they are against drug dealers.

Informants can be very difficult to detect and are relatively easy for security forces to generate. One of the main reasons that an intelligence operation is more secure the fewer people and moving parts are involved, is due to the possibility that one or more of the people engaged in an operation could turn informant or be one from the start. The spy can take some steps to minimize the possibility of their sources turning and the damage that any one informant can inflict on an operation by compartmentalizing them. The first step to keeping assets in line is to keep them out of the hands of the authorities. Many counter intelligence operations begin only after some pawn in an operation falls into the hands of the local police on unrelated charges and decides to save themselves by giving up something bigger. This is another reason why it is often a good idea for a spy to use their training and skills to become the sole conduit for sources into the black market and keep them away from other criminals. If a spy keeps tame sources within a company or uses others for operational work, always acting to limit and obfuscate information that any one person has on the existence and identity of others can buy important time in the event of detection. The less coherent a picture an individual source has about the operation as a whole the less likely the authorities are to believe their story or be able to act on it if they do believe them. If an asset is turned then compartmentalizing information becomes even more important.

A spy should always be attuned to the behavior of their sources and be constantly on the lookout for signs that they have been turned by the opposition. Some of these signs include a sudden interest in details of the operation that a source had no interest in before, demands to meet in locations or at times set by the asset and not by the agent and sudden nervousness or giddiness on the part of the source when meeting with an agent. If any of these signs appear or if the antennae of the intelligence agent start to twitch, for whatever reason, it may be time to begin a program of intensified counter surveillance and to run some surveillance on the source to make sure that they are still under positive control.

It is entirely possible to detect the opposition by running a program of surveillance on the turncoats that they might employ. Because the opposition considers itself on the side of apple pie and righteousness, they rarely will go out of their way to take precautions against surveillance themselves. If a spy can detect a potentially turned source and has the resources to follow them and keep the source under their own surveillance, it can usually be determined rather quickly just who else might be running them.

Dangles

Dangles are another favored trick of police and security services. A dangle is someone that is programmed and presented to the world and all of the spies in it as a great potential source and to offer their services for the express purpose of getting on the inside of an intelligence operation. Dangles can be used to detect an operation and also to feed false or misleading information to the spy and through them to the hiring party. Dangles are a favorite ploy of corporate counter intelligence since they do not have the power to arrest or prosecute the spy and since management will rarely give them the go ahead to approach the authorities. If a spy is not prepared to face this threat they can easily be taken in by the allure of a helpful dangle.

Spies need information, materials, tools and services which they can only get from the grey or black market. This limits their options for sourcing and provides the opposition with a ready-made introduction to clandestine operations. Always be wary of Greeks bearing gifts. This is as true today as it was during the Trojan War. The means of limiting the potential for dangles is by conducting as much of an operation as possible with the proven resources in the spy's possession. The more a spy has to rely on faith in others, especially coming from the black market, the greater the risks to operational security.

If a dangle is detected, a spy has the options of accepting their help and trying to control the opposition through their reliance on the dangle for information or rejecting the person and going deeper underground. State security services are more likely to use provocation agents than local police forces, because their goal is to detect and shut down intelligence operations, not necessarily to build cases. The means that the opposition uses to get close to an intelligence agent often gives the operative information about who is interested in their operations and what they have at their disposal to disrupt the work of the spy.

Direct Contact

Nothing can shake up a spy as much as an opposition member coming to their safe house and blatantly telling them that the game is up and it is time to leave town. Opposition internal corporate security uses this direct approach as a preferred technique because it inevitably stops an intelligence operation in its tracks and does not exceed their legal mandate. Scaring the spy directly often causes them to simply cut and run. This direct encounter does not require any form of legal sanction or potential compromise to the company. If a spy faces direct contact they can either go underground or run away. Exposure and confrontation of any operation is potentially fatal. The spy must question just how much of the information they received was compromised from the start and which of their agents or technical penetration routes were breached. A direct approach requires the opposition to be well informed about the agent, their operation and its infrastructure, but is a very high-result, low cost means of ending a corporate intelligence operation quickly.

Physical Removal

Physical removal of intelligence agents is uncommon in advanced countries, but is not unheard of in more volatile regions. This approach to ending an intelligence operation can include everything from roughing up an intelligence agent, illegal detention, deportation or even killing the spy outright. In most third world nations, if the spy cannot bribe their way out of detection, this is the most likely outcome. Which adds yet another reason why most spies do not like to work where the sun shines year round. In more stable environments, physical intimidation and direct actions against a spy and their operations are often conducted by internal corporate security because they have the least level of exposure. It is highly unlikely that a spy will go to the police and tell them that some toughs beat them silly to warn them away from future espionage activities. Also, an undercover spy might not even be missed if conveniently "disappeared" by corporate counter intelligence gun thugs. If a spy is discovered and captured while conducting private intelligence work, the possibility of very bad things happening to them exists and should never be discounted just because they are dealing with rival corporate entities and not Al-Qaeda. Companies have a lot to lose from corporate espionage and therefore hire some very ruthless people to keep them secure. Given the opportunity, one dead corporate spy can act as a very powerful deterrent to others.

Discovery

If a spy is discovered they have the option of running or diving deeper underground. Submerging under deeper cover and continuing the operation can prove a formidable challenge depending on the level of opposition the spy faces and the degree to which they have penetrated the operation. If the police find a lead while fishing and the threat level is low, then going deeper undercover is a viable option, but if the threat matrix indicates more serious opposition pressure most professional spies know enough to cut their losses and run.

Discovery does not mean that the operation itself necessarily is at an end. The opposition may have clued into the existence of an individual spy, but if the agent's sources are still secure the show can go on. Continuing the operation assumes the individual or organization running that inside source can move another operator into the theater quickly enough and without scaring away the sources.

More often than not, however, a compromised spy runs as far and as fast as they can. Means of evasion are dependent on how much a spy put into the infrastructure for exfiltration beforehand and the level of opposition resistance once detected. An experienced spy will prepare and keep means of getting away close at hand in a secure clandestine location and not hesitate to use them if the threat is manifest. Depending on who is after the spy, this preparation for an exit can make the difference between life and death.

After the Escape

Escape generally means relocating overseas where legitimate state security services will have a difficult, if not impossible, task of apprehending them. Once a spy goes private, it is always prudent to prepare a safe international haven available in case of trouble. Covert agents spend their time either undercover in the field or traveling to the next job, but establishing a secure and covered bolt hold provides piece of mind and safety in the event of real trouble. The best international hiding places are located in developing countries outside of mainstream international law enforcement activity that have inefficient police and internal security services and smaller expat communities.

The duration of a spy's hidden seclusion is in direct relation with the security service's degree of efforts to locate them. Escaping and hiding can be made easier if the spy has salted away some money from previous operations to live on while they are forced off the grid. One good reason to choose a developing country to hide away in is that the total amount needed to live well is greatly reduced. If there is no pressure to resurface because of money or loved ones, taking an extended vacation will often clear the slate and draw off most, if not all, pressure the spy might face.

When reemerging from time spent in hiding, a spy must consider all of the identities and other covert infrastructure used in the exposed job to be compromised. The covert agent needs to obtain new documents and cover identities before returning to the corporate intelligence scene. The spy should also pay very close attention to the people they work with since a single burned spy is often not worth the points a black market middle man or private intelligence group can get from the authorities for turning the spy over once they resurface. Past the grey line, loyalty among corporate spies is a rare thing and often does not transcend immediate business or monetary advantage.

The Grey Line: Modern Corporate Espionage and Counterintelligence

Part IV

Prevention

"Hope clouds observation"
The reverend mother Gaius Helen Mohiam

Introduction

There is an old saying about knowing your enemy and knowing yourself. This axiom is very appropriate for the practice of corporate intelligence as we enter the second decade of the 21st century. Every company has secrets. These secrets, proprietary information and technology, can be worth a great deal to a company's rivals if they can be uncovered. Protecting the sanctity of such secrets is the responsibility of the company itself. Only rarely will a company be able to rely on the defenses offered by their home governments to protect them from the threat of private espionage activity. It is therefore necessary for each company to take a long hard look at its own security situation and determine what steps they can take to better protect themselves from this threat. Misplaced hope can indeed cloud objective observation when it comes to modern corporate security.

Corporate espionage exists and is actively engaged in by a wide range of nations and individual companies at home and abroad. Because most corporate intelligence operations are never detected, let alone prosecuted, the true scale of such activity may never be known. One thing is known with certainty though, if a company possesses commercially valuable information or technology that can be of use to another, they are a target. Burying your head in the sand and convincing yourself that such action against your company is the stuff of Hollywood thrillers, is to ignore the simple truth that there are those out there who are professionally and actively working to penetrate companies to plunder their secrets for the benefit of others and themselves.

The instrument of private intelligence gathering is the corporate spy. Almost all corporate spies have previous state intelligence training and a wealth of experience penetrating groups much more secure than your average company can ever hope to be. These men, and increasingly women, are well-paid contractors doing a job they have been trained extensively to carry out. They are ruthless, cunning, experienced and hold no moral qualms about taking a company or executive apart to bleed them dry of secrets. This is the threat and the level of that threat is increasing annually.

Thousands of former national intelligence officers are entering the private sector each year. These people have one seriously marketable skill set, and a fearsome one it is. Coming from a national intelligence agency, a new corporate spook can earn more in a year of constant operational activity against unprotected companies than they could in a decade of working for the state. The lure of such wealth is tempting more qualified and superior operators out of the public intelligence sector every year. The operational environment is also more appealing, since they get to work in developed nations like the US against targets that pose little threat to life or limb and are considerably easier to penetrate than anything they ever had to target on behalf of their governments. Private corporate espionage also offers significant freedom of action that does not exist in the national intelligence world. Agents can recruit who they want, as they want, with little or no oversight and certainly without the mountain of paperwork and political correctness that went into such efforts in the public sector. For a spy, going private sector holds considerable advantages.

Corporations themselves are increasingly taking advantage of the availability of these trained private spies to develop an in-house intelligence apparatus or a relationship with an external espionage group. For a relatively small amount of money, companies can receive intelligence worth millions or even billions that there would be no legitimate avenue to procuring otherwise. The lack of effective detection, investigation or prosecution for corporate espionage means that companies, with little effort or risk to themselves, can engage in virtually any activity they wish to penetrate or actively disrupt the operations of rivals.

As an example of the advantage a company can gain over its rivals through active intelligence work image the following. Company A builds a deniable in-house corporate intelligence capability and targets their top three rival firms. Within nine months they have recruited and are actively running assets within each of their rivals' headquarters. Their espionage agents feed them information about the coming products, sales strategies, supplier costs, customer lists, corporate investment policy, research and development projects, marketing plans and any other areas that Company A seeks data on. What advantages does company A now hold over their rivals? From the stand point of Company A, their top rival firms are now conducting open business and most future actions are known. Total operational costs to generate this level of information dominance is likely amount to less than a few million dollars per annum. The benefits to Company A on the other hand, in their ability to out maneuver their rivals at every turn, could easily tally in the hundreds of millions. This is the calculus has driven explosive growth in private corporate espionage activity around the world and in the US in particular. The risks are virtually nonexistent for companies that engage in corporate espionage and the benefit to cost ratio is rarely less than 20 to 1.

Intelligence gathering activity aside consider the potential benefits of an active disruption operation against a rival firm. For example, Company A is releasing a new tablet PC and they want to undercut the market share of their main rival in a growing industry worth potentially billions of dollars. Now image a covert operation that successfully inserts a simple line of code into a secondary system of their rival's latest tablet PC model. This line of code lays dormant until about a three months after product release. Then a turned source inside of that company includes an activation trigger into the latest software update package which causes the internal cooling system to go offline. Every user who downloads the company's update now possesses a worthless burned out piece of expensive junk. A simple hacking action, using a single source inside of the target company and a mildly skilled computer programmer, has just cost the targeted company hundreds of millions to find the problem, fix it and replace the destroyed tablets. The secondary damage to reputation and existing client base likely means that it will be years before that manufacturer can regain their lost market share. The total operational cost to Company A to effectively destroy their main rival in a highly lucrative emerging market, less than one million dollars.

These are just a few examples of how corporate intelligence can be of benefit to those companies that engage in it. The new reality of business is that corporations are increasingly going to have to develop many of the covert offensive and defensive capabilities that were formally reserved to the state. Large corporations already hire private military forces all over the world to secure their assets and further their interests. Companies today engage in direct diplomacy with sovereign nations to secure privileged access to resources and markets. A growing number of multinationals have operating budgets and profit margins larger than the GDP of a majority of countries. There is a long history of corporate intelligence gathered on behalf of individual companies across the globe by the state and now through private firms. It is only by understanding the threat that corporate espionage and direct action pose to companies across the globe that they can have any hope of building an effective defense against it.

The Need for Prevention and the Real Limits of Prevention

Worldwide corporate intelligence operations, both state sponsored and private, target firms in virtually every industry. If a company holds any information or secrets that would be of use to its competitors it is a target, period. The ease of penetrating a company that does not take precautions, combined with the almost nonexistent level of protection that the state provides, demands that corporations take the matter of self defense and security into their own hands and take it seriously. Every company that stands as a target must take steps to secure their information and protect their operations from compromise or run the very real risk of being destroyed by their less than scrupulous competitors.

Even organizations like the CIA, that are purpose built for intelligence work, are penetrated by their rivals periodically. Companies will never be able to match the level of defense that an organization like the CIA can muster. The defensive goals of each company that finds itself targeted by corporate espionage should be realistic and tailored to the specific needs of that firm. Having no defense against corporate espionage, however, is simply not an option anymore for companies that wish to remain competitive.

The majority of companies already have some form of defense in place to protect their information. Unfortunately, the vast majority of these defenses are geared to the wrong areas to be effective against modern corporate intelligence gathering techniques. Firms believe that if they can secure their computer networks and data infrastructure against outside direct intrusion, they will be safe. This is a perfectly acceptable approach to preventing low-level hacking by poorly trained criminals or kids, but offers virtually no defense against high-grade cyber weapons or the cadres of skilled hackers employed by corporate espionage teams. It also does not recognize the reality that the simplest way to penetrate a secure network is to turn an employee who already has access to it.

Virtually every company in the United States, and indeed in the world, lacks two elements of critical defense against corporate intelligence efforts. First, businesses need a strong counter intelligence element inside of the company. It is not an option to just totally lockdown and compartmentalize operations within a company so that there is zero possibility of data leakage. There is too much need for easy access to data, open communication between sections and creative fusion for lockdown to be a viable avenue of defense. Major companies employee thousands, if not tens of thousands, of people around the world and cannot possibly guarantee the loyalty of each one who has or could gain access to sensitive information. The goal must be to place as many obstacles in the path of corporate intelligence operators as possible and engage in an active defense. Defensive prevention of infiltration can only be done by a strong internal counter intelligence apparatus within the company itself.

Counter intelligence within a company breaks down into two main components. The first part is monitoring employees and corporate operations passively looking for leaks and vulnerabilities. This filtering requires a certain amount of trained manpower and real access. A company can be hardened against attack by training the employee base on what to look for and how to resist recruitment by corporate intelligence agents. The first step to closing gaps in internal security is to identify vulnerabilities and examine the patterns of loss that will reveal an active intelligence penetration.

Active defensive operations are the second area of counter intelligence within a company. This method focuses on setting out traps for corporate spies and skilled hackers. These operations require a group of highly skilled counter intelligence personnel and technically adept white hat hackers with the will to engage in active measures on the part of company leadership. Actively seeking to disrupt and dismantle corporate intelligence operations can net the company a number of careless spies and also act as a deterrent against future penetration. In many ways, an active defense is the best course for companies seeking to dissuade invasion or at least drive up the costs of those who would work against their company.

The least palatable, but in many ways most important, element of an active defense against corporate espionage, is for the company to engage in covert corporate intelligence gathering of its own. Fighting fire with fire. This aggressive approach provides several benefits to the target company. From a defensive stand point, intelligence gathering includes the possibility of penetrating the corporate intelligence center of the rival firms to discover what operations are being mounted against them and compromise them at the source. It is impossible to completely secure a firm against penetration, but if a company can get inside of the groups that engage in corporate intelligence against them, they can create a very powerful barrier.

A further benefit of engaging in defensive corporate espionage is discovering what information has already been leaked by penetrating the centers of a rival firm and examining their take. If the targeted company can see inside of its rival and discover what proprietary information has already been stolen, it is a short step back to determine the source of that information within the company and thus to plug the leak.

Of course, using active corporate espionage measures against a company's rivals for defensive purposes will also allow the company to covertly gather information about its rivals which may have positive commercial value as well. There is a thin line between gathering intelligence for defensive purposes and using covert intelligence offensively. By no means does this suggest that offensive intelligence gathering is a bad thing. Legally it crosses the grey line, but as the need for good intelligence to conduct business competitively grows exponentially, constraining morality against covert operations will soon separate companies that are equipped to succeed from those that cling to the wrong side of that grey line and fail.

Technical Security

Technical security is the one area that companies have been investing heavily in since the advent of the information revolution, in many cases to the exclusion of all else. The sheer amount of data transmitted and held via digital communications, advanced computer networks, data sharing and external storage have made securing a company's digital defenses of paramount importance. People have access to practically every bit of valuable data and secrets a company has available and stored digitally, all ready to be downloaded and stolen by corporate spies.

Misplaced Technical Security

The unfortunate truth about network security is that it is usually pointed in the wrong direction. Corporate systems fairly bristle with high-grade defenses against outside penetration. These defenses provide adequate coverage against run of the mill hackers, cyber criminals and other simple nefarious types. Of course, this is not always the case, witness the numerous examples of companies that have their systems breached by unaffiliated hacker groups on a regular basis and suffer for it. Every time a story comes out about a corporate system being breached from the outside, other companies have their crisis meetings and revitalize their security measures. Yet eventually these new defensive barriers too are breached. The game of network security is one in which the line between offensive capability and defensive barriers is rarely in the company's favor.

These outward facing defenses certainly can keep most companies secure against standard threats, but provide little defense against military or corporate intelligence grade cyber attack. The key to securing a system against penetration is to not just focus on the exterior walls but on the internal aspects of computer security as well. While the outer protective wall is important, the company must plan on and expect it to be penetrated from time to time. This is why internal partitions, passive usage monitoring, encryption and access limitation technology are vitally important. Many companies believe that after all of the money they have thrown at computer security over the years they are safe. This may be partially true but most standard measures taken in corporate America today are rarely adequate to the task of preventing serious, professional and determined theft.

The most vulnerable aspect of any systems security program is the user. Cutting through external and internal corporate system ICE (intrusion countermeasures electronic) can require some serious talent and high-grade technology not always available to intelligence operations. Class A hackers, corporate intelligence grade cyber weapons and ICE breaking programs do not just grow on trees. But the one thing that is available to any spy is the inside individual user who already has legitimate access.

Corporate systems are designed for usability. It has to be this way in order for these systems to add value and efficiency to company operations. Company computer systems are set up in such a way that defenses act as gateways to keep the unauthorized users out and allow the authorized users free reign. Once an authorized user wishes to gain access even the most secure systems in the world will open up like flowers. This is where most internal and exterior corporate defenses fall apart. An effective counter intelligence program and a significant computer security redesign are both necessary to effectively defend against modern threats. By turning a single authorized user, the corporate intelligence agent has effectively rendered the entire multimillion dollar array of corporate cyber defenses, that companies are so proud of and utterly convinced are keeping them safe, completely impotent. Better internal systems defenses plugged into an effective counter intelligence operation are the best defense a company can realistically place in the path of would be corporate hackers and spooks.

Technical Penetration Areas to Watch

Corporate technical security cannot all be dedicated solely towards securing computer systems. Not when the threat is as broad and the means of gathering technical intelligence against a company include communication infrastructure, faxes, cell phones, VOIP programs, wifi and more. The need exists for corporations to secure against technical penetration of their communications, physical locations and the personal systems of their employees.

Communications

Tapping into the communications infrastructure of a company or the personal communications of its top executives is not as sexy as blasting away at their network defenses with hyper advanced cyber weapons but is still one of the most effective means of gathering intelligence that exist. Telephones, faxes, cell phones, VOIP programs and even the printers and copy machines that top level people use are all vulnerable to commercially available intercept technology. Securing these systems must be a priority for any company that wishes to keep their high-level communications secret.

Telephones

A regular sweep to detect clandestine bugs and telephone line taps should be conducted to ensure the security of this most common form of communication. There are a number of highly qualified people available to run these sweeps. A technical communications security expert is a critical asset to any counter intelligence staff. For high-level telephone systems, such as those used by top executives, encrypted units should be used exclusively in all locations where critical information is discussed. Training should also be given to all senior staff about the need to be wary of the information they discuss on unsecured lines and their habits with regard to using the phone to discuss important business dealings.

Faxes

An important tool in business, the fax machine, is an incredibly vulnerable piece of equipment. Common commercial faxes should be replaced with secure and encrypted fax machines as practicable throughout the company. This protection is most critical for research and development, executive suites and other areas that regularly send and receive classified materials.

Cell Phones

Most people believe that because of the inbuilt encryption on modern smart phones they are safe. However, it took all of a few days for a civilian to crack this encryption protocol during a recent technical conference in Europe. If some random engineer in Germany can do it in hours, then it should be realized that state and corporate intelligence groups have been doing it from day one. There are additional encryption protocols that can be applied to cell phones to increase the security of communications, but as with telephones, critical employees must be made aware of the limits to these defenses. Senior people should be trained to be aware of the potential for leakage from cellular communications and how to minimize the threat through changes in behavior and not just to rely on technology. Regularly issuing critical staff with new phones can act to reduce the risk of interception still further. All cell phones used by key personnel should also be swept regularly for physical bugging and malicious programs which can be serendipitously installed on them to monitor their transmissions.

VOIP Programs

Programs such as Skype and Facetime are increasingly used to conduct business with real time video conferencing worldwide. Commercially available programs are exceedingly vulnerable to interception and should be replaced with purpose built secure VOIP programs immediately. Additionally, all online information sharing programs, from email to the new cloud computing services, should be reviewed from a security stand point and regularly swept for detectable covert penetration.

Printers and Copy Machines

Wireless printers and copy machines produce signals which can easily be intercepted by a third party with commercially available equipment. Emplacing a signal intercept post close to a company's headquarters is a very effective means of generating large quantities of digital intelligence. This holds true for office internet wifi as well. Any system which utilizes wireless technology must be secured with additional encryption protocols or replaced with hardwired connections.

Wireless communications and computer systems have filled the air with a rich soup of potentially interception vulnerable signals. Corporate espionage agents regularly employee specialists to set up signal intelligence gathering capabilities around prime corporate targets. The amount of information that can simply be pulled from the air near an unsecured location is staggering. Securing the communications and wireless computer infrastructure in a company headquarters is a very important first step to take in order to reduce a company's vulnerability to clandestine intelligence gatherers.

Open Source Vulnerability

One area that many companies neglect to defend at all is the web and the open source information that can be gleaned from it. There is nothing whatsoever illegal about any information a spy can dig up off of the internet. Web based research about a company and their employees are a common first approach to developing intelligence on the operations of a target corporation. Open source information about a company can provide significant intelligence for a corporate spook and should be controlled. Materials issued by the company and those written about it by others should be examined by the counter intelligence apparatus within the company and steps taken to remove or make more difficult to find any materials which are considered a threat to corporate information security.

Data posted by individual employees is also a priority for security teams. Employees inside of the company write about what is happening there to their friends or others on the web all of the time. For optimal security, this open information sharing activity should be limited or censored by corporate counter intelligence. Training should be given to employees about the risks of posting personal and corporate data online. Not only will this awareness help reduce easy access to critical information for spies, but will also help place the individual employees in the right kind of mindset of defensive security towards the threat that corporate intelligence poses. Most people have no idea of the value that the little bits and pieces of information they regularly post online can have to corporate spies. Training to teach employees about the basics of information security should be mandatory. Make a few examples of employees who post too openly in order to drive home the seriousness of this confidentiality issue.

Corporate Network Security

Securing the company's digital infrastructure can be a very laborious and expensive task, but is absolutely critical to the security of important data. A good defensive strategy for corporate systems is one that includes outward facing defenses as well as internal access limitations and usage monitoring. A balance must be struck between ease of use and security when it comes to corporate systems, but security should never be ignored completely. An accessible and easy to use system does not have to mean open and insecure.

Defending Against External Attack

Building a wall around critical corporate systems is a necessary first step. It is beyond the purview of this book to detail all of the various effective defensive measures that encompass external computer security, but finding a high-end company to install and maintain up-to-date defensive barriers on a corporate system is absolutely vital to a company's defense. Every barrier that can be emplaced to defend against external penetration should be erected. Defenses include the need for more than simple password protection. Biometric access controls today are easy to use and have become very cheap and should be applied universally. A basic facial recognition scan via the built in web cam on home systems and laptops can be a very effective and easy to use barrier against clandestine access.

Another defensive area to consider is limiting access to secure information via smart phones and other portable devices. Such devices can be easily stolen and used by an intelligence agent to quickly access an otherwise secured system. By limiting the ability of such devices to access classified information, the user is only slightly inconvenienced while the system is made several orders of magnitude more secure. Whatever firm is selected to equip company defenses should also be contracted to maintain them against new threats and to run periodic penetration tests to ensure that barriers in place evolve to meet new attack vectors.

Limiting or securing corporate wireless networks is another critical step to take in order to better protect the systems. The final area that should be addressed in order to secure corporate computer and network systems is physical infrastructure. Limiting access to all areas that contain critical network infrastructure is important because it removes easy access to a spy attempting to place physical monitoring devices on core data centers to bypass other security measures.

Internal Defenses

Securing the network from outside penetration is only half, and not even the most important half, of a total network security plan. Corporate network and data security must be set up so that it protects from external penetration and also from unauthorized or suspicious activity by individual authorized users. A quiet passive security program to monitor those who have access to secure information can be used to detect unusual and potentially dangerous activity. The weakest element of any computer security program is invariably going to be the human user. By placing barriers to stop unauthorized users and passive pattern recognition programs in place to catch authorized users accessing suspicious amounts or areas of data, it is possible to increase the security of a system against bent employees and covert penetrations that have breached external defenses.

Passive monitoring should be total and based on the principal of need to know. For example, an individual user account in human resources, which is used to regularly access classified documents from research and development, can be detected easily if such a system of access monitoring is in place and can alert the counter intelligence section to a possible breach. Even with the most advanced pattern recognition system and controlled access protocols in place, this kind of a defense will yield more false positives than bent employees, but it is worth the hassle for counter intelligence to have this invaluable tool to help monitor employee activity.

Home Network Security

A company might lock down their headquarters systems very tightly, but if no steps are taken to secure the home computers of high value employees there will be a glaring hole in any security program. For the millions of dollars that companies spend each year on computer security, one of the most amazing oversights has always been the ability of an employee to access company systems from home or take data out of the heavily secured company system and use it on the same unsecured home computer that the employee uses to access sketchy web sites filled with Trojans, viruses and other malware.

There is often a valid need for employees to have access to their work from home. Ease of access and privacy concerns do not mean, however, that such systems should be ignored by corporate security elements just because they do not directly belong to the company. Any system used to access secure company information should be required to be protected to a standard as high as systems within the company. This can be done by either issuing the employees an already secured system for use at home or mandating the installation of a suite of security programs designed to secure the private home system to an acceptable level. Only systems which meet security requirements should be allowed access to the main company systems. Home systems used for work related projects should also be open to monitoring by counter intelligence as part of their internal network security program.

Top Ten Steps to Secure Corporate and Home Systems

1. Mandate regular password changes and use random long string passwords
2. Use biometrics for access to secure information
3. Limit access to secure information internally (compartmentalize internal systems)
4. Install and USE corporate grade antivirus programs on all systems
5. Passively monitor access to secure information and run pattern recognition to detect suspicious usage
6. Use DRM, copy restriction programs and encryption to limit data vulnerabilities
7. Conduct periodic security checks and mock penetrations on the systems to test for weaknesses and address problems as they are found
8. Never forget the human element in information security and focus on hardening the employee base
9. Educate all employees about confidentiality, data security and basic precautions
10. Make sure that systems security is always up to date and geared to protecting against the latest threat vectors

Personal Device Security

Employees tend to keep valuable company data on personal electronic devices. A smart phone, tablet PC or laptop can contain enough sensitive corporate data to make it a very tempting target for a corporate spy. Employees should be provided with a private suite of programs and training in their use for protection against malware and viruses. Encryption and biometric password security should be mandated for personal devices which house sensitive corporate data.

Securing personal devices is not just the private concern of the individual employee. Making sure that these vectors are secure is a vital role for systems security personnel.

Encryption

Much can be said for the value of encryption. Modern encryption algorithms are incredibly powerful and when used correctly can shut down easy access via signal interception, net based data theft, and network intrusion to all but the most technically capable spies. Both standard and purpose built encryption systems are available and can be made very user friendly. The key to effective adoption of encryption is ease of use. If the encryption program is too cumbersome most people will never use it. Finding a powerful and easy to use program and then training the company staff to actually use it can be both fun for the employees and a very powerful tool to prevent data leakage. Another aspect of encryption technology that can prove useful, is by making sensitive data readable only on designated internal systems and unable to be copied. Covering sensitive data under a layer of ICE (intrusion countermeasures electronic) can render it unusable if obtained illicitly and is an excellent defense against unauthorized transfer of information.

Hiring a Competent Computer Security Firm

Computer and systems security is a massive field with a wide range of firms to choose from. Some companies are obviously more competent and current than others. The company should look for a firm that has experience and comes recommended first-hand by others. Do not be too easily impressed with techno jargon and flashy security systems. The key is to find companies that will tailor their security solutions to match the individual needs of the client. Many computer security firms will oversell their services and try to provide a one size fits all solution.

The key focus areas are usability, flexibility, constant upgrade and a robust but realistic approach to system security.

The company should also build up a trained in-house computer security arm based around permanent well paid staff. A company's system security staff must be over paid, loyal, monitored and periodically tested. The most valuable recruit a corporate spy could ever hope to get is not a senior executive, but a member of the company's IT security staff. The keys to the kingdom literally rest in the hands of whoever is placed in charge of systems security.

Dealing with System Incursions

For day-to-day penetration attempts, a system should be set up to monitor the skill of the hack and to return the back trace data to the proper authorities. For more serious breach attempts, the systems security staff should include a skilled hacker of its own who knows the tricks and can trace the black hat and work with counter intelligence to identify and neutralize the threat. Handling incursions with in-house resources means that, if the invasion attempt is important enough, the company can send its own people out to deal with the problem and discover if the penetration attempt is part of a larger espionage operation. Handing investigation of computer intrusions over to the state often means that it will never again see the light of day and nothing will be either learned or solved.

Continual Monitoring

Companies should always be vigilant and on the lookout for corporate intelligence operations targeted against them. Constant systems monitoring and good communication between the IT security and counter intelligence elements can detect and neutralize hostile espionage operations early and decisively. A strong and integrated systems security and counter intelligence defense team is the best means of stopping and deterring hostile corporate intelligence operations against the company.

Staff Security

A corporation is nothing more or less than a group of people, a society in microcosm. The greatest security challenge this group of people working together for common cause experiences is securing its individual members. The weakest link in any security arrangement, particularly tech-heavy modern corporate security, is the human element. Individuals are weak, with needs and wants and are driven by deep cultural forces to never be satisfied. The monumental task of breaking corporate system security can be made much easier by turning a single employee with legitimate access to secure data. Despite all of the massive technological innovation of the past thirty years in the business world, corporate spies still target people as their main approach to penetrating a company's defenses because it works. The quickest path to uncovering a company's most closely held secrets is through its employees.

The challenges facing a company in its drive to secure workers are many, but a number of positive options do present themselves. The main areas every company should look at when developing a plan for staff security are education, awareness, contractual obligations and an active defense. Teaching a workforce about the existence of and dangers that corporate intelligence activities pose to a company is an absolutely necessary first step in building a credible defense against penetration. Most employees have no idea that there are cadres of professional intelligence agents specifically targeting them and their company. The reason this concept is so outlandish to most employees is that it is never presented to them as anything other than fiction. The consequences of espionage are rarely visible to employees and thus their ability to protect themselves or to actively monitor others is slight to nonexistent.

Internal corporate defenses cannot solely rely on a small group of counter intelligence personnel, but must include the employees themselves. Once a workforce is trained in spotting intelligence activities and potentially turned coworkers they can then act as the eyes and ears for the internal security apparatus. Informing employees of some primary signs that a coworker has turned and actively soliciting their input can significantly harden the defenses of a company.

The active defense part of staff security is by necessity the smallest, but often proves the most effective element of the overall security program. Active defensive operations include internal physical security, counter intelligence assets, IT security coordination and active countermeasures. These component pieces are a rare find in most companies, but provide an essential bulwark against malicious intelligence penetration.

Physical security is one area that companies expend quite a bit of time and resources on already. The emplacement of locks, barriers and onsite visible security staff is common practice in the corporate world. Because of the imposing semi-fortresses that many companies have transformed into, most intelligence activity does not involve actually physically breaking into a secured company building. Private security and guards are a necessary deterrent, but should be backed up by more specialized elements. Site security forces should focus on defense against technical intelligence gathering as well as more mundane threats. Defensive measures require a reappraisal of the role of the onsite security personnel and a revisit to the quantity versus quality arguments which have taken place at many firms concerned over such issues.

It is no longer enough to have a security presence in the lobby or a few night watchmen wandering the office building after dark. Particularly when these watchmen are themselves underpaid and extremely susceptible to be turned by a corporate spy. Employing an efficient counter intelligence group is a critical element in the defense of key corporate interests in today's security environment. Spies target people and it is the role of counter intelligence to protect the people who work for a company against corruption. An active counter intelligence program may seem like an extravagance to most companies, but with the ever rising threat of corporate intelligence, such a program can make the difference between real security and inexplicable failure.

In many smaller companies, there does not exist a need or budget for a large cadre of trained counter intelligence professionals. However, if a company has potentially valuable commercial secrets it must face the reality that it is a prime target and respond accordingly. If the resources do not exist to create a fully fledged counter intelligence effort, then at the very least, retraining for the existing security personnel to make them aware and capable of handling light counter intelligence operations should be undertaken.

For larger companies the necessity of a solid and empowered counter intelligence group cannot be overstated. Such programs can often pay for themselves many times over within a very short period. Disrupting a single corporate intelligence operation can save a company tens of millions of dollars. Considering the growing penchant for direct active measures, such as sabotage, cyber attack and black propaganda in corporate intelligence, and the dangers as well as savings grow exponentially.

A strong deterrence factor exists when an active counter intelligence program is in place within a company. The risk versus reward ratio may be deeply skewed in the spies favor, but every step that is taken to harden a company against attack moves that ratio further back to the target's side. Spies are risk averse by nature and presenting them with a visibly harder target is one of the best defenses that a company can mount. If a company is perceived to be better protected, many spies demur from attacking it and the price of engaging in intelligence activities against it for their rivals will increase thus potentially deterring the intelligence operation at the source.

Screening Employees

Companies already screen potential employees thoroughly for education, ability, references, criminal activity, background and credit checks and many other criteria. In order to weed out potentially weak, easily turned employees before they are hired, candidates should also be screened by counter intelligence. It is certainly not unheard of for an intelligence agent to plant their own already turned employees within a target company or even themselves masquerading as an employee. Security reviews that cover an employee's finances, lifestyle and mental state should be conducted periodically. Such reviews should be carried out on high value employees and those with direct access on a regular basis. Counter intelligence may be able to use these checks to spot a turned employee quickly before they can do much damage. Regular security screening will also help to make the employee base more aware of the threat posed by corporate intelligence.

Signs a Potential Employee May be a Plant:

- Over qualification for a desired position within a critical area
- Inexplicable gaps in employment history
- History of moving from targeted company to targeted company
- Keenly developed computer or technical skills not apparently connected to their employment history
- Too great a familiarity with personalities and structure of the hiring company
- Obviously coached responses to security questions during the hiring process

- Signs of tradecraft training or an overly developed sense of situational awareness

Monitoring Employees

The majority of corporate intelligence penetrations target employees who already work for the company in critical areas. This is why it is necessary to employ a skilled counter intelligence team to continually monitor these employees for signs of disloyalty. There are many motivations for an employee to turn on their employer. Looking for signs of budding corruption can help to remove incipit threats to the company before they can be fully exploited by rival intelligence. Once an employee has been turned by a corporate spy they will often display major personality and behavioral changes. Having a professional team of counter intelligence agents on site to monitor for the following changes can help to detect penetrations early:

- Sudden unexplained wealth or expensive possessions beyond pay scale
- Dramatic, indeed manic, improvement in job performance
- Mood swings and irrational behavior
- Paranoia
- Hiding their activities and schedules from coworkers
- Operating after hours with greater frequency
- Working weekends and nights for no reason
- Signs of light intelligence training and increased situational awareness
- A tendency to smug silence and wearing a knowing look
- Developing new friendships with employees working on critical projects
- An increase in drinking or drug use

- Increased marital or relationship problems
- A tendency to ignore their assigned work but appear to be busy
- New and inexplicable interests at work or off-site
- Unexplained international travel or time away
- An increase in petty deception and lying

Present Staff Reviews

For companies that choose to build a counter intelligence capability, one of the first acts the new team should engage in is a top to bottom review of the present staff. No employee is above suspicion when it comes to corporate espionage, from the longest serving to the most seemingly benign, all are potential intelligence assets. Main areas in a company that corporate intelligence agents target are the IT and systems management staffs, senior and mid-level executives, research and development teams, legal staff, and other personnel with access to critical systems and materials. Counter intelligence reviews should examine these employees first and others in secondary and tertiary positions next. Spies take the path of least resistance. They will target outliers within the company. Trained counter intelligence agents will quickly be able to key into those employees who present the highest degree of risk. The weaker employees should be culled or at the very least hardened against attack.

One very good policy for counter intelligence to communicate with the staff is blanket amnesty for employees who have been turned or approached by corporate spies. Convincing the staff that they will be rewarded for bringing to the attention of counter intelligence any approach made by a spy will give the employee a means of turning in spies that work against them, without fear of reprisal. This is a main concern for staff members that are targets of recruitment. They believe that if they are targeted and bring it to the attention of the company they will be punished or distrusted. If this can be overcome the employee base becomes much more secure. Whether or not the company actually follows through on its promise of amnesty or fires anyone implicated in espionage is another matter. As long as the employees believe that they have a choice this will be a very effective measure to take against covert conversion of the staff.

Risk Factors

A number of factors draw a spy to certain employees over others with similar levels of access. Identifiable risk factors make employees who display them likely targets for recruitment and such people should be monitored carefully by counter intelligence personnel. Spies go after the weakest links in any organization, the outliers. They do not target strong and stable people, they look for those employees with problems and grievances such as:

- Money problems
- Marital or relationship problems
- Significant recent emotional trauma
- Drinking, drug or other addiction problems
- Emotional instability or manic depressive personalities
- Deep ties to a home country or foreign ideology or group
- Deeply held leftist or anti-corporate views
- Stalled career prospects
- Underemployment
- Feelings of insecurity or under-appreciation in their position
- Feelings of inferiority and of being slighted by their coworkers

Employees that display any of the listed personal vulnerabilities need to be periodically reviewed and monitored carefully. It is up to the employer whether or not security concerns about such employees merit their termination, monitoring or additional training. Removing the weakest links in an organization can go a very long way to making the secrets held by that company more secure and hardening the staff base as a whole. Remember, it only takes a single turned employee with access to bleed a company dry.

Using Staff to Monitor Each Other

As the Soviet system and China's neighborhood control groups show us, the best way to monitor people for signs of disloyalty is not to rely on state agents but to use average citizens to watch each other. Educating staff about characteristic signs of disloyalty and what employees who are turned commonly act like is a necessary step to increase the defenses of a company against corporate espionage. Creating a means for employees who see suspicious signs or activity to share this information with the counter intelligence team can provide a strong system of mutual surveillance and early detection. Employees must have a safe and anonymous system to share suspicions with counter intelligence. Having the counter espionage arm take steps to recruit their own sources inside of the company to directly monitor others is another effective step to generating actionable intelligence.

Employees should be provided with a means to contact counter intelligence directly if they are approached by a spy. There should be no penalty for going to counter intelligence in the event of contact and indeed these actions should be rewarded. Employees should be made aware that counter intelligence assets exist in the company and that they are available if anything untoward or suspicious should happen.

Employee Access and Internal Movement

One of the most basic means of controlling access to information is to control the physical ability of people to move about the facilities. Creating secured areas with physical barriers and control points is a tried and true means of effectively compartmentalizing access to data. Secured areas and access are important with regard to internal computer centers, executive offices, and critical R&D areas. Physical access should also be strictly controlled not by easily stolen key cards but rather with biometric systems. A tight system of information compartmentalization needs to exist in conjunction with strict physical controls on access to critical areas.

Creating an Employee Base Less Prone to Betrayal

The best defense against human intelligence penetration that a company can possibly have is to simply make their employees feel appreciated, valued and happy. Employees who like their company and enjoy working there are not going to act in a way that threatens that positive work environment. Use both the carrot and the stick. Employees who are overpaid are less likely to be swayed by offers of money and since they would not be able to receive the same salary elsewhere are more prone to fierce loyalty. Benefits are also important. Medical bills can be a major source of stress and financial woe for employees. Massive unpaid debt and the knowledge that the company wasn't there for them is an explosive mixture and makes an employee extremely easy to turn. Companywide employee activities are also a very positive way to build loyalty and a sense of identity with the firm. A greater degree of interaction between management and the common employees will help to remove a lingering sense of "little guy versus big money" that exists in many large corporations.

The stick in this case is a process for quick removal of potentially soft target employees. The ability of a company to get rid of its potentially disloyal employees before they are turned is critical to increasing the overall defensive stance. This is especially important for potentially corruptible employees who work in critical areas of the firm. Additionally, the awareness that there are strict security measures and a strong counter intelligence presence within the company will act to dissuade a potential traitor if they are approached.

Personal Prevention

Securing Yourself Against Attack

There are numerous steps a company can take to secure itself against penetration both human and technical. For the individual employee, securing themselves comes down to recognizing their vulnerabilities and taking the time and effort to change bad habits. Employees are to be encouraged to review their personal and office security situation periodically. Employees with the tightest security, who pay the most attention to these vulnerability matters should be rewarded and those who do not penalized.

Technical Security

As part of a comprehensive corporate security plan, all employees need tools and instruction on how to secure their home and office systems. Place emphasis on effectively securing these systems and teaching the most common technical penetration methods used by spies. Basic steps such as installing and using a quality antivirus program, firewall software and a periodic home system security reviews should be encouraged if not mandated. For higher value recruitment targets, basic computer security procedures should be mandated and checked by the counter intelligence and IT security groups regularly. Blocking easy access to a home and office systems should effectively keep class B and below hackers out of the computers used by employees. Home system security also hardens them against easy detection of vice and compromising activities conducted on their home machines that spies might use to gain leverage over an employee. Encryption and wifi masking are highly recommended. Teaching employees how to do cool technical security actions can be both fun and, if the company provides the tools, wide spread.

Office systems security responsibility rests with the counter intelligence and IT security personnel to keep systems clean and security up to date. A regular sweep for bugs and other technical intelligence collection measures is to be routinely conducted at all corporate locations. Securing important conference rooms and offices against bugs, laser microphones, cameras and other more exotic technical intelligence gathering techniques is a critical task for serious security personnel. Test penetrations should also be carried out on a regular and surprise basis to test the security of company systems and plug any leaks that are detected.

Personal Device Security

As more business critical information moves over to portable computer systems and smart phones, securing these personal devices has become a priority. What makes these devices particularly vulnerable is the fact that so few people even realize they are at risk. Personal cell phones and portable computers both require up-to-date security and antivirus programs. Password protection and the use of biometrics are also highly encouraged. In the case of laptops and tablet PCs, the hard drives can be encrypted as well. A company can ensure that individual employees, particularly high value employees, follow personal device and computer security protocols by providing the tools and training them in their use.

Theft of personal devices is a common method for an espionage agent to get quick access to corporate data. People "lose" portable devices and cell phones all of the time. Some of these losses are attributable to theft by intelligence agents targeting the company. While smart phones are still less of a risk than laptop computers and external hard drives, given the sheer amount of data that can be held on such devices, they do pose a significant new attack vector and require effective security measures. Employees use their cell phones all the time to check email and to engage in other tasks that were once the preserve of larger, harder to steal devices. Because cell phones can't identify the operator, a spy can often gain access to sensitive data and email by simply lifting an employee's iphone and using it to remotely access a corporate system or to scan through its message data and net viewing history. Giving employees tips on theft prevention and providing the tools and training on how to secure their data on personal devices is of growing importance to a strong defense. If a laptop with company data is stolen, but the contents of the hard drive are properly encrypted, the spy who took it will not be able to use the information or will require significant resources and time to open it. When it comes to securing portable devices, the key is to make them difficult if not impossible for a spy to access. This is why encryption, password and biometric protection are vital.

Basic Office Security

Keeping offices secure is the direct responsibility of every company. Having on site guards in addition to internal access controls is a very good first step. For high value areas, such as executive offices, R&D facilities and important data centers, further technical measures should be taken to add enhanced layers of security.

Basic Home Security

Employees should feel safe at home and companies must provide the means of securing homes that contain important company data. Below is a list of eight basic security precautions that employees can take at home to protect themselves, their loved ones and company data.

1. Install an alarm system that includes motion activated silent video surveillance measures and armed response
2. Have quality locks on all doors and windows
3. Leave physical or technical tell tale marks to indicate if a home is covertly accessed
4. Get a safe for important documents and external hard drives
5. Secure important computer systems with passwords, encryption and if practicable biometrics
6. Get to know your neighbors for an additional set of eyes and ears
7. Keep a gun and learn how to use it
8. Buy a dog

Security when Traveling

It is extremely common for high value employees, carrying vast amounts of sensitive company data, to travel domestically and abroad for work and pleasure. Training employees to keep themselves and any valuable company data they are carrying safe, especially when traveling overseas is a critical element of a strong defense. Many state as well as private intelligence programs specifically target high value business people when they travel abroad and the rewards for such actions can be dramatic. Some basic travel security tips include:

- Keep luggage safe and light
- Read up on any area that you plan to travel to know the danger areas
- Always secure important travel documents such as passports and ID
- Do not engage in illegal activity. If harassed by state security forces contact the embassy immediately
- Transport important company data on encrypted mediums

- Never assume that a hotel room is secure
- Assume that anywhere you stay or conduct meetings is bugged and act accordingly
- When traveling in high risk areas, keep to well traveled locations and always vary your routine to lower the risk of kidnapping, theft and assassination
- If possible assign local security assets to protect high value personnel
- Be aware of your surroundings
- Be proactive in your defense

Life Monitoring

A very valuable service that a company can provide, through its counter intelligence arm, is life monitoring. This service should be mandatory for high value employees and subsidized for others. Life monitoring will allow the counter intelligence group to monitor the various aspects of an employee's life including credit, computer security, travel, finances and legal matters. Having this service in place will allow the counter intelligence team to alert an employee if any abnormal activity is detected. Banks and other financial service providers already offer a limited form of this service to their customers, but it is one that should be extended by the company internally to protect and monitor its most valuable employees. Broadening the scope of this kind of protection will allow the employee to have a much higher degree of safety and security. It will also allow counter intelligence to actively monitor the critical employees for signs of subversion and disloyalty.

Physical Safety

If there is a need for active physical security measures, such as body guards or defensive tactics training, the company should provide everything necessary to ensure employee safety. This degree of security can be very costly, but is often required if an employee has to travel to or live in a high risk area. For high value employees, various degrees of physical security should be provided at all times. This can include physical protection and also covers covert surveillance by the counter intelligence arm of key employees. Encouraging employees, or better still subsidizing them, to take self defense courses not only makes them harder targets but also builds physical fitness and morale.

Cultivating Vigilance

The key to security of any kind is constant vigilance. Maintaining a secure workplace, home and personal security is a direct concern and priority for every company. A little bit of prevention can go a long way towards making the personnel and data of a company safer and hardening your company against attack.

Part V

You are a Target

"Once is happenstance, twice is coincidence, three times is enemy action."
Ian Fleming

Companies are targeted by corporate intelligence agents because they possess information, knowledge and products that are of value to others. Companies must realize that if there is a single competitor or individual anywhere in the world that places value on what they make, how they make it or the composition and direction of their activities, there exists the distinct possibility that they will be targeted. The growing cadre of trained corporate intelligence agents throughout the world is merely a reflection of the ever expanding use of these covert professionals by other companies. Sovereign states, companies and individuals, target corporations and attempt to steal their secrets regularly. More often than not they succeed. Penetration and theft are the results of lack of knowledge, misplaced defensive measures, lax security, lack of interest from the home country and the nature of employing many potentially vulnerable people.

Companies are hit all of the time. In most cases, they never know that they have been penetrated and that their valuable information has been stolen until it is too late. If companies, particularly in the US, believe that they can rely on the authorities to defend them they have already lost. There is very little interest on the part of the state to defend corporations from covert operations even though such attacks cost domestic businesses hundreds of billions each year. The vast majority of corporate espionage activity taking place in America is conducted by foreign state and corporate actors but even this fact has not moved the government or local law enforcement to take effective action.

The argument has been made that devoting scarce resources to counter the threat of corporate espionage would require a lower level of defense against terrorist and other areas critical to the national defense. However, the pervasive and massive scale of corporate espionage regularly conducted in the United States in economic terms is the equivalent of a 9/11 happening every year against American industry. The costs, even by most conservative estimates, are in the hundreds of billions. It is not just the straight costs of lost contracts, stolen technology and data theft, but the human costs can be dramatic as well. Think of the price that society pays when ordinary people working at target companies are turned and begin committing crimes. Breaking the law and getting away with it creates a wave of secondary illegal action as people lose respect for the rules and the ability of law enforcement to uphold law and order.

The greatest trick the devil ever pulled was convincing people he doesn't exist. This parallels the problem of corporate espionage in America and across the globe. In the minds of everyday citizens, espionage is something that only happens in the movies and on television. The lack of media coverage, public awareness and pressure from law enforcement has made corporate espionage one of the most lucrative yet misunderstood illegal acts in the world. The scale of covert corporate intelligence gathering taking place every day in America and abroad is truly massive and the players are legion. As global competition increases, the frequency and severity of corporate intelligence actions, both theft of commercially valuable data and more direct actions, are going to increase. Companies must be prepared to defend themselves against covert penetration and attack. The most important step that every company has to take first is to acknowledge that the problem of corporate espionage is indeed real and from there seek effective solutions.

Signs That a Company Was Hit

How does a company know if it has been the victim of corporate espionage? Because of its very nature, corporate intelligence is conducted clandestinely and only a fraction of companies that are successfully struck even realize that they have been hit. Without adequate security measures and counter intelligence assets corporations are wide open to easy penetration.

Signs that a company can use to determine if it has been the victim of a successful corporate intelligence operation include:

- Other companies begin to use very similar if not identical technology
- Contracts and orders are lost to a rival for no obvious reason or by small margins
- Company market share is lost for no obvious reason
- Clients and suppliers are lost by very small bid margins
- The company begins to hemorrhage valuable staff, particularly in research and development
- Rival firms seem to constantly be one step ahead of the company
- Rivals know more than they should about a company's proprietary processes, products or services
- Overseas investors seem to know when a company has good or bad news before the company releases that information
- Rival companies release exceedingly similar, capability wise, products or slightly better versions designed to one up the company's products

- A rival's actions occur at particularly bad times for the company
- Suppliers seem to know the company's exact maximum bid threshold on procurement

All of the above are common enough occurrences in business, but a combination of several of these can quickly negate the coincidence defense. The ease with which rivals can conduct intelligence activities against a company and the lack of defense and deterrence means that if a company has a vague suspicion that they have been penetrated, they are most likely right.

What to Do When Your Company is Attacked

There are options available to companies when they are hit by corporate intelligence operations. Unfortunately, most of these options are bad news for senior management and the company as a whole. One rarely hears news about espionage activity. One reason that many companies never report or even acknowledge intelligence attacks upon them is because if a company were to report a breach the management would most likely be labeled as incompetent and fired. The perception is that if corporate espionage only takes place rarely, then any company successfully attacked must be exceedingly poorly run. The lack of immediate and effective recourse against the attacking company, even if it can be determined, means that in the minds of executives and share holders, reporting an incident of corporate espionage does little more than damage the company twice for little or no gain.

If it is discovered that the company is the victim of a successful corporate intelligence penetration, first conduct a thorough damage assessment. If the penetration took the form of a turned employee, it must be discovered quickly exactly what they had access to and how much they passed on to whoever was running the operation. What many companies learn at this point is just how wide open their internal data systems are and the unfortunate extent of access that a single authorized user can have across spectrums of information.

If the penetration is technical in nature, say a bug in the CEO's office, then the nature and extent of the information leak must be determined and countermeasures put in place to prevent the spy from simply replacing the bug a week later. If, however, the penetration compromised the computer infrastructure of the company, the degree of damage may be irreparable. The computer network at most major companies form the heart of operations in today's world. If these systems have been compromised to any significant depth, the amount of time and effort required to repair the breach and secure the system may be intolerable.

Police and Legal Options

The extent of a company's legal recourse in the event of compromise depends on how much evidence exists and how far back through the looking glass of fronts and cut outs they are able to go to actually prove who it was that ordered and carried out the attack. Just because you think you know who did it does not mean that this can be proved in a court without significant amounts of evidence. If a spy is caught in the act, they can certainly be prosecuted. Espionage itself is a crime, even against a company, as are many of the constituent elements that make up the act of intelligence gathering. In order to prosecute a spy, the company must take what they know and can actually prove to the police. The police then investigate and turn over what they find, assuming this takes the form of actionable evidence, to the prosecutor's office. From there the process proceeds slowly through a rather cumbersome legal process. Even if the prosecution is successful, the likelihood of a corporate spy receiving much jail time for his actions is relatively low. Spies can afford lawyers too and individual acts proven against a spy are generally considered minor nonviolent crimes.

Government prosecutors are more apt to chase after quick dramatic cases that involve physical harm to others, than take on a drawn out hard to prove corporate espionage case. Additionally, if the case did go to trial, a distinct possibility exists that a jury would acquit the spy on principle if given half the chance.

A number of corporate spies have been known to create their own anti-corporate, green, fight the man fuzzy whale NGO, costing less than a mid range car to build a convincing one, to use as cover in the event that they are ever caught. Proving that a spy was conducting their operation for simple greed and not to save the fuzzy whales can be made a very complex task. Spies can be rather ruthless when it comes to coning sympathy out of juries to stay out of jail.

Trying to prove the complicity of a rival corporation in the act of espionage or direct action can be a nearly impossible task. In virtually every corporate espionage operation undertaken by one company against another, the hiring firm hides their hand behind so many individually questionable links that proving their direct involvement can be next to impossible unless everyone of those links can be found and flipped. Even if every element in the chain can be brought over to the prosecution, no company keeps a division of corporate espionage on the books. This is where the practice of data laundering comes into play. A company will contract a legitimate business intelligence firm who fronts for the illicit intelligence gatherers to clean the data before it is ever passed on. What this does is almost totally insulate the hiring company since they can, almost legitimately, claim that they were buying the information from what they believed to be an above board intelligence company. The front intelligence company takes the fall, folds up shop and restarts a few days later in another country. In a perfect world where damning evidence can be brought together to connect all of these covert dots, there is always a convenient junior executive or two to take the fall.

Using the civil legal system means a lower evidentiary threshold, but the instigating company, the victim, is going to get caught up in trying to prove the case for more than a decade if not longer when you add in appeals. This process will cost millions and the company still has to deal with the press fall out for being breached, the likely firing of its senior executives and the stock drop all of this would entail. The rewards are often minimal as well. After the decade or so that it takes to go through the legal process and the penalty award phase the cost of legal action, not to mention the secondary costs of damage to image, often will exceed any reward from their rival. It is a wonder really that corporate espionage cases, criminal or civil, are ever brought at all.

Defense After the Fact

A more tolerable and common approach for victimized companies and senior executives, whose jobs and reputations are on the line, is to detect the leak, plug it and engage in active defense to determine if there are others internally without recourse to law enforcement and legal sanction. Working internally to rid the company of moles and intelligence assets is actually infinitely more efficient and quicker than any conceivable legal action. The reason for this is that no real burden of proof is necessary for internal sanctions within a company. The investigating group looking at a case inside of the company does not need to develop judicially relevant evidence to terminate a turned employ or chase after a corporate spook. They do not have to obey the Constitutional and precedence scruples of investigatory practice that the police and some security services are held to. Because there will be no trial, internal security can get to the bottom of a penetration more quickly and simply fire or remove those involved. As for the spy, extra judicial justice is not unheard of, but more a common practice is simply to burn him or her and make them run.

Mole Hunts

Conducting a mole hunt can be an extremely expensive, time consuming and uncertain process. If a penetration or technical compromise is suspected, the process of determining the actual vector of attack is best left to seasoned counter intelligence professionals. Done by amateur sleuths in-house, a mole hunt can cause a great deal of ill will among employees wrongly suspected and lead to even greater vulnerability and defections. If there is nothing but suspicion, the company can expect a long drawn out investigation process. If, on the other hand, a penetration is caught out, the process is generally quite short and more akin to housekeeping. This can be done in-house easily in the same way that people caught forging their expense reports or embezzling small amounts are generally handled, simple termination for cause.

When counter intelligence agents start looking for a leak, they have an entire bag of tricks and long proven strategies that they can employ. One of the more common active search methods is to use barium meals. A barium meal ploy involves the counter intelligence group concocting a number of different pieces of important intelligence and feeding these individually distinct morsels to the various suspects. After this is done counter intelligence watches the competition carefully to see how they react. When the competition makes a move that can be directly traced back to a specific piece of intelligence which was fed to them via their source in the company, that person can be identified.

Another, much more direct method, is to sweat the different suspects individually to see who breaks down. Normal employees are not trained covert operators and they certainly do not know how to stand up to intensive questioning from counter intelligence professionals. Even turned employees who are completely converted to the spy's cause will often give themselves away quite readily through their behavior and the inconsistency of the lies that they tell to cover themselves. This is an extremely common police tactic. It can be useful in corporate counter intelligence because there is a very strange quirk of human nature at play with almost every intelligence source. Those who spy willingly for others in the end almost all want to be caught. They want recognition for their cunning and acknowledgement for their audacity and brilliance in evading capture for however long they were at work. Many sources proudly confess to counter intelligence agents right off the bat, somehow perversely seeking approval for their actions. Then comes the inevitable and ceaseless wave of self justification.

Once a mole has been caught, there are a number of interesting options available to counter intelligence and the company. A covert source can be fired or they can be used, and then fired. Putting a mole to work, or doubling them, can be a very cost effective means of deriving some extralegal revenge against the rival company that hired the spy. By having the mole feed the rival company false data or intentionally misleading information, the target company can now, to a degree, control the actions of its rival. If done properly, a turned mole can actually cost the attacking company vast sums of money and a great deal of time and frustration. All of this occurs with no court, no police and most importantly no media exposure. Running a double agent is almost identical to running a normal asset in place except for the extra degree of caution and tradecraft that is necessary to fool the spy and his paymasters.

This is a good place to mention that corporate spies themselves can be turned by the target company if they can be found. Corporate spies, after all, are doing this for money. If the target company can offer more money then it is entirely possible that a spy, or even an entire espionage team, can be turned to work against the attacking company. If this can be done the possibilities for revenge against the attacking company are nearly limitless. Ultimately a double game against the rival firm using their own spies can be conducted for long periods of time and used to inflict significant damage on the rival and to gather large amounts of information about the sources and methods of the rival's intelligence operations.

A more proactive step that corporate counter intelligence can use to defend the company is to use dangles. A dangle is someone who is made to look as enticing as possible to spies so that they will get recruited, but is actually under the control of counter intelligence. Dangles are double agents from day one. They are not just useful for the reasons that double agents are such powerful tools, they can also be used as an active defensive measure. By offering potential corporate spooks the perfect readymade source, a dangle can work to identify those intelligence agents who are out there actively recruiting in a company and keep them away from other employees. Knowing who, how many and other pieces of useful information about the degree of the threat facing a company is an excellent first line of defense.

Retaliation

The best defense for a modern corporation is a good offense. Every company has its competitors, generally a manageably short list of major ones, so a preferable and more proactive defense a corporation can mount is to penetrate the intelligence programs of known rivals first. Knowing how and where a rival company is planning on attacking, can take the guess work out of counter intelligence. Perfect penetration of a rival company's intelligence gathering apparatus is a rare and priceless thing, but is possible. Even partial penetration of a rival company's intelligence operations can give the target company an idea about their intent and capabilities.

Proactive defensive steps against rivals should be taken, even if corporations have no wish to become involved in the murky, illegal world of direct corporate espionage. Think of it as the corporate version of spy versus spy. By targeting only a rival company's illicit intelligence gathering apparatus, a company can legitimately claim the moral high ground while at the same time engaging in an effective proactive defense. Best of all, the rival most likely will not go to the police or even the media if they discover an attack on their own covert intelligence teams because they started it (sounds childish but then it is all about media perception and when it comes to that sophistication of message is rare) and arguably have more to lose if the action was ever exposed. Another positive form of active defensive is to conduct active intelligence gathering within the rival firm itself to determine what, if any, information is being leaked from your own company. This is real corporate espionage but conducted for defensive purposes.

The reality and degree of corporate intelligence activities within the US and abroad are just beginning to be understood in the American business world. A particular mind set prevails within the United States that forces companies to disregard any intelligence activities that might seem questionable despite their obvious benefits. The problem with playing fair is that America is the only country in the world that is even trying anymore. Over and above the state run corporate intelligence programs of America's allies and strategic competitors, the tide has long turned and now corporate espionage is being run mostly for profit by individual companies against their soft American rivals.

The fact that US companies make the easiest and most sought after targets is nothing to be proud of. The prevalent and smug attitude in America of "let the poor foreigners come and steal a few scraps. America is an unstoppable dynamo" is ignoring three very simple facts. First, corporate espionage is mostly conducted by other developed first world national intelligence organs and their domestic companies. Companies in Japan, Israel and the EU do not require any additional help to compete effectively with American firms and the use of corporate espionage is just tipping the scale further in their favor with no reward for fair play to stripped American businesses.

Second, the value of those economic scraps from America's table can be counted in the hundreds of billions. These are not isolated events costing a few companies a few bucks here and there. Corporate espionage is a massive attack on American business across virtually every industry there is. By not even participating American business is already losing the covert global economic war, and losing badly.

Finally, the utility of corporate intelligence and massive advantages a company can gain is already driving an ever growing number of American companies to engage in covert operations themselves (mostly targeting other American companies). Companies are forced to develop capabilities and resources that previously only states had need and recourse to. It is an inescapable fact that in the modern business world, corporate intelligence is here to stay. No one begrudges a nation for employing intelligence gathering tools, even direct action if it serves the critical interests of the nation. Companies certainly have access to the necessary resources, the need for these tools. They certainly have more to lose by not actively engaging in espionage than a country.

It was once said by an American Secretary of State that "Gentlemen do not read each other's mail". This kind of starry eyed sentimentalism is dangerously, almost criminally, unrealistic for a nation and should be even more so for a multinational corporation, where the margins are so much finer. How companies in America and throughout the world learn to protect themselves and harness the power of covertly obtained intelligence for their own ends will determine their place in the future. The game has already started.

Part VI

Corporate Espionage in Practice

"The first quality needed is audacity."
Winston Churchill

The real world of corporate espionage is extremely complex and difficult for most readers to come to grips with. Covert operations are filled with an exceptionally diverse cast of characters driven by murky and often unseemly motives. Intelligence work, because of its very covert nature, is often portrayed in fiction and nonfiction with terrific inaccuracy. The wildest untruths have taken hold in the popular mind which turns those involved into James Bonds or Jason Bournes. To better offer the reader a more complete picture of the realities of modern corporate espionage the following case studies have been provided.

This section, while fictional in nature, is included to provide a summation of the key elements discussed in the preceding chapters as they are actually applied to corporate espionage activities taking place today. Fictional as the character of Alex and his cohorts might be the actions and targets involved in each of the following assignments come from real corporate intelligence operations conducted in the past few years. Do not let the format of this section fool you, all of this has happened before, is happening now and will happen again.

Alexander's Story

Like many private spooks, Alexander is a product of the state intelligence system. After September 11th, he, like many others at his university, applied to work for the CIA hoping to be able to do his part to defend the country. He had lived overseas, spoke several languages fluently, was an intelligent and fairly upstanding citizen and considered himself to be a prime candidate for this kind of work. After he submitted his application Alex heard nothing back from the CIA for over nine months. After long months of anxious waiting Alex finally gave up on his desire to become a spy and took a position with an international investment bank to pay the bills. Unbeknownst to him, the state intelligence apparatus had been interested and was just going through its normal cumbersome security evaluation process. What the CIA regularly neglects to tell people is that virtually everything it does, from recruiting spies like Alex to turning even the most mundane sources, takes huge amounts of time and requires a veritable mountain of paper work. After being provisionally accepted into the covert operations arm of the CIA, Alex passed through the Farm, the CIA's covert operations training regime, and was assigned to his first foreign posting, Colombia. Interesting because, although he spoke several other language, he did not speak Spanish nor had he ever traveled to South America. But he went willingly, hoping for an assignment to a part of the world he had some interest and experience in next time around.

After three rather uneventful years in Colombia, with any real covert recruitment activity denied him in order not to embarrass the government in the event of discovery, his tour ended. Alexander was assigned next to the Counter Terrorism desk at CIA headquarters, a necessary step up the promotion ladder post 9/11, but not back to the field as he had hoped. An additional three years of shuffling papers and learning to format cables was about all of the excitement of working for the CIA that Alex could take. Operational impotence and bureaucracy in the third world followed by still more paper pushing in the bland suburban nightmare that is beyond the beltway rural Virginia was not the professional life Alex had been looking for. He was still young, but with no real marketable skills after leaving the CIA, he made do with a series of mid-level domestic financial service jobs and so the days pasted.

One day, two years after leaving the agency, Alex got a call from a friend who had also recently left Langley. Mitchell, one of the best operators he had known while working for the government, had worked counter terror with Alex for a few years before going over to Iraq. After a dispiriting tour there Mitchell had also left the service of the state. Alex hadn't heard from Mitch since moving back to Seattle, but now he came with a very interesting proposition. Mitchell wanted to know if Alex could get access to the secured server farm at the investment bank where he worked. The answer, of course, was yes...but. Over drinks one night on 2nd Avenue, Mitchell handed Alex an envelope filled with ten thousand dollars cash and a non-descript flash drive. All Alex had to do was insert the drive into the investment company's system as described by Mitch and there would be another twenty thousand waiting for him. After working 90 hour weeks for very little money and near zero recognition in his cube, Alex was more than willing to do something exciting for a change. Thus on a quiet Saturday afternoon Alex used an ID card he had lifted off the IT tech who came up to fix a "problem" with his computer to enter the server room. He took out the small drive and within thirty seconds had made thirty thousand dollars.

When Alex met his friend two days later to turn over the memory stick, he asked if the people he worked for were hiring. Two weeks later Alex arrived home to a package waiting for him. Inside was a prepaid cell phone and charger. Within minutes of turning the phone on, it rang. He was asked if he still wanted a job. Yes, most certainly. Would he be willing to fly overseas to meet some people? Absolutely.

Two days later Alex was in Belize meeting with a man who called himself George. If you saw George on the street you wouldn't blink. He was in his mid 50's, 5'10" brown hair and as nondescript as a person can be without standing out for being too plain. The man was a pro. He had obviously put in some serious time in the black back in the day with some European intelligence agency. Alex guessed the DGSE, French intelligence, but it was impossible to tell since the man varied his accent ever so slightly from moment to moment. It was as easily possible that George was former CIA, Mossad or even from an Eastern European intelligence arm for that matter. Not that it really mattered or that Alex would ever be able to check but he had been well trained to pick up on such little signs.

In any event, after six hours of conversing with George in a hotel room, Alex got a test and another envelop with cash. Fly to Dubai and turn a junior VP at Morgan Stanley based there. It took Alex all of five days of surveillance and a bit of judicious computer hacking to discover that the VP was gay and given his internet viewing habits, a regular on the Thailand little boys' circuit. Alex broke into the hapless VP's flat, made his pitch and had him onside in an afternoon.

Test passed, Alex was given a six month apprenticeship in corporate espionage working a number of assignments as George's guy Friday. This new life started with a folder containing three solid new back stopped identities, a dozen numbered accounts in four countries and a signing bonus. Welcome to the world of corporate espionage Alex.

Assignment 1

Alex awoke to another blustery morning in Macau. He had chosen China, or at least the gaudy casino filled former Portuguese colony part of the one country-two system new China, as a base for several reasons. China is a beehive of activity these days and expats there are as common as chopsticks. It is an exotic ever shifting sea of people from all over the world in which one can easily sink below the radar. Because Macau is not a recognized center for crime and most importantly subversion Chinese counter intelligence tended to focus the majority of their efforts across the bay in Hong Kong. They mostly used Macau to trap dissidents who thought they were safe across the magic line and drunken foreign businessmen at the brothels and high end casinos downtown. The cops were more than a little susceptible to monetary persuasion and the organized crime groups there were local in flavor but highly capable and not too penetrated by intelligence groups, foreign or domestic. Given the international stature of the mega city Macau had become he could travel from there to anywhere in the world with no one giving his passport stamps a second look.

With his background and training Alex blended well with the local expat community brimming with thirty something foreigners hoping to cash in on the explosive growth to be found in China. He had a strong and innocuous cover as a consultant working for various international clients with operations on the mainland, of course all front companies and wholly owned subsidiaries of Alex himself. His flat was held in the name of another wholly owned but untraceable subsidiary of his consulting company on a long term corporate lease.

Alex slowly woke up this day and went to check his email. He had purchased a flat a few hundred meters down the road with the proceeds from one of his first operations and leased it to a very nice older couple from New Zealand. Little did they know, it also housed a state of the art wireless set up which Alex used to access the internet from his safe house down the road. Just part of the hundred and one little things that Alex as a spy did to build interlocking layers of operational security around himself. There it was, after nearly two months of down time, a quick status update posted to a Facebook group that he followed under a front account. The group was dedicated to the actress Natalie Portman who, like most famous people, had hundreds of unofficial fan pages, most with only a few anonymous followers. One thing Alex had been taught early in his career was that by far the best way to hide anything on the internet is to place it in plain sight. It is just not possible for any group, even the mighty NSA which vacuums up and scans every bit of data moving around the web, to review even a micro fraction of a percent of everyday innocent activity online. What they do ping to is that small sliver of traffic which is encrypted, secured or otherwise made to look enticing. Best place to hide a tree? Why, in the forest of course. Looking at the cutesy fake status update, he used the simple substitution code of letters for numbers to get the new phone number of his handler. Alex never really knew who he worked for or when they would call, but that was all part of operational security for the client, which he understood and took in stride. It was, however, always the same handler. This was for his security and something that he was quite adamant about. Work with people you know, and never trust the people who know you. Corporate intelligence tradecraft 101.

Alex stepped out into the dying gusts of this week's latest typhoon and went to one of Macau's vast electronics street markets to go shopping. He picked up an acceptable disposable cell phone for about thirty bucks from a skinny Indian kid and went to the park to make his call. It was answered on the second ring. A slight distortion on the line when the call was picked up told Alex that it was most likely being routed through an Eastern European hacker service which took international calls, covered them in a massive impenetrable layer of ICE, bounced them around the internet and then connected them to a one time VOIP account. The man who answered, Alex's control, could have been sitting in the café across the street or in a cave in Afghanistan for all he knew. And good luck trying to trace that call, or listen in, those kids in Belarus knew their business.

"Ready for some work?" Alex's control was all business today. But Alex was restless. The gaps between operations had become longer as the recent recession wore on. It would seem even the world of covert corporate espionage wasn't totally immune to the economic downturn. "Rush job, just came in and they want an American to pull it". Usually control wanted to talk about some fake old times and stories that had been worked out in advance to check to make sure that Alex hadn't been turned and was talking with some counter intelligence spook breathing over his shoulder. "Sure I'm ready. I have been sitting here on my ass for about as long as your marriage to that girl from London lasted." Control grunted in response. It must be early where he was it. Sounded like he could use some coffee. "I should have married the tart from Madrid, at least she could cook." Procedures are procedures and all was clear. "Rush job? Aren't they all?" Alex asked. "Details will be sent via FedEx, arriving in three day to the Boston office". Control meant a very nice little bed and breakfast in Victoria, Canada. Three days to travel securely from China to Canada ready to work, no problem. Alex hung up, disassembled the burner phone, broke the sim chip and left the dead phone in the cup of a very scruffy looking beggar with no legs.

Next morning Alex was on the early flight to Lisbon, Portugal. One evening in the city of good red wine, then the commuter flight to Glasgow and a Virgin Atlantic flight to Vancouver. After a long two days of travel Alex alighted in Canada. Taking the roundabout way of getting from point A to point B when he was operational had been grilled into him early on. It was also safer to travel through airports that were not major entry ports for terrorists and drug smugglers, but always filled with hordes of tourists. Alex took a bus from the airport downtown and then a ferry to Victoria. Always better to use public transport when the opportunity arose. Aside from the counter surveillance options, it also left no record and could still be conducted in cash without having to show ID.

The package arrived at the front desk as promised three days after the phone call in Macau. Inside was a single heavily encrypted memory stick tucked inside the spine of a cookbook and an innocent post card from his "auntie". Alex had been on the local Craigslist and had just purchased a very nice six month old Sony Vaio laptop from another causality of the recent recession. After downloading the freeware he needed to decrypt the memory stick online using the free wifi at a local Starbucks, he open the file and began to read. The job was a rush alright. He was tasked with conducting a rather elaborate penetration program against one of the largest computer companies in the world before the launch of their latest soon to be monster hit product in four months. Alex quickly returned to the bed and breakfast and booked a flight to California.

The beautiful tactical thing about California for spies like Alex is that the state is filled with high-end migrant labor. Since so many people come and go in town, another new face never stood out. And anyway everyone in California is convinced that their neighbors are probably serial killers or rapists, so no one bothers to get to know the new guy. Thank you American television! While in Victoria, Alex had used one of the clean corporate accounts that were included in the operations packet to set up a rental for a two bedroom flat in Palo Alto. The rental agreement and keys were waiting for him when he arrived the next day from Canada. The agent had been kindness herself over the phone and assured Alex that if he required any further assistance while he was in town to call her personal number. Of course, he would use different brokers to arrange the other safe houses and office space that he was planning on renting, but it never hurt to have a smitten local on tap. Besides, her pictures on Facebook looked alright and informed him that the real estate girl had attended a local high school and was single. Because this was America Alex also needed to get some kind of transportation. He decided to go with a very sleek motorcycle he found for sale by owner online. Easy to hide, difficult to follow and simple to check for tracking devices a high end bike was Alex's preferred mode of transport when in the states in spring time.

With his housing and transport issues sorted Alex's next order of business was research. He scanned through a wide range of internet sites via the wifi at a local library on his new laptop to create a list of the various offices located in the area of the target company. Next he built a list derived from people's Linked-in profiles and a very useful link to the full corporate directory an employee had posted up a few months ago for some long forgotten reason. The list was full of employees who might fit the access qualifications he was looking for. This list ended up being hundreds of people long. The first part of the assigned project was to turn an employee of the computer manufacturer and grab the proposed technical details of their super secret next generation phone. Not the one that was going to be released soon, but the one coming down the pipe eight months after that one. While the second half of his tasking was to steal the supplier data base. Both of which could be done technically via a good computer hack but since Alex's computer hacking skills were still fair to just enough he decided to go with a source recruitment approach first and if that failed then call in the class A hackers his group kept on retainer. Always better to go with what you know and try the easiest approaches first. Besides hackers can be very difficult to work with and were breathtakingly expensive sometimes.

The morality of corporate espionage rarely bothered Alex, but when he had the opportunity to go after a company like this one who really screwed the public herd with annual planned obsolescence and fear marketing of their obscenely overpriced digital toys, it became something of a pleasure to do the work that he did.

Because this was such a rush job, control was sending over a helper. Her name was Eliza and she arrived one week after Alex. They met at a new anonymous bar downtown he had found online. After running a quick surveillance detect run (SDR), they went back to the building, also down town, where Alex had leased a small office on the same floor as a number of upscale boutique law firms. Police hate lawyers and lawyers always love to use their wit, such as it is, to dick with police. Housing an operational center in a building full of lawyers was just another layer of security. There they reviewed Alex's plan of attack and made up an initial shopping list for Eliza to cover over the next few days. The list consisted mostly of computer equipment, office supplies and some basic surveillance gear.

The first order of business for the new intelligen shorten the list of potential targets down to a dozer concentrate on digging further into their lives. First th long list of possibles that Alex had assembled at the lit through their social media profiles, Linked-in professional autobiographies, personal websites, match.com accounts and a myriad other online open source nodes. The sheer amount of data that people put up about themselves always fascinated Alex. He only rarely came across a potential target that did not seem to want to give their entire life story and opinion online about everything from the Virgin Mary to Obama for the world to read. He mused for a minute thinking that in all likelihood the only people who would ever show even a glimmer of interest in the poorly written and pointless online drivel of these corporate nobodies were private spooks like him.

After three days and ten espresso runs they had a list of 17 men and 6 women who looked promising. These potential targets worked in the research and development, accounting, supplier relations, marketing and executive areas of the company. After a bit more research into the company, it was determined that they fire-walled the technical specs for their products rather fiercely. This massively useful piece of information came from a series of exchanges on Facebook between one of the potential target employees and their friend about the lack of easy access to certain data and how the company was more like a police state now than the free and easy start up they had joined years ago. This eliminated the accounting people as well as the very promising guy from marketing. Three executives they were considering, were also discounted when they found that each had been with the company for over five years and all had just returned two months before from an executive level security seminar provided by the target company's new counter intelligence arm. This new counter intel team posed a very big potential problem for Alex and Eliza.

The company was a major target for corporate intelligence collection efforts and had finally hired a consulting firm to help up their internal security. Unfortunately for the company, the counter intelligence budget was raided to boost the earnings numbers before the latest shareholders meeting and all that had been done to this point was a series of short seminars for senior and mid-level executives. Although Alex and his girl Friday had no way of knowing it, the counter intelligence consultants had also royally pissed off the in-house IT security people by running them through a series of near interrogations and recommending that half of them be fired as "security risks". Apparently the fact that most of the IT security staff had dabbled at one time or another in black hat hacking, bothered the former FBI trained counter intelligence guys. On paper, the defenses looked stiff, but as so often happens real life was much more scattered and random.

Alex and Eliza had looked at a number of the IT security people at the company, always the best catches, but ended up going with one woman in research and development and a man in supplier relations as their primaries. Always better to go after the softer more easily controlled sources when operating against a major company with the resources to possess serious internal counter intelligence assets.

The woman in R&D was named Candice and had been with the company for ten years. She was very smart, graduated from MIT, made a good salary, was reasonably attractive, but single, which indicated a very serious and stable worker. However, she seemed to have stalled in her career. She had occupied the same position for the past four years and according to her tax returns had been getting very limited raises for the past two years and was not receiving stock options anymore. Eliza had a personal source from her days in government who could call up enough data on an individual to make Orwell blush. She had the source run the female target, the male target and about a dozen others in the company from the original list. Once he emailed her the information, she sent him his usual five grand via PayPal.

Alex decided that the best way to turn Candice was to dig into her personal life and remake Eliza into the perfect new best friend. She would give Candice a shoulder to cry on and a sounding board for her frustration at her coworkers and lack of career progress. Turns out, this was easier than it should have been. Candice took zero personal security precautions. Her email password was her favorite band from college (one of the only groups she followed on Facebook) plus her birthday. That took the two of them all of twenty minutes and a quick scan of her online profile to figure out. All of her passwords were the same as well, even for her corporate email account. An afternoon spent reading several years of back emails, banking records and old blog entries give the team a fairly broad picture of this woman. As Eliza went to work becoming the perfect Candice trap, Alex began the process of digging into information about the man from supplier relations for the second part of their assignment.

The man, his name was Steve, was a go getter. A wanna be jet setter and a big partier. He regularly played golf with management types, had an appetite for cocaine and mindless young women and had just bought a new red Porsche. His email password was pantiesdown6969 to give an idea of what kind of person this soon to be middle aged weekend warrior was. It was Eliza that came up with the approach the team ended up going with for his recruitment, the honey trap.

Alex called a former Special Forces guy named Charlie who had opened a rather high end strip club in Los Angeles after a few years out of the service. Charlie had done a lot of black on black spec ops work during the global war on terror and now kept his hand in the game training the more clever girls he had dancing for him to act as swallows for corporate intelligence types. For about ten grand he sent up Brandy, a stripper slash college student who looked all of sixteen, to work the honey trap on poor oblivious Steve. After hacking into Steve's personal email the team found half a dozen subscriptions for teen porn sites that good old Steve regularly renewed. Looking over his favorite video lists on these sites, Brandy had been chosen as just his type. They set Brandy up in a one bedroom flat close to the local university and spent the afternoon decorating her new room with pop music posters, IKEA furniture and three hidden HD video cameras.

Checking Steve's bank account information using his purloined password showed that every Saturday night he went to a set of downtown clubs to do his snorting and hunting. Alex showed a picture of Steve to Brandy, explained what they wanted and operation "Pants Down" commenced. When you stop having fun at this kind of work you are half way down that burnout bottle and nowhere is it written that operational code names have to be boring. As expected Steve went right after Brandy. She acted suitably impressed with his fake sophistication, cheesy lines and flashy new car. When they went back to her flat, as directed, Brandy told Steve repeatedly that she had skipped a grade in junior high and was only 17, but dear horny Steve brushed that aside and the deed was done. After an hour of creative video editing the team had a rather good sex tape of Steve knowingly debauching a seventeen year old college freshman. Brandy was not really seventeen, of course, but Steve couldn't know that. When possible Alex always preferred to break as few laws as he could get away with.

Alex waited until Steve went to the gym on Sunday morning and then broke into his apartment. He had the apartment alarm codes because Steve emailed himself with important little bits of information like that so that he wouldn't have to remember such mundane things. Just like that Alex was sitting on Steve's couch drinking a highball of his fairly decent single malt scotch when Steve returned. Right after a good workout is a great time to approach a target. They are filled with endorphins from the exercise and are calmer than they would be after work or coming off of a hangover. Steve was at first shocked to find someone in his house and after a few seconds of bluster and threats finally noticed that his oversized flat screen TV was on and playing a piece of loud porn. The crash came seconds after Steve recognized his own voice. Alex's pitch was simplicity itself. Unless Steve agreed to lift and send Alex the information he asked for, this sex tape was going to the police and Steve was going away for statutory rape. Hard to keep up those payments on a new sports cars after you get put on the registered sex offender list, especially in California. Because the appeal of anal sex only went one way with Steve, he was understandably eager to cooperate and not go to jail. The team now owned their first source.

Candice from R&D was proving to be more of a challenge. The gut feeling that Alex had about Candice, and her vulnerability, was not playing out. There was also now a serious problem. After accidently running into Candice at her gym and using the coincidence of carrying the same book (courtesy of Candice's Amazon.com account) Eliza had quickly struck up a very nice friendship with the target. They had been going out to dinners, to charity events and gallery openings together for two weeks. It was the day after the team's recruitment of Steve that Eliza discovered why Candice was still single. Candice was a closet lesbian and Eliza, being a rather confirmed heterosexual woman, had not responded positively to her clumsy inebriated advances the night before. The source was considered too good to just give up on so another tact was decided at the crisis meeting held in the operational office that night.

It was decided that Alex would cold approach Candice and appeal to her bruised ego. Using the false flag of a head hunter for the main rival of the company where Candice worked now, Alex would offer her a serious pay increase and the direction of an entire R&D section there. All she would have to do is provide a bit of a bonus to her new employer to prove herself. Not really stealing you see, think of it rather as helping your new company and by extension yourself. Taking some cutting edge tech off of the pack of jerks she worked for now would give her a measure of revenge to think about and savor, as well as ensure her a big signing bonus. The pitch went well, after all Alex had used this approach a number of times before over the years and had the tone and jargon down pat. Candice was still more than a little reluctant, she had never done anything even remotely illegal before, and who did she call for advice that same night but her new best friend Eliza. After patching up the awkwardness of the previous evening before Alex made the pitch, the two were now thick as thieves. The near disaster of Candice's late night groping was actually a blessing in disguise because few things deepen a relationship among friends like shared secrets admixed with a dose of mutual embarrassment. Eliza told Candice to ask for some kind of proof that the offer was genuine before she agreed to anything but that the offer was too good not to at least consider. Such a sensible suggestion brought Candice back to the table and within two days Alex had arranged a fully documented job tender from the rival firm, forged of course, contingent on the successful completion of certain "consulting" duties on Candice's part. As an added incentive and to show that the company was serious about recruiting her, Alex presented Candice with a brand new Rolex watch. Carefully chosen based on Candice's internet shopping habits and Amazon.com wish list. Candice was floored, no one had ever given her such an expensive gift before and she was sold heart and soul.

Steve's assignment was easy, he was to copy the supplier data that he had ready access to and send it via email from his home system to Alex. He was not to use the computer in his office because Alex was afraid that this vector would be monitored by IT security and counter intelligence. Sending gigabits of data that you are not supposed to from your office is a very quick way to get caught and Steve was already mentally unbalanced enough to make him a significant security risk if pressed. Because the shock and docility of a recently turned source caught out in a honey trap tends to wear off quickly and drive the asset to find a means of getting out of the deal, Alex had Steve retrieve the information the very next day. Alex pressed Steve to work fast because he also did not want time for counter intelligence to doctor the file in case Steve had already broken down and was working with them. Before Steve had returned home, Alex had installed a tap on his phone and number of covert video pickups in his apartment to keep an eye on the guy after the pitch was made. So far Steve was behaving according to profile but it never hurt to have a little extra insurance. Steve went into work sweating like he had just run a marathon and got little done aside from copying the entire supplier database and future needs projections onto a sleek new external hard drive provided by Alex. He went home in the afternoon telling his secretary that he didn't feel well. A completely understandable reaction when ones world has just been turned upside down and they think that they are facing serious jail time. But the bluff worked and Steve sent gigabits of data to the anonymous ftp site that was set up overseas by control for just this transfer the minute he got home. In fact Steve completed his mission so fast that the site had only been up for 20 minutes before the data came streaming over the internet. After the file was received the site went down again just as fast. Steve heard nothing for two very long days while the information was passed on by control to the client and they sifted through the data. After Alex got the confirmation email from control that the material looked genuine he called and told Steve that he was going to bury the tape but that he should learn to behave himself and do all of them a favor by destroying the external hard drive and going back to his life. Steve's story does not end here but this did prove to be the end of his beginning.

Candice took another week to assemble her data but when she turned it over it proved to be well worth the wait. Due to a lack of internal systems controls for personnel with high level access at R&D, Candice was not only able to provide data on the device that Alex and Eliza were tasked to discover, but a mountain of data on the entire range of that company's personal electronics and computer products including all future products in development and planned upgrades. She delivered this gold mine to Alex in the tasting room at a small winery in the back country two hours out of town. Eliza was posted off the road to conduct counter surveillance in case Candice had been discovered or turned and the hand over was a trap.

Candice was not followed or compromised. However, now the team faced a pretty significant problem. The take from Candice was worth untold millions to the right people. One of Alex's golden rules was never to double dip an operation unless it was absolutely risk free. Unfortunately this information carried with it a number of very big risks. There were only a handful of companies in the world who would pay top dollar for this data and his group had worked with most of them. Trying to move the data, even through a fence would be too difficult because of the sheer value of it. Few people will begrudge a simple corporate spook a couple hundred thousand dollars but ten million or more makes people very greedy and prone to rash action. Instead of taking the risk of an independent side deal, Alex talked it over with Eliza and then contacted control and let him know what they had in their hands. He passed it up to the next level and told him that he and Eliza expected a nice chunk of the resale value of this treasure to the present client or another interested party when this was all finished. He and Eliza may have walked away from untraceable millions, but the risks in trying to flip this data themselves were just too great. Better to send it up to people like those that his control worked for that could more easily move that kind of rich sauce and take the bonus when it came back than to risk his neck and his job.

There was another problem with Candice. She was expecting to move over to the rival company now that her end of the deal was done. She had even prepared her going away speech or rather diatribe she was planning on screaming at her bosses in front of everyone. It was a very seductive fantasy and had Candice all smiles during the hand over and for days afterwards. Of course, there was no dream job waiting for her at fantasy corp., but Alex had something of a plan. Another of his little rules was to never leave bad blood in the water if at all possible. He hated wasting valuable assets like Candice if anything could be done to keep them happy and in place. He talked to control about his plan and within a week had an affirmative from him to give it a try.

By this point Candice was frantic, she had stolen the company's crown jewels and passed it off to someone she had met all of twice and hadn't heard from for two weeks. When Alex invited her to a meeting she nearly choked with mixed rage and hope. She showed up, again Eliza was providing counter surveillance and again Candice was clean, at the prearranged spot. After she had waited for about ten minutes and Eliza and Alex had determined that Candice was not being followed, Alex called her and told her to meet him instead at an address which he gave her. There he made his new pitch. The plan was simplicity itself, the truth. Few things in life are more searing than simple honesty. Alex told Candice that he was in fact a corporate spook working for a competitor and that there was no new job. He gave Candice a few seconds for that to sink in and then sprung the other half of the plan.

Instead of a new job how would she like an ongoing and rather significant tax free stipend deposited into a secret account overseas. To sweeten the pot Alex gave her the best part last. He would get her a promotion at her present company and make her a star in the R&D section to boot. The money would come through a series of shell companies from a covert operations slush fund that the company which had hired Alex and his team maintained in the former Soviet Union where such things are as common as cheap vodka. The promotion would come from a quick bit of black propaganda that would be created to make it seem that Candice's boss had stolen a portion of the information that she herself had taken. This little gem would be fed to the new counter intelligence team hired by Candice's company. Because they were a new hire presenting them with such a big win would likely mean that they would not look too deeply into it or be too suspicious of its source. Even former FBI counter intel spooks are only human. The promotion would be sealed and her star elevated because Alex had just received a valuable bit of intelligence of his own. The company that had hired Alex's team and would continue to run Candice in place had agreed to provide a simple work around that they had developed in-house to a problem which Candice's R&D team had been struggling with for months. Removing the fake mole from R&D made laundering the stolen product data easier and by placing their own asset in an elevated position within the target company's R&D section she would have access to still wider fields of valuable information like software integration and marketing plans. It took Candice all of an hour of venting to come around and Alex hadn't even had to use the stick of exposure to bring her onboard. Eliza took over the frame job of Candice's superior and would eventually take over running Candice in place for the rival firm at a very nice stipend for the next two years.

Alex still wasn't finished with Steve as he received the next portion of his assignment against the by now thoroughly penetrated target computer company. The client wanted Alex to convince Steve to help switch the present Taiwanese supplier for digital camera components in their next generation phones to a subsidiary in Japan. The price was higher but then so was the quality and the deal might actually make sense from the target's side. Steve was understandably reluctant because this request meant actually having to continue to work with the man who had set him up and was holding serious felony charges over his head. Alex took another tact with Steve. He flew Steve to a "secret meeting" for five days in Thailand. Alex indulged Steve's every whim and through the haze of sunshine, drugs and nubile women cultivated a certain bond with Steve. Turns out that Steve had some rather deep seated issues and his aberrant behavior was merely the outlet that he had for his anxieties and fears. Alex understood, after all it was a rather unfortunate but necessary part of his job to build understanding and rapport with people like Steve. If a few days of watching Steve coke binge and screw around while picking apart his soul was enough to bring him on board and stabilize him then it was a dirty part of the process but something Alex was capable of delivering. It worked, Steve went back to his office a new man. Steve used his not inconsiderable charm and connections to frame the change in supplier as a brilliant move which would save the company millions on the back end. Who knows, it might actually at that but none of it was any of Alex's concern. His job was finished, or so he thought.

Control was absolutely delighted with Alex and his team. They had achieved their mission goals nearly a month and a half in front of a very tight deadline, in the face of a supposedly strong counter intelligence program and had even brought in a few golden eggs with Candice's data flood and Steve's supplier shift. Alex and Eliza were now going to be a victim of their own success. A final tasking came down from control. The client company had just put together a very dirty piece of code that they wanted placed into the operating system for the new phone that was going to roll out shortly. The program itself was harmless but combined with a second piece of code to be delivered by tailored virus, it would cause a certain fraction of the units to seriously malfunction. Nothing dangerous but debugging, replacing the damaged units and the losses to the brand name could seriously hurt the target company and the client really wanted to spike this new model.

Unfortunately, with a bit of research it was discovered that the product testing procedures would almost certainly detect the bit of extra code. Programmers are lazy and the code could possibly be left in if they couldn't figure out what it was. But it would have to go through a number of computer specialists and the probability was for detection. After a few more weeks on site and having run the research, talked to a number of people (including Candice from R&D) about the procedures involved it was decided that in order to inflict this kind of direct action sabotage there would need to be a minimum of four people recruited in key positions and there simply was not enough time to bring it about before the launch of this latest version. The ground work was, however, laid for this operation to take place later with the next version. Didn't matter to Alex all he had to do now was clean up the operational locations and then jet off home, his work was done.

While Eliza took the assignment to stay on station and run Candice, Alex decided that he had about enough of California for one job and took another round about trip back to the Far East and home. Waiting for him there was a very nice low seven figure bonus in addition to the fee for his time on the west coast. Looking at the new balance in his Commercial Bank of the Lesser Antilles numbered account Alex decided not to invest in a certain major California based computer company, no matter what the market analysts might say about unstoppable growth potential and market share dominance.

Assignment 2

After only two weeks downtime, Alex received another Facebook update from control. You can never be too careful especially with the people who hire you, and it is never wise to let a calling pattern indicate where one actually lives. After first flying to Germany, Alex made the call. This time his target was located in the Northeast United States. Not his favorite part of the world, he did after all, live close to the equator for a reason. It was still spring time, so only a small chance of snow. Flying direct from Germany to New York's JFK airport, Alex used a very solid US passport to dodge the pictures and fingerprinting that was getting more and more common at border check points and was someday soon going to prove to be a real problem for people in his line of work. Not for the first time, he considered buying a medium range sea plane. He could park the plane in Canada and just fly South into a local seaplane port where dangerous border security checks were far less common. The day would certainly come but not before Alex could retire, with any luck.

Alex rented a car in New York and drove to New Jersey. Here he acquired for cash a six year old Jeep Cherokee from a very nice lady whose son was serving in Iraq. It just sat there while he was deployed and so she had decided to post it online for a few thousand dollars. Alex told her it was worth more than she was asking and that he didn't mind paying its real value, he still had a battered but serviceable amount of patriotism left in him, and walked out with a fine cover vehicle for the next assignment.

The target was a small chemical manufacturer that had just developed some new means of making soap soapier. Obviously valuable to someone out there, though he could not image how, Alex began his research. The mission was to steal the chemical formula and turn it over before the company could patent it. This gave Alex a window of approximately six months. There was a very serious problem with this operation which Alex discovered within his first two days on site. The company's research and development staff consisted of just three guys, two of who were brothers. It seems that they had just stumbled upon the miraculous discovery of soapier soap. The company was family held and the only people with direct access to the formula could be counted on one hand. Every one of these people had a direct personal stake in seeing this product get patented and onto the market. They were thus going to be difficult, if not impossible to turn. Alex went through a few weeks of research and surveillance just to make sure none of the potential direct access targets had any significant skeletons in the closet or other issues that could be exploited. He discovered exactly nothing.

There are of course a wide variety of tools available to a trained intelligence operative and during the period of surveillance Alex did discover that the owner of the company kept a disc with the formula on it in his home safe. He found out this important piece of information in spite of the fact that few of the old guys who ran the company used the internet or even had cell phones. Because he could get almost nothing from an email and home wifi hack, he decided to go old school and physically tap their phones. Bless the company president too for using an ancient cordless phone that was almost as old as Alex was and one he could actually tap himself. It took Alex a trip to the local radio and electronics store, a couple hours online to review the designs (utterly unbelievable what people post on the internet. You could make anything with the right tools and a net connection) and an afternoon to assemble the necessary equipment to eavesdrop on every call the president made. Alex placed a signal interception array, little bigger than a football, at the edge of the wood near the president's home and sat in his rented flat taking notes for a week.

One conversation set in motion what would turn out to be a very daring and successful bit of field craft. The president was talking to the head of the development team about some tests that were needed to satisfy the upcoming patent process. The development team had made a slight refinement in the proportions used in the formula for super soapy soap and the president told him to put it all on a new disk so that he could keep it safe in his home vault.

Rather than targeting the company itself, which was located all of three blocks from a police station in a small town, Alex decided to call control and bring in a second story man to snatch the disk from the old president's home safe. Alex had always been risk adverse. Despite what he did for a living taking dangerous chances and conducting operations he was not trained for had always been something that he avoided at all costs. Control was at first a little reluctant to authorize the cost and inconvenience of hiring a professional thief, but as it became apparent that the low tech nature of the defense surrounding soapy soap meant that it was actually better able to stand up to the modern espionage threat that Alex represented, control finally relented.

The man that control sent in was a pure joy to work with. The reason, Alex never met him and he did his job perfectly. The National Security Agency keeps a group of black operators who are little more than highly trained cat burglars. It may sound like fiction within fiction but the reason for the existence of these patriotic thieves is that the US government, even an organization with as many resources as the NSA, often finds it easier to physically steal the encryption ciphers used by foreign governments rather than go through the hassle and expense of actually breaking their codes. Most codes used by third world nations are about as much defense against an attack by the NSA as a two dollar bike lock is against an industrial laser. For these codes the acres of high powered super computers sitting underneath NSA headquarters and their thousands of super high end mathematicians are more than adequate. Sorry Egypt, Nigeria and Brazil, you are conducting open diplomacy in the eyes of the US. For allied first world nations, who do you think provides most of their systems expertise and even individual codes? This leaves countries like China, Russia and Iran. All of which stubbornly insist on using codes that are both reasonably advanced and not provided by US intelligence agencies. They do, however, have embassies around the world. Some of which are more secure than others. Thus the employment of government sanctioned thieves. Obviously former NSA cat burglars are not the only source for high grade second story men and few if any of these corporate burglars will ever give you a true answer as to exactly where they did pick up their trade but the trail is warm.

In any event, control sent a pro to solve Alex's little problem. All Alex had to do was find a good dead drop. This he did, right in the bathroom of a freeway rest stop 30 miles away from the target. Easy to run counter surveillance on and at most times of the day all but deserted. Free coffee and 24 hour access, it was ideal. Alex sent the details to control and they sent them to the thief. Five days later the thief signaled that he was ready to make the break in happen. It occurred during the President's routine Saturday evening dog walk. The thief had received a full copy of Alex's meticulous surveillance notes. The thief broke in, disarmed the security system, such as it was, opened the safe, removed the disk, copied it, replaced it back into the safe and walked out rearming the security as he left. An hour later Alex received an email telling him that the drop was full and proceeded to pick up the stolen data.

The target never found out that their soapy soap had been stolen until a rival overseas company came out with the exact same product a few months before their patent was filed. While the company itself did not fail as a result of this action, their core business lay elsewhere. They did try for a legal solution by claiming that the foreign company had stolen their design. Their overseas rival countersued using a veritable army of high end lawyers in the US as well as some not too subtle lobbying in DC. Added to this blizzard of counter attack were a number of tame journalists at home and in the US used to poison the press and US government officials against the small American company. Against such odds the poor little company never really stood a chance in court. In the end the company with the soapier soap dropped the lawsuit for lack of evidence, the rival had covered its tracks well and had a whole room full of chemists who insisted that they had been hard at work on the world changing soapy soap problem for years. After spending their corporate life's blood on legal fees and the endless process that is international litigation they had little to show for it in the end save an ulcer or two and an empty corporate bank account.

Assignment 3

Alex's next assignment was a bit more dicey than the last, where the danger came more from boredom and frostbite than small town America's nonexistent opposition forces. In this case, he was tasked with penetrating a rather large manufacturing concern to steal the secrets of a new chemical treatment process and then to infect the automated manufacturing robots there with a stuxnet like virus developed in-house by the client that would cause them to ruin themselves, spectacularly and untraceably. Ideally the robots would damage themselves beyond repair and the company would be convinced that the new process was flawed and stop using it. Double points for stealing something that works and making the inventor believe it was a flop, while at the same time wrecking their productive infrastructure for months. This was a very bold proposition on the part of the new client. This single covert action could give them a valuable chemical process and perfect market share in the space of a few months. Not to mention deal a significant blow to their rival both physically and financially.

One thing that Alex had noticed over the years operating in corporate intelligence was the increasing number of missions he was getting which involved some form of direct attack in addition to the act of data theft. Most of these attacks were based around what can only be described as cyber weapons developed by the clients or somehow obtained by them. Alex had been copying each of these weapons as he received them and kept his collection on a massively encrypted black server he had set up in Dubai years ago. Hey, some people collect guns. Alex himself was now a rather avid collector of corporate intelligence grade high yield cyber weapons.

Alex began his routine by moving circumspectly to the new target location in Japan. Alex hated operating in Japan for some very specific reasons. The main cause of his desire not to operate clandestinely in Japan if he could help it was mainly because companies there love to spy on each other and they are very good at it. That means that companies operating in Japan work in a much more hardened environment than almost anywhere else in the world and have ready access to some of the best covert corporate espionage operators in the world, not to mention a first rate state security force. Japan also has an incredibly insular culture which can unmask the activities of a non-Japanese spook quickly just because people actually pay attention to what foreigners do there. The fact that the target company was owned and operated by a French concern operating in Japan would, Alex knew, make no difference whatsoever since they were partnered with a Japanese company and most of the employees were locals. The other reason that Alex did not want to muddy any pools in Japan was that he was very uncomfortable operating in a country where he physically stood out so much. He could and had blended in perfectly well in the EU, the US and as an expat operating in a number of different countries, but Japan was different. Running an operation in that country would be doing so with a very big neon sign on his back that read "see me, I am different, watch what I do!" But a job was a job and since he was operating against a French company that employed a good number of American and British engineers, he had high hopes that he could be in and out before the sign on his back got too bright.

If there is one place in Japan where a foreigner can conceivably operate clandestinely in relative security it is Tokyo. The vast majority of foreigners who call Japan home live there and it is such a vast metropolis that if done carefully a good spy can sink quietly beneath the radar. The target company had their headquarters in Tokyo and their foreign staff was all located in the city. This made getting at them much easier than if they had lived out at the actual plant in the hinterland. Even still Alex was cautious by nature and unwilling to take the risk this assignment called for without a significant increase in his normal fee. Control agreed and the client ended up paying twice what the operation would have cost to run in France or the US.

Alex lucked out after a month researching and keeping a covert watch on the imported engineers. While most of them went out together to go drink in Roppongi and chase Japanese girls on the weekends, there was one who stood out because he was seemingly never invited. The engineer in question was a second generation Chinese American named John. The Japanese have a rather peculiar and ever so slightly negative view of people from other Asian nations, American born or not, and John had managed to alienate his coworkers with his ceaseless complaining about how terrible life was in Japan and how much better everything is in California. His loathing of all things Japanese soon had him ostracized outside of his peer group which can be a very lonely place indeed, especially in a foreign country that you do not like much. This opened John up to any number of approach vectors and conversion tactics. It was now just a matter of finding the right lever to pull to bring John onside.

So now Alex had his mark. At first he was going to approach John under a false flag as an agent of the Chinese government and get him to cooperate that way but after reading his collected private emails over a few days it became apparent that John, far from being pro-China, was in fact as American as apple pie. He had near zero connection with China, no relatives that he kept in touch with there and little grasp of the local politics of the region. Here was a 100% California kid who read tech blogs and watched cheerleader porn, as American as disco. So discarding a false flag approach to appeal to John's inner love of Mao, Alex went instead with the straight up money and ego combination. He first introduced himself at John's local expat bar. Knowing his dislike of the country, it was easy to strike up a quick bond by doing a good round of Japan bashing.

Alex tailored himself to be the best friend that John could wish for in such a lonely place. They shared many of the same interests (all courtesy of John's easily hacked home computer) and had even read a few of the same books (Alex had stolen a peek at John's Kindle while he was at the gym).

It is strange that even in the midst of tens of millions of other people one can still feel so isolated and alone. Perhaps the sight of so many other people that you will never have the occasion to meet, befriend or fall in love with trips some kind of circuit in the mind and activates the crushing loneliness spiral in some. This is certainly not true for everyone, but more than a few souls have been eroded by too long spent in the endless metropolis that is Tokyo. In any event, Alex befriended John quickly and soon they were inseparable. When Alex finally pitched him, after a whirlwind bromance of less than a month, John was more than ready to strike back at all of those who in his mind had rejected him. John hoped at the chance and from the first viewed the money, in this case about $10,000 US per month, as a measure of his worth and power. Alex had grown to dislike John intensely during the run up to his approach and was more than happy to limit their meetings after John was turned based on "operational security".

John was quickly able to assemble the information relating to the new treatment process and passed it over to Alex since he had direct access to the data as a part of his job. The actual exchange took place in a posh hostess club in Ginza. John had insisted on the spot and Alex had agreed. Not something that he usually did, let the source dictate the location of an important exchange, but John had become increasingly resistant to Alex's control. The initial approach as a friend had skewed the control dynamic between Alex and John. In John's mind he held more power in the relationship then may have been warranted by the facts. This was, to Alex's, dangerous but manageable. Alex had not been able to detect any opposition pressure on John so he had tentatively agreed to the hostess club meet. Worst case here was that Alex got caught and deported within a day. His cover was solid and he felt confident at this point. He nearly bolted, however, when he arrived at the club and saw half of the senior staff from the target plant sitting two couches away having a birthday party. John thought that it was the coolest thing he had ever done, passing along the big secrets right in front of his bosses. This manic and unsafe behavior by John should have set off big flashing lights in Alex's mind, but at the time he was focused on finishing this project as quickly as possible and getting home. Everything seemed to be going very well, too well in fact. John was on side, if a bit unstable, and had all of the access and motivation that could be asked for. It was typical of sources that are no longer under the positive control of their handlers to act like John was, dangerously reckless. Once a source takes control of the spy-asset relationship, one can usually expect serious danger ahead.

Once the information was received and sent on, Alex was ready to have John install the virus in his factory's robots. He wanted to get this done and be finished with this project as soon as possible. However, as is often the case in intelligence work something unexpected happened. There was a delay of about three weeks due to a programming error at the client's cyber weapons development center. It turns out the virus liked to turn itself on during the middle of the day when there were workers all over the place. Because the client did not want the mess of death and dismemberment to bring the massive investigation that was sure to ensue should there be fatalities, it was decided to wait until the error could be sorted out. During this operational pause John did what every out of control source tends to do and just kept taking chances. The hostess bar memory stick pass was bad enough, but now John was taking it to new levels. He began to pilfer information which he was not asked to and tried to sell it to Alex for more money. Alex was also convinced that John was trying to contact other rival companies directly to move his stolen information, though John denied it when Alex asked. He even offered to personally set fire to the factory one night when drunk and took to spending the money that Alex had provided him for the initial information in very flashy ways. What finally gave him away, however, was a simple everyday bit of forgery and expense account fudging.

When John walked into his boss's office the next Monday to find most of the senior staff staring at him with grim looks, he broke down instantly before they could even speak and told them everything. The shock in that room can only be imagined. Here they were about to hand John his walking papers for getting caught taking a bit of money from the cookie jar, but instead they are handed a major case of corporate espionage with the potential to cost the company millions. Because Alex had given John a copy of the first robot virus, which John had copied for himself of course, before the flaw in that program had been discovered the entire operation was now wide open. The senior executive on site, having no wish to lose his job over this fiasco, did not report the breach to home office in France. Instead, having worked in Japan for over a decade, he went straight to the Japanese joint venture partner and asked them to take over, quietly. The Japanese company having some degree of experience in such matters, as the foreign executive well knew, had their own intelligence group they kept under the skirts of a deep subsidiary company and soon the tables were turned on Alex and his paymasters.

The in-house Japanese intelligence group went to work extracting every bit of information that John had on his handler and were soon able to locate Alex in his supposedly safe flat. From there they kept him under round the clock surveillance using ten or more Japanese watchers and technical hacks of his phones, computer and any other device they found. They bugged his flat with a laser mic set up across the road, tapped his calls and hacked his wifi. They didn't enter the flat because they knew after watching Alex for a few days that he was more than a little security conscious and have undoubtedly taken measures to defend the inside of his house against direct penetration. What they were rewarded with a whole lot of nothing. When operating in a known hostile environment like this Alex took extra care with his communications and tradecraft. He never called control from anything but a brand new cell phone picked up expressly for that reason and never used the internet in his safe flat for operational purposes. Besides he was waiting for the debugged robot virus to come and had nothing operational to do.

So for several weeks, and at the cost of a few hundred thousand dollars, Alex was a rat in a cage that he didn't even know existed. That is until the day that the watchers made a simple mistake. According to their rotation roster one of the female watchers was listed as not having been observed by the subject, that is Alex, for several days. She came in wearing the same red rain coat that she had the last time he had seen her and as soon as he spotted the pretty girl walking on the opposite side of the street in the other direction but giving him a very subtle eye that he had seen before in a totally different part of town, his antenna twitched. When the only defense a spy has against getting caught and all of the terrible things that go along with that are their instincts and anonymity, they learn very quickly to trust their spider sense. At this moment Alex's mental alarms were singing. It is a very common surveillance trick to run a waterfall pattern (keeping eyes on target by running people in the opposite direction the target travels) on a security conscious target. This is difficult to detect because most people, even trained ones, rarely consider someone walking away from them to be a threat. With enough people and a few cars in a busy mono ethnic city like Tokyo surveillance teams can run the waterfall all day with even the most experienced agents never pinging to it. Alex added a few jack moves to his daily SDR, nothing too gratuitous just little things, and sure enough he began to spot repeat faces. His living in an Asian city like Macau paid heavy dividends now as Alex was able to spot the distinct features of his Asiatic watchers, where most non-Asians have a difficult time telling individuals apart from that part of the world. Now Alex began to sweat. He could go to ground or change safe houses easily enough. He did have totally sterile extras laid in for just this kind of an emergency. But could he really be confident of having shaken his tail? What would his watchers do if he bolted? How long would it take the kind of resources he had detected watching him to reacquire his scent even if he was able to go to ground in the city? Was the operation completely blown? The answer to this last was fairly obvious. He had received none of John's normal whinny texts or invites out to play darts for many days now, which was unusual, and the flavor of the watchers said private intelligence not government to Alex. This meant that his source was most likely blown and so was he. It was time to start implementing his contingency escape plans.

But first he had to shake the watchers long enough to buy a new phone from the seedy street vendors in Shinjuku and contact control to let them know what had happened. The first step was to retrieve the bug out kit that he had buried in Yoyogi Koen, Japan's answer to Central Park, and get close to the river. After that he bought some new clothes and headed towards the Sumida. A little pleasure craft is an easy thing to hotwire and steal. In any city with a river, a lake or ocean front, and Tokyo with its Sumida River had no shortage of riverfront tie ups, such craft are plentiful and can be grabbed with a minimum of fuss. Stealing the little speed boat and careening upriver for twenty minutes, he slipped his watchers and after dumping his old clothes, GPS trackers are very small these days, he headed via express train back to Shinjuku. Once there he picked up a cheap disposable phone from a Nigeria street vendor hawking hip hop clothes and "you know, other stuff, mon" and made the emergency call.

Control was not happy, to say the least. This was a major operation and the robot virus had been developed and tested at great expense by the client. To give up now would cost the intelligence group that Alex worked for a lot of future business. There was one last chance to complete the assignment before Alex ran. As part of his preliminary research he had bought a secretary at the company to get information on the target engineers, a rundown on internal security and other details about the company. Alex had only used her one time and that at the very beginning of the assignment. He calculated that it was unlikely that she was burned. Alex decided to take the chance. Because he felt that he was facing internal corporate counter intelligence and not the near limitless resources of a fully fledged state run operation, he rolled the dice and contacted the bent secretary. Then he decided to get off of the grid.

Control contacted the client company and had them rush the virus rewrite. Alex was told that it would take at least three days to get the new virus ready. He hit the local camping store and tooled up. After he had some gear he took a series of local trains to get to the suburbs and from there a nearly empty bus for a few hours to the mountains. Once he was alone on the bus he got off on a random stop by the side of the road and hiked into the wilderness. He had decided to throw any pursuit that may have followed him this far (Alex had no idea if the opposition had recourse to drone surveillance aircraft or other means of tracking and it never hurt to be through) by taking the three days to walk across the mountains to a medium sized city he had found on Google Earth. Alex was in very good shape and this would give him the chance to be absolutely sure of having lost his tail. He got out a new compass (old school is the best way to get totally off the grid these days) and started walking.

Alex had been very careful when he was riding the series of trains around town to cover with a cap and mask his face from observation by the numberless cameras mounted all over the city. Tokyo has the greatest number of surveillance cameras in a single city in the world. They are omnipresent and most are nearly invisible among the lights and architecture of the city. And scariest of all for Alex they are almost all linked into a central system that uses cutting edge biometric and facial recognition software to track people. The system was also open to outside penetration (Alex knew of at least one hacker who had breached it and used it to digitally stalk a famous actress there) and who knew if the corporate intelligence team that was tracking him had their own back door. Not many people in Japan have any idea that such elaborate and effective tracking capability exists in their capitol city. What possible use it could serve in the lowest crime country on Earth, Alex had no idea.

The fact that he was up against corporate intelligence and not the state played a major role in Alex's decision to stay and finish this mission. Because in Japan the state will actually pursue corporate spooks and the police and internal security there are quite good if given a reason to move (not to mention the crazy scary tools they have at their disposal).

After three days Alex returned to the city via a similarly circuitous route. First he bought some new clothes and went to a public bath (one of the few benefits to working in Japan is their fantastic bathing culture which Alex thoroughly enjoyed). After Alex washed the dirt of three days climbing mountains off he stopped at an internet café and stole a memory stick from some hapless gamer when he went to the bathroom, emptied it and downloaded the new and improved virus. The next step was to meet the secretary for drinks and pass on the stick. Alex ran a three hour SDR, face covered all of the way, and met up with his new last best hope shortly before 10pm. He promised the secretary that she would receive a significant bonus if she installed the stick exactly as he told her to. Because the senior staff had kept the entire affair quite for the past few weeks and the secretary was from a different section, she had no idea that there was a hunt underway in Tokyo or that she was to become an unwitting tool in this spy drama. She happily took the memory stick, thoughts of Prada bags and other luxury goods soon to be hers after this little chore was done dancing through her head, and went home. Alex, having done all that he could needed to crash for the night. He chose a love hotel and told the old lady behind the screen that he was ordering in his companion for the evening. Love hotels, where they exist in the world, are very discreet, plush short time establishments built to provide inexpensive temporary shelter for amorous couples in overcrowded Asian cities. It suited Alex's needs perfectly, especially the discreet part.

In the morning after he got word from the secretary that she had uploaded the memory stick he took a local train to an outer suburb of Tokyo, rented a car with a sterile identity and drove north all day until he reached Sapporo in the northern island of Hokkaido. Taking his chances that the target company did not have the resources to stake out every international airport in the country, he bought a ticket to Korea and from there on to Italy and whence to ground in Turkey.

What happened with the secretary and her destructive virus? She did exactly as she had been told to do and had uploaded the virus perfectly. Unfortunately for Alex's client one of the first precautions that the target company had taken as soon as they knew such a virus existed was to take their manufacturing robots offline to scan for any infections and allow time for an anti-virus to be created. Of course the several weeks of down time served the competitor nearly as well as destroying the line would have, with none of the inevitable blowback from such a spectacular operation, but they were only partly mollified. Apparently whoever was running the operation for the rival company was something of a Michael Bay fan and had their heart set on the fantasy of renegade robots destroying his competitors for him with fireballs and all of the rest.

After escaping from this last assignment Alex was put on a forced vacation while some damage assessment was carried out. As it turned out, the Japanese joint venture partner that had sent their in-house spooks against Alex had been more than a little impressed, especially when they discovered the secretary and her little plastic poison pill almost a month later. They asked around and hired him and his intelligence group a year later for a series of penetrations against targets of their own in the EU and America. As for John, after the debriefing he was held in a small house in Western Japan by a couple of thugs while the chase was on to track Alex. After the whole thing was over, he was give a quick drubbing and put on a flight back to California, coach. After this, I doubt there was a person in his life that did not get bored to tears listening to his fantastic stories of kidnapping and espionage in the wicked orient.

The Grey Line: Modern Corporate Espionage and Counterintelligence

Assignment 4

After the mess that was Alex's assignment in Japan he went on vacation. Time spent away from the game more often than not lead to sun, good drink and some kind of additional training. Alex headed to a small seaport in eastern Mexico where he took a month's worth of flying lessons to learn to operate a seaplane. Never hurts to plan ahead, the ability of most spies to work corporate usually comes with a limited shelf life and having a separate skill set or two lying around is considered good insurance. The ability to slip into and out of most countries with little hassle is also a very good one to possess in this line of work.

Control decided to ease Alex back in after his run from Japan by giving him what was considered to be an easy assignment next. Though this was not to prove to be the case it was nice of them to have at least tried. Spies can break down too. Exposure to stress, especially a close escape like Alex's, can be very corrosive to a spy's mental well being. Thus, the extended vacation and supposed soft ball assignment.

Within the corporate intelligence world, one of the fastest growing areas is in personal use spies. Companies have vast resources that they can throw at intelligence operations, but so do certain rarified individuals. One of Alex's best friends at the CIA had gone corporate a few years before and now worked in the shadows behind a very popular Hollywood starlet. He worked covertly with the corporation behind the star's publicist to turn certain key people in the media and had significantly boosted her career. He aided the other security elements around her in tightening up her defenses, especially against hackers and rogue fans. But what he mostly did was cover ups, scandal mitigation and generally kept her image in the right light. The reality is that most intelligence operations that do not involve direct action or deep penetration of a company can actually be rather cheap to mount. This puts the services of a trained spy well within the price range of a wide variety of individuals.

The next person to hire our spy Alex was no shadowy element hidden within a vast corporation, but rather a very ambitious executive named Nathan. The long time star at his investment bank, Nathan, was the product of old money, good schools and fierce competition with those who he considered socially inferior. The problem with Nathan's career at this point was that he was finding it ever more difficult to outshine those grubby, but hungry, state school kids. The financial crisis had hit a number of his old family friends hard and many were neither willing nor able to slide big bucks into his care every few months or so as they had before. This was weakening his portfolio just as a new batch of wunderkinds was taking over at his firm.

Nathan's main rival at the moment was the epitome of all that he had been brought up to abhor. Not only was the guy from Brooklyn and had gone to, gasp, NYU on scholarship of all things, but he had a real gift for the markets and was shining where Nathan was seemingly on the downward swing. Not that Nathan actually had to work, but the pleasure of winning was addictive and the old money and power of finance is a great means to measure your success against former college buddies. It was from just such a former Ivy League college friend that Nathan was introduced into the shadowy world of corporate intelligence. His friend mentioned to Nathan one day that he had used a company that did shadow work for his father's firm to create a brand new tax shelter for one of his clients which had gone over like gang busters. He had also heard that this firm did other, murkier, things besides set up impenetrable offshore accounts and introduce new tax havens. Nathan was intrigued. He read up on the subject a bit and decided that hiring his own personal spy was just the means to destroy his enemies, real and imagined, regain his role as top dog in the firm and perhaps for a few other chores as well. Contacting the company proved easy enough, but waiting while the company checked him out was tedious and frustrating. Finally he met with a man who claimed to be a senior executive with the private intelligence firm and who was willing to listen. Arraignments made, deposit received and a week later Alex was on his way to Miami.

The first surprise for Alex was that his new client had actually listened during their brief chat online about basic operational security and had not sent a flashy Rolls Royce to pick him up. The next was the sheer scale of opulence that he found himself surrounded by at Nathan's home away from home. Old money can be just as ostentatious as new and having inherited young, Nathan played the rich single guy well. Coming from a culture of secrecy and constant security consciousness it was something of a shock to be acting in the light of day as an advisor to someone so willing to overtly display and use their money and power. Working in the light was something that Alex did all too rarely these days.

Those first days in Miami, Alex explained exactly what he could and could not do for Nathan. Nathan may well have been full of ambition and pride, but as a ruthless aristocrat, he hid his faults well enough for Alex to develop something of an attachment to his new master. Of course it did take some hours to convince Nathan that Alex did not normally repel down buildings or shoot whoever looked at him funny. After that reality check, the two spent days crafting a realistic strategy to achieve Nathan's goals.

Principal among those goals was the destruction of Nathan's main rival in the company Peter. The enemy, as Nathan saw it, was a man who lived for his work. It stung that he was also much more intuitively better suited for it than Nathan. Be that as it may, according to Nathan the man had few enemies, aside from himself, was recently engaged, didn't do drugs or party and was not a closet homosexual. The last is still a very black mark to have in certain rarified circles.

Being a through spy, Alex double checked all of the information that Nathan provided on his rival at work. What he found confirmed much of what Nathan had already told him. The man was clean, had a happy stable heterosexual relationship and worked nonstop. On a long enough time line that addiction to work would likely turn Peter's life into a stress filled ruin all on its own, but since the client wanted that destructive cycle to begin immediately if not sooner, it would likely have to come down to the invention of fault. There are many ways to slander a fellow man in the eyes of his peers, many more if you cross the grey line and do so illegally. The question became to what degree Nathan wished to ruin his rival. The narcissistic answer was simple, utterly. This meant framing the target for a crime. Now most people when they consider something like this will immediately turn their minds to murder, Nathan certainly did. The problem with murder is that you need someone to actually die. You need to craft forensic evidence just so and plant it in such a way that your fingerprints are not all over it but the target's are. Murder and other serious physical crimes require some extensive expertise to tie to someone who did not commit them. There is also the pesky issue of believability and motive. For someone like Peter it just didn't make sense to go for something like murder which would be heavily investigated and easily proved false.

The solution to this framing problem was devious and ties deeply into the mass hysteria about a finite number of crimes which exists in America. Not to say that those who commit these crimes are in any way redeemable, but certain offenses such as drug possession or child porn are open and shut and can be used by a spy to quickly and totally remove anybody. There is no need to do anything too deep to prove such crimes, since they are rarely investigated fully and there is no mitigating defense for them if physical evidence is found. Even a hint that such an act on the part of the target is true is usually enough to destroy their reputation. Despite what television may tell us, the criminal justice system is rarely used maliciously by one to frame another. This means that police and prosecutors are very difficult to convince that they are being used. They have heard it all before and every criminal, especially perverts and drug fiends, was invariably "framed".

The matter once again devolved down to evidence. Peter, who never took drugs and certainly never sold them, would be able to make a pretty potent case that any found in his home had been planted. Add in the phalanx of lawyers that the firm he worked for would certainly throw at such an obviously untrue allegation, bag of heroin in his kitchen be damned, and the choice became clear. Alex held his nose and contacted a very discreet class A hacker he used rather extensively, located god only knows where, to begin the frame job. And a remarkably quick and easy process it was.

First a bogus child welfare and human trafficking monitoring group was created based in Europe. These kinds of NGOs come and go and with a bit of masking tech, appear completely legitimate for the period they need to be. Next the actual materials were assembled. Unfortunately this took the least amount of time and effort of any of these steps down this dark road. Then Peter's home system was cracked, well for the hacker perhaps this was the quickest step. After that the images were uploaded and a program was inserted to make it read that such images were accessed regularly and had been downloaded by that machine over a period of years. Then a tip was sent from the bogus watch group to the FBI and Interpol who takes these kinds of matters very seriously. Within a few weeks Peter was rounded up with a host of other unsavory characters around the world in one of those great big sweeps one reads about in the papers every so often. Much to the consternation of everyone who knew him, Peter was arraigned after illegal sexual materials were found on his home computer. With anything involving hidden sexual practice, Americans are willing to believe almost anything about anybody. After nearly a year, Peter's lawyers did manage to prove during his trial that the images were indeed uploaded by a third party and that he was innocent of the charges. However, the cost for the lawyers and computer experts used at trial took most of his acquired wealth. The trial itself led to social damnation (most of his peers were never really convinced that he was truly innocent) and for the purposes of this operation to his immediate and unambiguous termination from the firm. Nathan was ecstatic. Within a matter of weeks and for less than he usually dropped during a weekend in Vegas with friends, he was now once again the golden boy at his company.

While this little bit of direct action was in the works the client, Nathan, became rather concerned at just how quickly and easily it was possible to infiltrate and destroy the life of another person. Not for any moral reasons, but like all people who taste power derived from covert means he began to worry about the same thing happening to him. Infiltration and malicious subversion are valid enough concerns in the modern era where data and its manipulation have such a powerful and pervasive impact on everyday life. Nathan wanted his own life to be airtight. Thus Alex began to look at his client as only a trained and hardened spy can. First he tightened up Nathans home security. Alex had a good safe installed, his home computer systems hardwired and firewalled by a team hired out of California who had built some of the better systems security that he had run up against. He made Nathan buy a dog. Never hurts to try and humanize a man a bit. Next the office, where Alex put in covert motion activated cameras and a biometric security system for his door and computer as well as a high grade safe. Nathan even when so far as to insist on physical security measures such as bullet proof glass in his penthouse and an armed response silent alert system in each of his rooms. Paranoia, after all, knows few bounds once unleashed in a fertile mind. Alex was able to put together a rather detailed dossier on many of the people Nathan worked with regularly, which Nathan thought was the most entertaining thing he had ever read, and even ousted a doorman at his building who had been busted twice for breaking and entering tenant's flats while they were on vacation.

With the removal of Peter from the immediate scene, Nathan next set his sights on other potential threats inside of the company. He wanted and got illicit phone taps on five other executives in the firm and a corporate intelligence grade computer activity monitoring program sent over from Alex's faceless hacker. Nathan spent an evening going from office to office installing the program himself.

Alex had always been a bit wary of dealing with class A or better hackers. As integral as computer experts are to so many modern covert corporate espionage operations, they take extreme measures to keep their identities and activities secret. Par for the course in an illegal market place filled with spies and other assorted criminals, but it does raise some serious trust issues no matter how often you may work with the same one. Alex was very careful to explain to Nathan the fact that in all likelihood any programs that were installed on those machines included a number of very discreet backdoors built in which would allow the hacker who wrote them to have full access to everything stored or connected to the systems. Sometimes a person will open the gates of Rome to the barbarians to spite a single senator. The immediate concern that Nathan felt about his place in the company clearly outweighed any questions he may have had about the wisdom of allowing a hacker to install, through his hand, corporate intel grade penetration programs on the firms systems.

In any event, Nathan was very satisfied with the level of information that the phone taps and computer monitoring programs were feeding him daily. Alex began to prepare a kind of Presidents daily brief (PDB) of the activities of others each day at the company for Nathan to go with his breakfast. It did make from some interesting reading occasionally, but much of the recorded conversations and email traffic was too technical for Alex himself to really derive much meaning from. Alex did, however, unbeknownst to Nathan also feed the information to a bent broker he kept overseas and that person understood the content well enough to make a series of short trades which helped to build up Alex's nest egg quite a bit. The daily intake also revealed a great deal of personal information about the activities of the other employees at Nathan's firm. Only a fraction of which Alex ended up passing on to Nathan. The rest he wrote up in detailed files for future use. Some of the things that fund managers, stock brokers and senior financial service executives get up to on any given Tuesday made them easy targets for future recruitment.

As the weeks became months Nathan came up with a new task for Alex. The client had an ex-girlfriend, model/actress, who he wanted to destroy next. Pure petty vengeance and completely personal but it was not Alex's place to dictate to his client what he should and should not do with his money and power. He was there for a job and took the assignment, without a great deal of enthusiasm, but for a very large private payment arraigned to look like a commission on one of Nathan's numerous investment programs. Alex did his homework and found out that the girl was actually a rather good actress and had even recently secured a decent role in an upcoming summer blockbuster. She was, however, completely unprotected by any kind of physical security and had zero defenses in place for her online life. He toyed with the idea of just leaking some of the more salacious texts and photos she had on her phone and home computer, Rep. Weiner style. But knowing his client's preference for high yield and very public disgrace Alex took another tact. In this case it was decided by Alex that he would let the media do the real work of destroying the girl's career for him. Through a connection in the massive drug market that is New York Alex bought a potent concoction which would make the model/actress act visibly high and out of control for a short stretch. Having already hacked the target's cell phone he simply sent a text supposedly originating from one of her friends to meet up at a busy outdoor cafe in an hour. He had scouted a number of locations around the city to find one in a CCTV blind spot with lots of traffic and the right kind of image. When she arrived Alex, in light disguise, simply walked by and distracted her with a quick bump while spilling the drug into her drink. Sure enough, within a few minutes the drugs began to take effect. Alex used a burner cell phone to grab some very damaging minutes of video which he promptly sent to a number of celebrity web sites and new organs. By one that afternoon the model/actress's career was done and a few days later her agent, in full on damage control mode, was announcing her admission into a famous rehab clinic. It didn't matter that the girl was not actually addicted to anything. The videos that Alex and other patrons had taken and through the media gestalt shared with the world demanded a pavlovian response and the target was out of the picture. Nathan was smugly satisfied with the virtually imprisonment of his ex and the splashy end of her budding career.

Just when Alex was getting used to serving a master he could put a face to and living above board for a change, control tapped him for a very interesting mission back where it had all begun, South America. This time around though the stakes were much higher and Alex was no wet behind the ears first year case officer.

Assignment 5

In most, if not all of the developing countries it had been Alex's fate to operate in, both for his country and then as a private spook, it had always come down to graft. If his backer had the money and stomach to use it effectively, there was little that could not be vampired out of the bush with a little bit of cash and bling for the local dictator of the month and his cronies.

In this assignment, Alex's story had an interesting twist. The company that had hired him through the normal screen of cut outs and brokers was losing influence with the host government at an alarming rate and because of this, some very large contracts and potential billions in mineral concessions were in the balance. Due to the fact that there was only one company with their name plastered about town, a number of the more standard filters between Alex and his employer were done away with. Not to say that this would have made it any easier for Alex to directly tie his activities to the client company, he still got paid through a dozen ghost accounts, but it did limit the pretense a bit.

The most obvious reason for this sudden loss of power in country that Alex could see, was the utterly high handed treatment that the onsite executives meted out to the various local grandees and government officials. But the right bribes had been sent to the right people, so despite the neo-imperialist attitudes of the corn fed corporate suits, there had to be another reason for their sudden and dramatic loss of power. It was an intriguing problem, but not one that would normally require Alex to be pulled from an ongoing assignment, even with his local knowledge.

He came using a cover as a private security contractor, which in the third world among corporate types will leave the average visitor with as many business cards carrying that title as plastic surgeons in Beverly Hills. Alex spoke to the company representatives and their private military contractor people. He spoke to the government officials, who were as always charmingly vague as to their motives and masters. Finally he tasked a cadre of off-site intelligence analysts that his group had on call to look for movement from other foreign companies into the region. There he hit pay dirt. The head of the overseas development branch of a large European mineral consortium had recently given a speech hinting at the possibility of expanding operations into areas such as, wouldn't you know it, the one Alex now sat in. So it was discovered that the cause of his client's woes was a semi-national EU based mega corporation that was making moves to replace the dominance of his client in this charming country filled with flies, poverty and vast profitable resource reserves. Facing a company like that in the field meant that he was going to be facing a directed effort on the part of the national intelligence services of the controlling members of the consortium. One thing that no corporate spook worth his salt wants to do is get in the way of a first world national intelligence service hard at work for god and country in the wild South. But since Alex was not getting paid to give up and leave, it was time to start considering his options.

The first thing to do was to create a targeted black propaganda campaign to try and frighten away the rival consortium. It is a bewildering fact of our modern world that a simple press campaign, as fleeing and fickle as they tend to be, can sometimes scare even a state run operation and major corporation away from billions in easy foreign plunder. His first efforts using the resources available to him via the intelligence group he worked with, meaning about a hundred bent journalists around the world, were stymied and soon overwhelmed by the massive response the state agencies were able to mount using their own hundreds of bent media faces. And now the rivals were awake to the fact of another player out there working to thwart their ambitions for the region. After all, it is not every day that the media anywhere in the first world wakes up and decides to run screaming press on a place like where Alex was working without some significant outside prodding. So the combined in-country national intelligence assets came sniffing around or rather their local hires did looking to out their competition. Since Alex had yet to spread his presence around too much and still maintained the bought loyalty of some of his old contacts, he did feel relatively safe for the moment. This was not to last.

Smelling opposition, the EU consortium upped its game and began a local press campaign against Alex's client company and also a further round of bribes. In conjunction with this was a smattering of guerilla attacks against remote pipelines and some weakly held jungle facilities belonging to the client. This was meant as a not too subtle warning to Alex and his people not to get in the way. At least now Alex knew that the Euros were talking to and likely funding the rebel forces in country. These revolutionaries amounted to little more than narco gangs masquerading under the banner of quaintly antique Marxists groups that had been around since Alex's father was young. Nonetheless, the use of revolutionary terror and assassination, while not unexpected in an environment like this, certainly did up the risk factors and allowed for a proportionate response.

After several months in country, Alex had a much better grip on local politics than when he first arrived. It would seem that the EU rival company had spent quite a bit of money turning a certain senator, fancy ribbon sash and all, and through him was funding a substantial and growing clique of party in power members within the government. These servants of the people were all of a sudden absolutely convinced that the resource concessions granted to Alex's client were better off in the hands of the masses. Of course, actually developing these resources would by necessity fall to the helpful and benign EU consortium. When one wishes to change the policy of a developing country you generally have to look no further than its leading one half of one percent. Alex's client had become too complacent in this particular kleptocracy and had lost positive political control. The client was about to reap the whirl wind of that complacency in the form of having its assets nationalized and scooped up by a more dynamic, and liberal with their money, EU based group. The Euros had a massive intelligence advantage and resources in the form, not only of their own largess, but of a number of their national intelligence services personnel in country as well. These spies had been busy tapping the phones, computers and offices, not to mention apartments of mistresses of the senior staff of their main obstacle to great wealth, namely Alex's client. These gringos had gone about their business blithely unaware that they were the target of a sophisticated surveillance and monitoring program carried out by some of the best corporate spooks in the world.

Alex could not hope to match the outlay of resources that the state players could bring to bear, but he could try to slow them down a bit. He brought over a technical sweeper team and had the offices and homes of the most critical personnel swept top to bottom on a random and ongoing basis. He began a program of anonymous emails and phone calls to the senior administration people at their homes to try and trick them into thinking the CIA would mount a coup if they went forward with the plan to nationalize. Government officials in South America are so conditioned by history to believe the CIA all powerful and ready at the drop of a hat to remove them that this seemed to actually work for a few days. This was put to an end when the local CIA station chief was sent by the Ambassador to grovel in front of the President for life after rumors of a CIA backed coup finally reached him. "We desire nothing but stability and progress here in the glorious country of X, an invaluable ally of the United States in the global war on terror". To run a coup, even in a total back water like this, would require the States to actually care about the activities of the country in question. No such luck and the Ambassador himself was appalled at the very idea of disrupting his happy retirement present from the President, who he had supported for several years, with bloodshed and bombs. It had been worth a try though.

The final move Alex made as part of this series of stall tactics was the tasking of a hacker team to attack and crash a few local banks to give his client some more overt leverage when dealing with the government. Deploying high yield cyber weapons strategically against a country and not a single company was something kind of new to Alex and he wanted to see how effective it would be. This kind of covert cyber warfare was the wave of the future and he was very curious to see it in action up close. Of course, those in power did not keep their money in country and so were totally immune to the attack. They dismissed as fantasy any suggestion that the collapse of three major national banks was the result of a covert strike, after all banks fail all of the time in the third world, even big ones. What these actions did do was to buy Alex some time to bring a few more special resources to bear. First he attempted to impress upon the local executives working for his client that they needed to spend money to shore up their little remaining support in the government and try to reverse the gains of the Euros. When this appeal failed and his other direct measures didn't work he contacted control to discuss options for more permanent solutions.

The meeting took place between Alex, the head of his intelligence group, a senior representative from the client and a very menacing looking former soldier. On a boat sitting in international waters near Martinique the intelligence and direct action teams got the green light to move against the senator who was leading the charge to nationalize the client's interests and turn them over to the Euros. The actual killing would be carried out by the tough looking soldier and his own handpicked group of former spec ops guys. It would be Alex's responsibility to provide in-country resources for them and to build their infiltration and exfiltration routes. It is an interesting thing just how much terminology and style in corporate intelligence circles is actually lifted directly from Hollywood movies. The real dirt and blood involved in an operation to remove a problem government official in a back water country to keep the bottom line high is far removed from anything that is ever shown on the silver screen but when comes to ridiculous "spy speak" like "to sanction an individual...with extreme prejudice" people actually do talk like that. Even old intelligence hands have been known to start spouting Hollywood generated "spy-isms" from time to time.

In this case, a completely deniable go ahead was given Alex and the Spec Ops team for "an executive action to draw down the threat profile" of the local problem Senator. In other words, the corporate type did not want to spend the money bribing back the Senator and his friends since it was cheaper to just kill the man and be done with it. So a few nods later and with three discreet wire transfers, the death plan for Senator X was put into play.

The grisly soldier flew his five men in over a period of three days sheep dipped with fake EU passports and visas issued through the auspices of a well known humanitarian NGO whose email server had been breached. Hackers and their twisted sense of humor never cease to amaze. Once in country Alex met with the Major, as he had taken to thinking of the soldier type, only once to pass along contact information for an underground arms dealer who would sell them explosives cheap and to provide details on the planned exfiltation routes, both primary and emergency that he had worked out. They met out of country at a dirt strip of an airfield in the middle of nowhere. Two light aircraft with no flight plans in the middle of the jungle. Just like the local drug dealers. Again hiding trees in the forest. About as secure an environment as one could get in this part of the world. Alex had recommended staging a false flag raid on an explosives depot used by the rival company as part of their mineral exploration contract to smoke screen the operation, but was turned down due to time constraints. Once someone decides that they are going to "sanction" another person, they invariably want it done double quick. Whereas, in every case that Alex had ever heard of measuring twice and cutting once was the best policy in the long run. But the kinetic part of the operation was in the hands of former Spec Ops guys now and Alex had to assume that they knew their business well enough to get it done and get out in one piece. He made his own preparations to flee quickly just in case.

In the end, the GI Joes got their bomb, affixed it to the target's car and within a few fractions of a second the march of the EU Mega Corporation into this part of South America took a huge backwards step. An hour after the explosion, the five men were on a fishing boat headed north to proceed at a leisurely pace to the nearest neighboring country and fly back home first class, job well done. The local media screamed about fallen heroes and the need to crack down on terrorists and rebels for nearly a week. The story didn't even have legs enough to rate more than a page six mention in the neighboring country, let alone displace the latest LiLo meltdown in the Western media. The funeral was a very somber affair with a lot of very nervous government types and a few smiling corporate executives.

The only blip on the transnational radar was from an actual NGO staffer in the target country who blogged about the bombing in English for a few months. Her theories of corporate responsibility for the attack did get a micro degree of traction in the blogosphere. Nothing a bit of creative hacking and link blocking didn't severely retard though within hours of each post.

One aspect of corporate intelligence that is beginning to get a great deal of play these days is information control on the web. Crashing web sites and blogs, controlling traffic, rigging search results, redirecting IP addresses to effectively erase sites and virus mining target content is a rapidly growing field. Companies who don't want their name dragged through the mud or wish to silence critics, now have ready high end cyber assets available to do just about anything they need to stomp out limited net memes before they go viral. Even without an active information suppression campaign run on the web, the likelihood that such unsubstantiated wild conjecture, especially coming from the source it did, would have ever had more than an eye blink of viral fame online was extremely remote. But protocol in the information age necessitates a degree of post operational informational awareness and suppression as needed, so another blogger got stepped on.

For Alex, the mission was wrapped a few weeks after the explosion. He did after all have to monitor the remaining members of the late senator's faction to make sure they got the message. He had helped to reset the balance and preserve the client's dominance in country, just like he was paid to and now it was time to move on to the next assignment.

Part VII

The Future

"We have no future because our present is too volatile. We have only risk management. The spinning of a given moment's scenarios. Pattern recognition."
William Gibson

This book has been about spies. What they do, how they hunt, who they target, how they turn employs and penetrate networks and what all of this means for individuals and companies in America and throughout the world. Burying the issue of corporate espionage under layers of infotainment myths and rare but uninformed speculation in the media has provided this industry with all of the cover they could have ever asked for. Corporate espionage has become a massive multibillion dollar a year enterprise covering dozens of nations and actively penetrating thousands of companies. What the emergence of private covert intelligence activity means for companies around the world, and particularly those in the primary area of operations America, is that now this power, once reserved to the state has become a vital part of corporate operations. Like it or not, question the morality of using spies or not, corporate espionage and direct action is here to stay. Companies have two choices now, fight back or fall victim.

If you work in the corporate world and think that spies are out there using their skills to go after others, but never you, think again. In all likelihood you have worked out next to one in the gym, stood next to one in line at Starbucks and hit on the same girl at the club. If you are working in a strategic position within your company you may even have one of more as a "friend" on Facebook. Corporate espionage is conducted not by a small cadre of shady spies but by literally thousands of professional intelligence agents around the world. Corporate espionage is widely engaged in by states and even more widely by private firms operating on behalf of some of the largest names in business. By a number of estimates corporate intelligence activity now generates revenue in line with that of the drug trade. That is a lot of zeros which means a lot of covert activity utilizing a stadiums worth of professionally trained intelligence agents from virtually every country on Earth.

One of the more interesting facets of the modern corporate espionage world is that many of those who are now in the private sector conducting these activities are in fact Americans. Patriotic kids who watched the towers fall and wanted to make a difference are now out there in the private sector trying to pay the mortgage and survive the market crash using the skills which they learned during the global war on terror. Corporate spies are not monsters, they are not evil ruthless beings bent on destroying American industry. The modern corporate spook is a professional, well trained and experienced in doing one thing which now has value only in the private sector. Instead of toiling away in the Stan or the Suck to no apparent purpose for 60 grand a year (yes, CIA salaries are in line with MacDonald's managers) a trained intelligence officer can make millions working in Miami, Seattle, London or San Francisco. They can operate as they want, recruit who they need and live without having to submit hundreds of pages of cables to Langley to justify each action. They work with others from the same background (for many it was a revelation to work with intelligence operatives trained by other countries for the first time after going corporate) who share a common purpose and desire for effective action and good pay. The siren song of the easy corporate life has drawn out some of the very best from the state sector and the more entrenched and successful these private intelligence groups get the more appeal they will have for others.

Corporate espionage has proven to be one of the few industries that were recession proof during the recent economic crisis. The demand increased so dramatically over the past decade that there was even a program of incentives put in place at a number of American intelligence agencies in an attempt to keep trained and experienced operators from leaving en mass to the private sector. A number of those spies who left the state agencies and went into the private sector ended up returning back to their old jobs at CIA, DIA and NSA as consultants and contract workers making three times as much but doing many of the same things they did before (how the government justifies that to Congress each year exactly is still a source of mystery). Many did not. Included in the group that went over to corporate intelligence are some of the finest officers US and allied intelligence agencies have produced. Facing this tidal wave of highly skilled covert operators is an entire world filled with soft corporate targets and easily recruited employees.

Having gone through the proceeding chapters the reader should now have a better understanding of what corporate intelligence is and how it operates in the real world. Despite all of the Hollywood distortions of intelligence work, one thing that they did get right is the power of the threat. Not in a world threatening villainy kind of way, but in the fact that intelligence agents are highly trained and capable professionals who go about their work with dedication and purpose. And they are very good at what they do.

Of all the myriad emerging threats to businesses at the beginning of the 21st century few have a better chance of still being around and pervasive in fifty years as corporate intelligence. The very utility of intelligence gathering and direct action targeting rival companies will ensure that they remain a potent threat across the globe well past the relevance of this book. Spies are useful and present a very sharp threat to modern business operations, made all the sharper by universal lack of understanding of the dimensions of their operations. They come from all walks of life and from nations around the world. Their one motivating factor is greed and their sting is in their ability to turn employees, break into corporate data systems and employ extra legal means to affect change on behalf of shadowy and well insulated elements inside of rival companies. All of these actions are carried out covertly and well under the notice of today's media. Even well informed security specialists have had a difficult time coming to grips with the dangers posed by private intelligence operators.

The vast majority of spies work for companies, either directly or through private intelligence firms. The reason for the existence of these firms and their ever increasing growth is that privately funded and run intelligence operations are yielding those companies that hire them untold wealth and advantages over their rivals. It is not possible to stop the emerging threat that private intelligence organizations pose to corporations by attacking these groups directly. The very covert nature of their existence and degree of training that spies have makes them much more difficult targets than lay criminals. And we all know how well the war on drugs and crime is going. The sheer scale of money to be made in this industry will ensure that the ranks of private intelligence organizations stay full and the services that they offer remain for companies to engage well into the future.

The key is this, spying is unfair and it works. If there were ever a single thought that could sum up the American attitude to life in general and business in particular it is "fairness". The use by competitors of such underhanded and unfair tools as spies cuts against the grain of the American psyche. Unfortunately this is very much not the case elsewhere. Criminals and spies are regular adjuncts to corporate operations around the world. The ability of American, and other, business entities to come to terms with this simple truth will determine how they are able to deal with the present wide spread and growing use of covert intelligence in business.

The Grey Line: Modern Corporate Espionage and Counterintelligence

The Japanese have a saying, "the best way to cure poison is with poison". In the realm of corporate espionage this sentiment is one to be remembered. Now that the use of private spies has sped well past the tipping point it will be impossible to remove from the modern business world. Pressure may be put on individual countries to curtail their state corporate espionage programs but this will only drive the consumers of that intelligence to seek similar power in the shadow private sector. Not engaging with the reality of corporate intelligence is simply not a viable option any more. And expecting ones home country and its police forces to come galloping along to the rescue is a long wait for a train that won't come. Companies now face a stark choice, either they emerge from beneath antiquated ideas of morality and take on those functions of the state which will protect them or fail quickly and inexplicably.

The emergence of corporate intelligence as a power in the business world was slow in coming but made inevitable by the advent of modern communications and net technologies as well as the creation of vast armies of trained intelligence cadres by states. Spies are not going away. In the short term a company can work to build barriers and defenses against espionage. This is an absolutely critical first step but will not prove to be enough as adoption of state like capabilities continues on the part of rival corporations around the world. A defense only approach to countering the threat of covert intelligence is setting yourself up to fail from the start. There is no way that a company can tighten its defenses enough to totally protect themselves against professional corporate spooks. The only way that companies are going to be able to effectively compete in a fast approaching future business world is by finding and employing a balance of offensive and defensive intelligence capabilities.

Companies need a strong internal counter intelligence arm. They need to harden their employees as well as their computer systems against conversion and attack. There needs to exist a cooperative approach between counter intelligence and systems security staffs to limit the potential for damage from intelligence penetration. None of this can begin until the threat that corporate intelligence poses to companies around the world is thoroughly examined and understood by management and private investors. Providing a starting point for that long overdue discussion has been the goal of this book.

State based corporate espionage targeting the defense industrial complex has long been understood. When one looks at the lengths which these companies go to defend themselves it is clear to see that there are sections of corporate America that understand the danger of covert intelligence. The next step now is to extend this understanding to the wider business world. There are several orders of magnitude more spies targeting non defense related industries today than there have ever been working against the defense industrial complex even at the height of the Cold War. And this number is increasing every day. The amount of money to be made and the invariably lax attitudes within core American industries towards security have made them inviting and easily penetrated targets. Private intelligence collection today ranks easily as one of the most lucrative illegal activities in the world. Considering that this trade is carried out by highly trained and generally ruthless intelligence operators and the dimensions of this problem become truly alarming. Add the growing penchant for companies to launch covert direct actions to damage their rivals and the damage caused by future covert corporate conflict looks set to spiral.

There are three critical steps that should be taken to engage with the problem of corporate espionage today. The first is to harden individual companies. Corporations in the US and abroad must be made aware of the dimensions of the threat that espionage and related activity pose to their well being. Solid actions must be taken inside of each company that wishes to remain relevant in the future to harden their defenses and create a barrier to easy penetration and attack. This calls for the advent of serious corporate counter intelligence and better

IT security. Taking a proactive approach to corporate security is also a must.

The second critical step to creating a viable defense against private corporate espionage is the deployment of US and other nation's counter intelligence and intelligence services to counteract the uncontrolled spread of these activities. The US in particular is guilty of doing virtually nothing to help defend her companies against the depredations of their competitors. Diplomatic and political pressure should at the very least be applied to halt the actions of ALLIED countries intelligence services engaged in economic espionage in the US on behalf of their domestic industries. If this kind of activity is to be tolerated from others then the US should begin to engage its own state intelligence apparatus to level the playing field a bit and target overseas firms. The fact that the United States is the only country in the world not engaged in corporate intelligence gathering on behalf of her domestic companies is nothing to be proud of.

The third and final step that should be taken is the development within individual corporations of their own intelligence capability. Whether this is carried out for purely defensive (targeting their rival's covert intelligence gathering infrastructure) or more offensive, positive actions is up to each company. Companies need intelligence, period. A positive covert intelligence gathering and even direct action capability is becoming an absolutely critical adjunct to a modern corporation's operational profile. Without such a capability companies are totally at the mercy of their less scrupulous rivals. With a covert intelligence capability the modern company will have the tools it needs to compete effectively in a future thick with spies.

In the proceeding chapters of this book I lay out what makes corporate intelligence tick, how and by whom it is engaged in and basic steps that can be taken to safeguard a company against the depredations of corporate intelligence agents. The next step will be up to businesses around the world. Like the US secretary of state who refused to read the secret messages of his country's rivals because it wasn't "gentlemanly" there will be companies who refuse to acknowledge the realities of private espionage. Over the coming years these will be easy enough to spot as they fail in droves. Those that choose to embrace the coming age of corporate utilization of previously state only tools such as intelligence will invariably hold a great deal of advantage over their global competitors. Companies around the world must realize that they are on a steep learning curve, one with significant penalties for failure. In today's business world future success will depend largely on a company's ability not to fall into the trap of morally superior complacency.

Acknowledgements

A great many people have contributed to the creation of this book. Few of who desire fanfare but I want to thank you all just the same. I would especially like to thank the many sources, friends and family members who had to listen to my endless dissertations on this subject while the book was being written. I only hope that they use their unsought espionage training for good. Haver, Jazeera, Bernell, Nori, Alice, Yuko, Em, Thomas and Andre in particular have my deep regards for their friendship over the years and their invaluable input on all subjects. My editors deserve special praise for their patience with the endless back and forth of rewrites and fine tuning. I will try to keep my sentences under half a page from now on, I promise. A big up to Kate, the design wizard, for her exceptional work. And all between trips to Portugal and South Beach. "I have nothing to declare but my genius", indeed.

I want to also thank the brilliant, eclectic and frighteningly global cadre of people who are the Amur Strategic Research Group. Their insights and perspective from all sides of the grey line provided this book with a firm grounding in reality. I wish to give a special nod to FT/Felicity for providing my bona fides into the Alice in Wonderland world of class A hackers. Thank you, all of you, out in the ether (especially NI/KyuMaru, AE/Warspite and PL/Minerva) who spent long hours explaining, in terms I could understand, what hackers actually do. What they can do with a few hours, Red Bull and a laptop is simply staggering.

To TM/Rasputin for practical insight on how to "shoot straight, blow shit up and run faster than the sirens." I am sure that you are right in saying that the vast majority of people who know how to do this stuff are well adjusted (although I am not quite convinced that it is because, as you say, they all own dogs). To AE/Coldstream, for the endless refined discussions on how people are turned and the myriad other subtle tricks of psychological manipulation used in intelligence work.

One thing though, you need to do something about the fact that you sound just like Anthony Hopkins's portrayal of Hannibal Lecter. It is just creepy. And finally, to AE/Stavka for sharing your knowledge of the international grey market banking system. The best part was your reaction to my short lecture on how a "normal" person opened a savings account at Bank of America. You can learn more about a system by looking at the differences.

You are all on my Cowboy Angel list, definitely!

This book simply would not have been possible without regular espresso breaks at Dutch Bros. coffee off Lancaster. You guys, and girls, are just too cool! I want to send all of my love to Sister Chill and the Nobi crew. One day soon I will be back to burn that Last Train to Lhasa CD and hit up Corubars again. I want to give a special thanks to Harvey Levine, Charles, Max and the rest of the staff at TMZ.com for getting me back into the popular culture mainstream. After a long stretch spent overseas I came back a bit jaded but found through your combination of exceptional journalism and wicked insight a new appreciation for the frenetic world of modern media.

To Charlie Sheen for being the one celebrity who isn't afraid of twisting the media gestalt's tail a bit to suit his purpose. Strip away the theater and apoplectic response and the message was deliciously positive. For throwing a bit of sand into the gears, I thank you, it was oh so fun to watch. To Hideko B., the world needs more people like you with the audacity to just BE that cool. To Barry Eisler for his fascinating discourses on modern publishing and writing in general (and of course, for his novels! I don't think that I am alone in anxiously awaiting the return of Rain). To my Aniki, the owner and fellow staff at Club 7th Heaven in Kabukicho circa early 2000's. It was there with you that some of the deeper lessons were learned. Nothing truly good in this life comes without cost but you guys were worth it. To the 9 Direction

Demons of Lin Shen North Road for teaching me how to cheat at Mahjong and other important bits and pieces. To Clark Speed and his course on the Anthropology of Power. Between the vast university library and your lectures I came out better than I went in. And finally I want to thank all of those who have made the impacts, large and small, which helped shape the lens through which I see the world. This book is for all of you.

For access and knowledge better left undefined:

BE/River Wind
AE/Tension
AE/Case
AE/Serendipity
BE/Slight
BE/Leito
LM/Athena
NE/Haruhi
NE/Yukimi
FX/Phalanx
PL/Forever
PL/Benjamin Stacker
RT/Sky Bright
RT/Conception
XE/Dreadnought
XE/Rising
XE/Fei Xue
XE/Nobel

You know who you are and how you have helped. You have my deepest gratitude.

About the Author

Andrew Brown is a corporate intelligence and international business specialist with extensive experience working around the globe. He has consulted and taught on the subject of corporate espionage and counterintelligence practice on four continents to an array of clients in the private and public sectors. His most recent work *The Grey Line: Modern Corporate Espionage and Counter Intelligence* is a summation of the experiences and knowledge he has obtained from years of working in the private intelligence arena. For more information go to Amurstrategic.com or follow him on twitter @TheGreyLineBook.